PENGUIN BOOKS

MY EAST END

Gilda O'Neill was born in the East End of London. Having left school aged fifteen, she later returned to education as a mature student and went on to take three university degrees. Since 1990 she has been writing full-time and her novels include *The Cockney Girl*, *Whitechapel Girl*, *The Bells of Bow*, *Just Around the Corner*, *Cissie Flowers*, *Dream On*, *The Lights of London*, *Playing Around* and *Getting There*, as well as her oral history *Pull No More Bines*, the story of East London women hop-pickers, and many short stories, articles and reviews. She and her husband John live in the East End, as do their two grown-up children.

My East End

Memories of Life in Cockney London

Gilda O'Neill

PENGUIN BOOKS

PENGUIN BOOKS

Published by the Penguin Group
Penguin Books Ltd, 80 Strand, London WC2R 0RL, England
Penguin Putnam Inc., 375 Hudson Street, New York, New York 10014, USA
Penguin Books Australia Ltd, 250 Camberwell Road, Camberwell, Victoria 3124, Australia
Penguin Books Canada Ltd, 10 Alcorn Avenue, Toronto, Ontario, Canada M4V 3B2
Penguin Books India (P) Ltd, 11 Community Centre, Panchsheel Park, New Delhi – 110 017, India
Penguin Books (NZ) Ltd, Cnr Rosedale and Airborne Roads, Albany, Auckland, New Zealand
Penguin Books (South Africa) (Pty) Ltd, 24 Sturdee Avenue, Rosebank 2196, South Africa

Penguin Books Ltd, Registered Offices: 80 Strand, London WC2R 0RL, England

www.penguin.com

First published by Viking 1999
Published in Penguin Books 2000

28   2006 000 522

Copyright © Gilda O'Neill, 1999
All rights reserved

The moral right of the author has been asserted

Set in Monotype Minion
Printed in England by Clays Ltd, St Ives plc

ISBN-13: 978-0-140-25950-6

For my family, who filled my
head with wonderful stories

Contents

List of Illustrations

25. A 'dock copper' checking that a dockworker isn't leaving with more than he arrived with.
26. The Royal Artillery unloading a ship during a dockworkers' strike in July 1949 at the Royal Albert Dock.
27. London Docks, 1961.
28. Royal Docks, 1942.

Section Three
29. Sheltering from the bombs for the night became a part of wartime family life.
30. The docks, vital to the life of the country, were continually targeted by enemy bombers.
31. Royal Docks, 1944.
32. 'Bombed out'. Lydia Street, 1940.
33. VE Day celebrations, 8 May 1945.
34. Women enjoying a chat in Whitechapel, 1938.
35. Teatime, Whitechapel, 1938.
36. Scrubbing the step ready for the Coronation party, 1953.
37. Coronation street party in Morpeth Street.
38. Attracting the punters, Petticoat Lane, 1936.
39. Attracting the punters, Petticoat Lane, 1998.
40. Likely lads, 1951, by an advertisement for the ever-popular Troxy.
41. A celebration knees-up at Bill Cannon's 'Pigeon-do', 1960s.
42. Girls playing in the street, *c.* 1950.

Author's collection: 11, 13, 18, 39, 41, endpapers; Hulton-Getty Picture Collection: 10, 26, 34, 35, 36, 37, 42; Museum of London: 9; Museum of London, PLA Collection: 28, 29, 30, 31; NMPFT/ Hulton-Getty/Science and Society Picture Library: 33; Private collection: 3; Springboard Educational Trust: 12; Tower Hamlets Local History Library and Archive: 1, 2, 4, 5, 6, 8, 14, 15, 16, 17, 19, 20, 23, 25, 27, 32, 40; The Whiffin Collection/Tower Hamlets Local History Library and Archive: 7.

Acknowledgements

First, my very special thanks to Rosy Fordham for all her help, and to Eleo Gordon for her support and advice, to Lesley Levene, Gráinne Kelly and to all the many people who shared their stories, thoughts and memories, by telephone and letter, in notes and conversations, as well as in the extended, formal interviews, without whom this book could not exist: Vivian Archer, Julia Ashwell, Mary Bacon, Reg Baker, Vic Baker, Sarah Baron, Ernie Bennett, Theresa Bennett, Eileen Berley, John Bond, Grace Clay, George Cooper, Len Crickmar, Harry Davies, Michael Davis, Vicki Diamond, Eileen Doe, Gwen Field, H. Field, Robert Field, Ken Fletcher, Sally Fletcher, Keith Gotch of the Metropolitan Police Service, Thames Division, Janet Greaves, Eunice Green, Brenda Hall, Marion Hancock, Stevie Hobbs, Fred Hodgkins, Irene Horner, Mrs Horrobin, Edward Inch, Rosemary Inkpen, Rezaur Rahman Jilani, Priscah Karanja, Vera Knights, Mr and Mrs Kurtz, Matthew Lagden and his mother, Gerry Leheup, Sheila Leheup, Elsie Lewis, Terry McDermott, Elsie Mackie, Rosa Moss, Edith Nailard, Diana Nicholson, Dennis O'Neill, Isabel Pam, Iris Perez, Carol Price, Mrs Procter, Lavinia Richardson, Cherie Rolph, Lil Rolph, Mrs E. Rose, Mary Rose, Pat Rutter, Peta Sandars, Lionel 'Sid' Sheldrick, Helen Sheppard, Bert Slattery, Val Slattery, Doreen Smith, Richard Smith, Jim Stevens, with the kind help of his daughter, Margaret Stone, Mr V. Stubbens, Mrs W. Taylor, Mr L. Townsend, Winifred Tyley, George Wainaina, Eve Wee, Pamela Whetton, Esther Wilson, Ken Younger and Benjamin Zephaniah, plus, of course, those who wished to remain anonymous.

My thanks as well to all the people whose stories appeared in *Pull No More Bines*, my history of hop-picking, on whose recorded testimonies I have also drawn for this book.

Thank you to the staff at the libraries, museums and information centres I have visited, for their patience in answering questions and for directing me to further sources of information. Details are listed in the bibliography and further reading section: Bishopsgate Library, Brentwood Library, British Library, Commission for Racial Equality,

Corporation of London Records Office, Guildhall Library, London Metropolitan Archives, London Museum of Jewish Life, London Research Centre, Museum of London, Newham Local Studies Library, Newspaper Library (Colindale), Public Record Office, Ragged School Museum and Tower Hamlets Local History Library.

Specific mention should go to Sarah Harding of the Newham Local Studies Library, Chris Lloyd of the Tower Hamlets Local History Library, Lena Martinez of the Tower Hamlets Advice and Information Centre, Tim Owen of the London Research Centre and Iris Perez of the Fern Street Settlement.

Thanks to all the local and regional newspapers around the country who printed my requests for information.

Finally, I'd like to take this opportunity to thank everyone for their kindness and understanding when I took a break in my work following our family bereavement.

Introduction

I was born in Bethnal Green in 1951 into a traditional East End family. My nan had a pie and mash shop, my grandfather was a tug skipper on the Thames and my great-uncle was a minder for Daddy Lee, the owner of a gambling den in Limehouse's Chinatown. My childhood was at the fag end of a world that is now mainly the constituency of history: hops were still being picked by hand; horse-drawn vehicles were used as transport, rather than as advertising gimmicks; trolley buses with their sparking, crackling, overhead rods ran past our street door; women, exhausted from childbirth because they were unable to plan the size of their family safely and reliably, were old before they reached their forties. It was a world before the silicon chip, mobile phones and the Internet; a smaller, less private world made up of your close neighbours, where children addressed the women in the street as 'auntie' regardless of actual blood relationships. Looking back on this past could be a barren exercise in, admittedly pleasurable, nostalgia, but it is also a way of deciding what the past means to us, what it says about who we are now and what we wish to be in the future, by allowing us to reclaim the best of what was, and is, important to us as social beings living in a world of sometimes alarmingly rapid change.

I chose to write a history of the East End because of the pride and great affection I have for my birthplace, and from a fascination with the cockney identity, which was once carefully hidden by those who considered themselves fortunate to leave the slums of their childhood but is now more often acknowledged as a source of great pride. Where once people would have been wary of discussing their working-class roots, with mothers telling their children to *talk proper* and to ape the ways of their *betters*, they are now more likely to celebrate such memorable beginnings. In the course of this project, I received letters and invitations to record stories not only from people in the East End itself but also from those as far away as Canada and New

Zealand, all of them keen to share their experiences and enthusiasm for their common birthplace. The words of one man who asked me to do a good job in telling 'our story' echo those of so many others who contacted me.

It was because of this desire for 'our' stories to be told in an appropriate way that I felt drawn to write the book in the way I have, beginning with a brief traditional history which provides a context for the oral testimony of East Enders themselves.

As the first parts of the book deal with times which are out of the reach of living memory, they are dependent on printed primary and secondary sources, including popular as well as more scholarly works, and archive materials housed in various libraries, public record offices, local history collections, museums and private collections. These sections are deliberately brief, an overview of events, as they are intended simply to put the creation of the East End into the wider setting of the development of London as a whole, and to provide a backdrop against which the main body of the book, the oral history, can be seen more clearly.

It is there, in the oral history, that big moments are recalled which still have resonance today. Stories are told of families struggling to survive during the hard inter-war years; and of another kind of bravery and determination, when the East End defied everything 'Hitler could throw at us'. Then there are smaller moments, such as the pleasures of getting together with your neighbours for a knees-up; the anticipation of preparing for the annual jaunt 'down hopping'; and simply looking back fondly on a time when 'we was all one' and you could leave your door on the latch without fear of being robbed, although it wasn't likely that you would have had that much for a burglar to have taken anyway.

As well as one-to-one interviews, I had discussions at day centres, women's clubs and retirement fellowships, many telephone conversations and, thanks to some wholehearted generosity, extended correspondences with a number of people. As was familiar to me from previous oral histories I have compiled, most conversations or letters would begin with something like: 'I used to live in the East End and I'd love to tell you some stories, but I think you might be wasting your time talking to me. I'm just an ordinary person.' I think there is no such thing as an ordinary person. There is something extraordinary about all of us, as the following stories of hopes and fears, desires and aspirations, loss and disclosure, longing and recovery, will show.

When researching, it is easy to become waylaid by such things as the cost of a whitebait supper at a Thames-side inn, or the exact rules of the children's game High Jimmy Knacker, but I don't dismiss these as insignificant. It is the recollection of the smell from Stink House Bridge, the sputtering of a gas lamp when adjusted by the lamplighter, the flick of a long, dusty skirt as a woman sits down on her street doorstep to shell peas into a colander, which give us access to other worlds, to our past, about which we seem to have such a strong need to know. A line of a song, a half-remembered tale from a much-missed relative, a sudden, fearful memory of that first day at school, all can make us weep. Not from nostalgia but from loss. Why didn't we write it all down, ask more questions, realize it was our past we would lose?

A lot of what we call history – the factual representation of the past – is as much to do with opinion, faith and dogma as any philosophical or religious system of belief. But through oral history, how we represent what we remember, we can explain the meaning of the past to ourselves, and thus the meaning of the present, and who and what we are, or want to be.

As we are separated from the past of our memories by the increasing number of years that, before we know it, have slipped by, so the barriers to understanding, knowledge and lessons that may be learned also slip ever further from our reach. Who was my great-aunt Mog's husband? Did she have one? Was she widowed? Does that explain why she was in the workhouse? Wanting to understand things can lead us to a realization that we can only ever have a partial knowledge.

I wondered why my dad calls what is now known as the Three Mills Heritage Site 'Long Wall' and discovered that that was the name of the defence erected to protect against tidal flooding of the surrounding low marshy land. Preventing a breach of the banks or walls of the river was a vital task for a community which depended on the Thames and the Lea as arteries, places where you lived, worked, that were life itself. But to my dad, a man approaching eighty, Long Wall would always be more than that. It was the name of the place where, as a child, he and his friends would sneak in and scoop molasses from the treacle barges that were moored there. Something I probably would never have found out without having access to his memory; a memory which evokes a time when trade on the river was thriving, when children were not restricted in the ways they are today, and when the chance of eating something sweet required risking a clip round the ear from a bargee, or a potential soaking in the river, rather than a trip to the supermarket with your mum.

As with any history, I have had to be selective. Just the resonance of a place-name can encourage a detour down one of the winding side roads of the past. Learning that Limehouse, for instance, recalls the lime oasts where Kentish chalk was processed to produce the lime needed by the increasingly demanding London building trades. Who worked there? I want to know. What sort of lives did they lead? Were they happy to be in the East End or had they come, as so many had, as strangers desperately seeking work in the big city? And discovering that Middlesex Street, close to my own home, was once known as Hog Lane for the pigs that were kept in the nearby fields and herded along it on their way to the slaughterhouses of Whitechapel; and that it was then renamed Petticoat Lane for its huge second-hand clothing market, the roots of which can be traced back at least to the Peticote Lane of the seventeenth century, which has now metamorphosed into a bustling general market that spills into the surrounding streets, and is closed only on Saturdays – a reference back to its once having been in an almost exclusively Jewish neighbourhood.

It is said that an average person living in the seventeenth century would not, in his or her lifetime, have encountered as much information as is contained in just one edition of a Sunday broadsheet newspaper. I'm sure that's so, but a lifetime of Sunday papers, complete with supplements, is nothing compared to the amount of information that can be had from a brief chat with my dad, or one of his friends, any of my aunts or even a willing passer-by in that East End street market. After a quarter of an hour your head will be filled with stories of cobbled streets, how people looked out for neighbours bombed out in the Blitz, what it was like to be a child when the Thames really was the gateway to the world, and how things were different then. The wealth of detail – poignant, surprising, funny, dark – could fill volumes on any single aspect of this history: Irish immigration; the extended cockney family; transport; housing; children's games; pearly kings and queens; worrying about having to pay the doctor; and so it goes on. This book is a compilation of such information, the personal views and reminiscences – the oral history – of East Enders themselves.

I have not changed the language in the testimonies to make it *grammatically correct*, but have made editorial changes to prevent unnecessary repetition and, more importantly, to protect the confidentiality of respondents. That is why names are sometimes omitted and precise areas sometimes undefined. I have included a selective bibliography, further reading suggestions and contacts for sources of additional information for readers who wish to pursue particular interests, or who want to find out more about the earlier history of the area. It would be useful, however, to remember the point made by Millicent Rose in her 1951 book on east London that, apart from 'sensation-seekers' writing about the criminal, bizarre or otherwise seamy side of existence, there is often no record of what she calls the 'common run' of people, and that many standard London histories have all but ignored the East End. Quoting from as far back as John Northouck's 1773 *A New History of London*, Rose cites his as a typical opinion that much of the area has no interest for the serious historian:

[As] these parishes, which are chiefly inhabited by sea-faring persons, and those whose business depends on shipping in various capacities, are in general close and ill-built: therefore afford very little worthy observation . . .

But some outsiders have continued to write about the history of the East End, and occasionally to raise the eyebrows of East Enders with what they have to say. The 'East End', for instance, according to a recent book on the regeneration of the area, written by a non-East Ender, is a phrase that was 'once used' to describe the area. *Once* used? The same book also concerns itself with whether Newham can be included in the geographical description 'east London'.

It does have to be admitted that there is a difficulty in defining what and where the East End is, begins and ends. The physical East End is as difficult to define as the spiritual ideal with which so many cockneys, wherever they now live, feel such connection. During my own childhood it was very clear where it was placed: it was where we lived, and Hackney was, according to us lot south of Victoria Park, very definitely in north London, and parts of what is now Newham were definitely much too posh to be thought of as being inhabited by rough East Enders – when an auntie and uncle moved to furnished rooms in Upton Park, they had 'made it'. But times and understanding, and meanings, change.

One boundary, however, was constant: that of its western edge, the City of London, the bounds of which have not changed significantly since the thirteenth century. But the same could not be said for the area beyond and to the east of the city walls. This is a topography which grew organically with intermittent spurts of development, changing yet still enjoying some measure of continuity for the generations who lived there.

The East End in its earliest incarnation can best be defined as the ancient Tower Hamlets, a name which was revived in 1965 with the creation of the London borough, which referred to the settlements east of the walls and west of the River Lea. But nowadays the East End seems to include not only Hackney, Newham, Redbridge, Barking and Dagenham, but much of urbanized Essex as well. It once seemed odd to hear news broadcasters referring to Romford as east London. As a child, that was the market town where I was taken as a treat to watch the cattle being auctioned. But claims to being from the East End now come from people as far apart as those who live in the shadow of the Tower itself and Essex cockneys right out in Southend – the result, no doubt, of all those families, like my own, that moved out to the new housing estates in the post-war slum clearances. Because of this self-definition of being cockney, the book is concerned with the areas covered by Tower Hamlets and Newham, staying north of the river, but also 'leaking' from within the boundaries of those boroughs northwards through Hackney, out to the easterly boroughs of Greater London, and, of course, through into Essex.

With its predominantly, though certainly never exclusively, working-class population, swelled by more or less exotic immigrants from both home and abroad, the East End has often alarmed its far more prosperous and highly regulated neighbours in the City of London, and the West End beyond, with its apparently ungovernable, ever-expanding sprawl nudging at the walls. A consequence of its seemingly limitless power to attract consecutive waves of newcomers has been that its history is also the story of an ever-changing series of communities. Cheap housing, the anonymity of the slums and, in its foul-stinking prime, its diverse opportunities for work (both legal and criminal) have combined to make it an area ripe to take the blame for all manner of ills. Not only has it been the focus of moral panics – being held responsible for everything from unbridled criminality to the very destruction of the British way of life – but the most recently arrived have found themselves the targets of such blame. Indictments have come both from outsiders looking in, who see nothing but the threatening stare of the poor, condemned to a life of squalor and immorality in the ghetto, and also from those already established in the area; those who were from immigrant families themselves, now taking the first opportunity to flee what they come to perceive as threatening, foreign, shameful even, leaving what was once their own place of sanctuary, the community which welcomed them. It is salutary to remember that people often believe this perceived danger – of the most recent newcomers taking away or spoiling *their* culture – to be a recent phenomenon pertaining only to them. But whether considering the earliest settlers from Europe, the desperate poor from rural England, or the Bengali, Somali, Eastern European and other new arrivals of the 1990s, immigrants have continued to be attracted to the great port of London, to the capital of what was once the British Empire, and have proceeded to band together to establish places to work, eat and worship. They may have different concerns in some ways, but they still share the need to survive, the desires and aspirations, the hopes and fears, that have to be a constant if we are to describe a society as human.

That is what makes this a living history. Yes, there are the crossing sweepers, the mudlarks and the flower-girls, the music halls and the mayhem, Jack the Ripper and the workhouse, but, more importantly, there is the present – a present made by that past. This is the oral history, the voices of which communities are made, the voices that speak to us, to each other, and which stop us being alone; the voices that can give meaning to our lives and all that we experience.

I can remember, when I was about eight, the shame of having the toes cut out of my shoes when I grew out of them and sulking because I couldn't have new ones. When, as an adult, I told my dad how I had not understood that there was no money for new ones, he told me about being made to wear clogs to school. He had hidden at playtime so the other children wouldn't see him and had preferred to walk home barefoot rather than be spotted wearing what was, for him, such humiliating footwear. But he then told me of a boy far worse off than him who had had to wear his mother's old lisle stockings under his ill-fitting boots. What other deprivations had he and his generation had to endure in their far harsher, less flexible world? This was a world where men queued on the stones in the despondent hope of getting a half-day's casual work at the docks, and women stretched their meagre budgets to feed their husband, then their children, and went without themselves; a world without the benefit of a welfare net – however inadequate – to stop you sliding off the edge and into desperation.

Now, as one millennium closes and another opens before us, the *idea* of the community we once had has come to be cherished as a nostalgic haven, a mythic projection of our longings. We look back and see a warm, cosy place where we were all once safe, where everybody shared and where we sorted out local wrongdoers with a fair, if rough, sort of justice – much the same place that we longed for when we watched the black and white, but sunshine-filled, Ealing comedies in the austerity numbed, Utility-clothed post-war years. But representations of this highly desirable location carry, of course, a great deal of ideological baggage, and 'community' has become a particularly slippery and politically loaded concept, employed by spin doctors and analysts from both the left and the right. For the right, there is the village with its warm beer and maiden ladies on bicycles; for the left, the glories of social housing and nurseries for all. While acknowledging the importance of the past in enabling us to construct meanings and desires within the present (a theme I have explored in *Pull No More Bines*, my book about hop-picking as a vanished way of life), I also wanted to question some of the myths, because as actual, physical communities – as opposed to a nostalgic fantasy land – are forced to change for a combination of social, cultural, economic and political reasons, no one has quite put their finger on what these changes mean in practice to those who live within them or those who choose to leave them. By looking at the changing history of east London, I hope that is what this book will do.

Like the woman speaking below, my family moved from the East End to a housing estate in Essex when I was a schoolgirl.

> I hadn't started school, so I must have been about four. I was sitting on the damp, warm ridges of a wooden draining board, swinging my legs, in a big, low-ceilinged room, listening to the sound of women talking and laughing over the din of them doing the weekly laundry. It was the communal wash house under my nan's buildings, the big block of flats where she lived. All the women had cross-over aprons on and their sleeves rolled up above their elbows. My nan probably had her slippers on, she usually did, and her stockings rolled down to her knees. It must have been hard work, when you think of it – they were scrubbing collars and cuffs on their rubbing boards, their hands all chapped red from the hot, sudsy water in the big butler sinks round the room. All that wringing and rinsing and mangling. Pulling all those heavy sheets and towels and napkins dripping wet out of the boilers. But, like I say, they were laughing, talking. They knew one another. They were friends, part of the neighbourhood. Probably related, a lot of them. Families

lived close to one another then. I don't know where my mum
was, she must have had to go out somewhere. But I was all
right, I was with my nan. And all the old girls made a fuss of
me. It was good. Why I'm telling you this is, the difference
when we moved to our new place. My mum, who had always
done her washing the same way as Nan, now had a nice new
kitchen. A Formica-covered sink unit and an Ascot water
heater, and a twin-tub washing machine that had the washer
and a spin-dryer attached. It must have been so much easier
doing the washing and keeping things clean, but I know my
mum was never happy there. It was lonely, you see. There
was no one to have a laugh with, no one to mind me if she
had to go out. She didn't know her neighbours and she
certainly never had her mum a couple of turnings away.
What I'm saying is, I know the house was a lot better than
where we'd lived in Poplar, which, to be honest, was no
better than a slum when you think of it, but we lost a lot
moving away from there. She was never happy. Never really
settled. It was never her home. Not like the East End was.

I understand what she means, as my own mum never really liked
Dagenham. One day, I was on a playing field near our new house
and I saw, high overhead, a plane trailing a banner declaring 'You
never had it so good', a message from the then Prime Minister,
Harold Macmillan, trumpeting the post-war affluence we were all
meant to be enjoying. But was it true? Were our mothers in their
Formica-clad kitchens really better off than their mothers 'up home'
with their scrubbing boards? I have spoken to East Enders of all ages
to find out and present here the stories of those so-called ordinary
people, the stories of those who helped create the geographical and
intangible place which we know as the East End, which I hope will
correct the idea that it is little more than a place of deprivation and
poverty. Because it isn't. It is a place of great and varied riches:
courage, warmth, strength, anger, humour and rebellion. I have
attempted, in my sifting and sorting of this complex and very human
story, to achieve some level of objectivity, but it is a history of which,
with my mongrel, English, Irish, Scottish, Welsh, Jewish, East End

background, I am very much a part, so it is as much about me and mine as it is about you and yours, them and theirs. And that history continues to be made, with cockneys starring in it as part of a strong, saucy, wild, often difficult continuum in which I am proud to play my part by telling some of its tales.

The first of which has been defined as liquid history, as it begins with the River Thames.

PART 1

The Makings of the East End

The Thames is liquid history.
John Burns (1858–1943)

The place that would become London, the centre of world trade and the pinnacle of the greatest empire ever seen, has been populated since the Ice Age, when people scavenged a living in the Thames valley. The river was far broader and shallower then than it is today and, without its artificial banks and walls, was more like a lake dotted with small islands.

The early settlers found plenty of clean drinking water, which came from rainfall filtering through the gravel subsoil and then, after being trapped by the base of London clay, eventually resurfacing on lower ground, forming brooks, streams and springs. Several of these springs have recently been discovered in the new Mile End Park. As well as water, there were plentiful sources of food, fodder and materials for building homes and fences, and for weaving baskets and fish-traps, all to be found by the river, among the rushes and sedge of its bank-side marshes, in its lush, grassy meadows and in the surrounding broad-leafed woodlands, all making it a desirable place in which the early farmers decided to settle.

Centuries later, in 54 BC, when Julius Caesar crossed the Thames on his way to do battle with the British tribal leader Cassivellaunus, it is recorded that he encountered settlements throughout what is now Greater London, and that, in AD 43, when the Roman invasion finally occurred, under Claudius, there were around 5,000 inhabitants scattered throughout the area. But it is still accepted that the kernel of the London we know today, and what would eventually become the largest town in Roman Britain, was established by the invaders in around AD 50, although their first attempts to create a Thames-side settlement were destroyed by Boudicca's avenging army in AD 60.

The port rapidly developed as a centre of commerce and trade, with slaves and commodities being shipped to and from the rest of the Roman Empire. By AD 100, Londinium had a population of around 45,000, and had replaced Colchester as the capital of the Empire's most northerly province.

The farms and hamlets to the east of the city's defensive walls provided food and services for the Roman metropolis, but, with trouble brewing in other parts of the Empire, the occupying population began to decrease and, in A D 410, the Romans finally abandoned London altogether.

The tribal Britons, who had lived alongside the invaders for 400 years, were now facing invasion from Germanic tribes, the Angles, Saxons and Jutes, who took advantage of the soft, almost undefended target. Despite the signal towers on the Thames to warn of their approach, A D 457 saw the Saxon victory in Kent just across the river. This marked the beginning of another period of foreign occupation.

These new arrivals seemed, at first, concerned more with cultivation than with administration, clearing much of the forested areas in what is now Newham and farming land right up to the Roman wall, but, as the raids continued, their numbers increased.

During the fifth and sixth centuries the Saxons and native Britons were locked in battle over land ownership, with the Britons generally coming off worst. New kingdoms were established by the victors, including Essex – the kingdom of the East Saxons – which had London within its boundaries.

By A D 600 around half of all Britain was under Saxon rule, and an Anglo-Saxon culture was evolving, and with it the Germanic language of Englisc. The new Saxon population revived the abandoned city, establishing a trading settlement known as Lundenwic, and returning it to prominence as a base of political power within occupied Britain. A bishopric was also founded, the head of which would have authority as the manorial lord over almost the entire district to the east, the area which would eventually become the East End of London.

It was also at this time, almost 600 years after the Roman occupation, that the creation of the Saxon settlement of Stebenhythe or Stibenhede – covering most of what is now Stepney, Poplar and Bethnal Green – saw the area becoming increasingly populous, and indentifiable signs of the East End's future characteristics came into existence. Trade and manufacture began to flourish alongside the traditional activities of fishing and farming, and, with the prevailing eastward winds blowing any unpleasant smells downstream towards the estuary, the ruling patricians were happy to live upwind of the so-called stink industries, such as the slaughterhouses of Stratford, which were to rise to prominence after 1371, when the messy and smelly business of medieval slaughtering was banned from within the city walls. Other businesses, such as metalworking, brewing and leather trades, were joined over the centuries by a whole variety of crafts and activities which were unwelcome further west. Still today, if the wind is blowing in the wrong direction, the stench from works close to the river can be detected from as far east as the Millennium Dome, and most local people who have worked in or around Carpenter's Road, Stratford, will wrinkle their noses in recollection of its own, special pungency.

London's fortunes prospered throughout the next two centuries, and Bede could describe the eighth-century port of Lundenwic as an important centre of international trade. But battles between the Saxon leaders saw London again being left vulnerable to attack. By the last quarter of the ninth century, the Danish were occupying the city.

The English king Alfred, who in 871 inherited the kingdom of Wessex, engaged in a series of attacks on the Danes which culminated in his taking London. In a settlement with the Danish leader, he declared the area to the east – the present-day East End – to be under the control of the Danes.

The Scandinavian presence had considerable influence on trade and politics, and in 1016 a Dane, Cnut, was crowned king of all England. On the death of his sons, however, the English king, Edward the Confessor, returned in 1042 to take the throne, and the invaders' power ended. Once again London became the most important town in England, a position strengthened by the building of the abbey and royal palace at Westminster. But it was not until the coming of another wave of invaders that the next major change would occur in the East End.

When Edward died, in 1066, there were three claimants to the English throne; William of Normandy, of course, was victorious.

Not only did William the Conqueror build one of his impressive castles to the east of the city walls – the White Tower, which would later form the heart of the Tower of London – but Stepney, including in this period what is now Hackney, became the most important manor of the Bishop of London, an office which made the holder a man of national consequence. The people who lived in the hamlets beyond the wall found themselves the feudal tenants of their new episcopal lord, although they still owed military loyalty to the Tower, hence the name Tower Hamlets – an obligation retained until the nineteenth century.

By 1086, the time of the Domesday survey, the hamlet dwellers were occupied in providing food, fodder, fuel and building materials for the bishop's manor, much of it from the great forest between Hackney and Tower Hamlets, and even creating sufficient surplus to sell for the profit of their master.

Further east, the Normans had taken an interest in the land between the forded rivers Lea and Roding, giving it the name of Hame, which would later become the separate communities of East and West Ham. The River Lea, important as a power source for the mills of Bromley and Stratford, and as a navigable route linking Hertfordshire with the Thames, was also prized for what its marshy riverside lands could yield to the city and the bishop's estate.

In the early twelfth century, by the reign of Henry I, the settlements at Bromley and Bow experienced further expansion linked to the building of Bow Bridge. This opened it up as the major route through to the eastern parts of the country. But although industry was expanding, with milling and cloth fulling, baking and dyeing, the landscape was still one of river-side meadows, where boats passed grazing cows and roaming sheep.

During the next 400 years, medieval London rose to prominence as one of the most powerful cities in Europe, prospering culturally, economically and politically. Parallel to this transformation, of a place that had once been distinguished merely for providing an easy river-crossing into a major capital, were the changes taking place further east. With the increasingly hotchpotch development outside the safety and commercial protectionism of the city walls, what would one day be the East End continued along its own path of commercial development, the ongoing process of land drainage and clearance providing space for housing and workshops alongside the still-important business of agriculture.

Whitechapel became an early example of ribbon development, with the tiny hamlet expanding to service passing travellers in and out of London. By 1250, it would be sufficiently affluent to begin work on its eponymous chapel and, by 1338, its traders and craftsmen were worshipping within a parish in its own right.

Further east still, development continued at a more gentle if no less successful pace. The monks of the Abbey of St Mary, Stratford Langthorne, who had begun farming the land in the West Ham area in the twelfth century, had managed, over the course of 300 years, to swell the abbey's wealth until a large part of what is now Newham was under its authority.

Other religious houses also prospered. The Abbey of St Clare, familiarly called the Minories, a corruption of the name Sorores Minores – Little Sisters – by which the Franciscan nuns were known, whose estate almost butted on to the city walls, were gifted with many endowments and lands, and, although they took a personal vow of poverty, they became the richest order in all England.

The lack of restriction in this comparatively free eastern sector did not apply only to locals; there was also the opportunity for newcomers to settle and ply their trades close to the all-important river. These immigrants were of a rather more peaceable kind than the earlier invaders, often bringing with them new skills and trades, as well as making a willing addition to the labour force. They came as workers in the cloth and other craft industries; as merchants to trade; and as financiers to deal with the City.

This latter group were Jewish and had originally been encouraged by the Norman rulers as, unlike Christians, they were permitted to act as moneylenders. This, along with the taxes levied on them, did much to bolster the depleted royal exchequer. Yet, despite their usefulness, they still faced, as would generations of immigrants after them, constraints and prohibitions under which they were obliged to live and work. Although London never had a formalized ghetto as such, the Jewish newcomers were unable to own land in their own right, nor were they able to bear arms. Being visibly different in clothing and customs, they were easily targeted and experienced hostility which at times escalated into mob violence. There were those jealous of their financial success, angered by the rates they charged for their services or simply vexed by their supposedly favoured position. If any preferential treatment did ever exist, it rapidly disappeared once the Jews had been bled almost dry of their assets. Their usefulness at an end, they were finally expelled from the country by Edward I in 1290.

Prejudice against newcomers was not new, was not restricted to anti-Semites and was not exclusive to the thirteenth century. Leff and Blunden quote an eighteenth-century East London clergyman's opinion of recently arrived Protestant Huguenots:

This set of rabble are the very offal and beggary from which they fled, and are to be fattened on what belongs to the poor of our own land and to grow rich at our expense.

And, a century after that, there was widespread fear that the 1851 Great Exhibition's promotion of free trade with the world would result in 'floods of aliens' swamping the capital.

But, whatever the welcome, there are always newcomers eager to take opportunities in new lands, and the place of the expelled Jews was not left vacant for long as financiers from Lombardy – remembered today in Lombard Street in the financial sector of the City of London – rapidly took over as the principal moneylenders of the time.

Other peaceful arrivals also came to London: some as a result of royal or political allegiances, some because of imperial influence or command, but most because they were attracted by the trading and commercial opportunities in a city with an ever-widening sphere of influence.

German merchants were to become a group of particular consequence in medieval England, rising to great influence through the Hanseatic League, a unified trading consortium. This gave them, among all foreign traders, dominance in the highly valuable wool business, which, during the medieval period, was largely responsible for the capital's thriving economy.

This massive increase in commercial activity was, however, not being matched by a growth in the pool of available labour. The East End, which would one day provide the major share of the labour force to work for their wealthier neighbours to the west, was still a very mixed community, with the working poor living alongside the likes of the eldest son of Edward III, the Black Prince himself, in his great palace at Poplar. Then, with the depletion of the population following a wave of epidemics, particularly the terrible Black Death, labour was at a real premium.

This novelty of being in such high demand saw those who survived the contagion questioning their traditional lot as goods owned by their lords. The disquiet grew and, when the king levied a poll tax to pay for the wars in France, dissatisfaction boiled over, encouraged by the likes of John Ball, one of the so-called hedge priests. His famous cry,

> When Adam delved and Eve span,
> Who was then the gentleman?

echoed round the land as Ball, and like-minded priests, spread their message of equality and resistance. It was in Kent that Wat Tyler heard a speaker declare that freedom would come only if people took it, and it was up to them to refuse the tax collectors who threatened them with penalties and punishments.

When Tyler's wife was the target of such a threat, he decided to take the priest's advice. He gathered a crowd and led them to Maidstone Castle, where they freed John Ball and the others being held for their subversive sermons. They then headed for London. It was June 1381 and the Peasants' Revolt, commemorated to this day in a mural at Mile End, had begun.

The word spread and many thousands joined them, all with the shared intention of pleading with the new king, Richard II, to put an end to the impossibly high taxes and to their exploitation by the lords and nobles.

The rebels pitched camp on Mile End Waste, close to the site of the old Mann, Crossmann and Paulin Brewery, and waited. Richard, then a fourteen-year-old boy, eventually rode from the Tower to meet the rebels' leaders: Wat Tyler, Jack Straw and John Ball.

Over the next few days negotiations were attempted, but the crowd was still inflamed and the clash which followed resulted in the deaths of Wat Tyler and other rebels. But the rebellion was a success in that the poll tax was abolished and the people discovered that even lowly peasants, if they banded together, could take over the streets of London itself. It was a lesson learned, and remembered, by both commoners and lords alike.

The reputation for rebelliousness among those outside the authority of the City was further enhanced in later years by the cockney taste for rowdy, popular entertainments, and in the area's accommodation of wanton playhouses and brothels, but it was a reputation that was not always justified. In reality, the history of the East End has been one less often of anarchy than of hardship and struggle, in which filling empty bellies and finding shelter for the night took easy precedence over insurgence.

The Thames, having played a leading role in the creation of the capital city and the birth of its eastern suburbs, continued to influence developments in the hamlets downstream from the Tower. By the mid-sixteenth century, increasing industry on the river contributed to the emergence of Ratcliff, Limehouse, Wapping and Blackwall as significant centres of ship-building, and, as complementary trades and services evolved, more traditional waterside occupations such as milling and fishing began to wane in importance.

Although it had originally been Stepney, with its port at Ratcliff, which was predominant among the riverside hamlets, when the newly founded East India Company – a commercial enterprise, chartered in 1600 by Queen Elizabeth, which was to form the germ of the British Empire – dug its ship-building dock at Blackwall Yard, nowhere else in the East End, for the next hundred or so years, would be so closely identified with trade on the river as Poplar-and-Blackwall, the most distant of the hamlets from the City. Here, all life revolved around the East India Company: school, work, worship, homes and even, towards the end of the employees' lives, the company's own almshouses.

Incongruously, the East End was gradually emerging as a focus of massive international trade. At this time, however, it was still only an embryonic version of the predominantly urban character with which east London would become totally identified during the coming upheavals of Empire and the Industrial Revolution.

The still-essentially agricultural nature of the majority of the area was reflected in the records of crimes committed, such as theft of wheat and crop damage, although, with the increasing prosperity coming from the new industries on the Thames, opportunities were beginning to present themselves for more urban categories of crime.

Pickpockets, and the more violent footpads, robbed unwary passers-by in early instances of what we would now call street crime or muggings, part of the illicit way of life, of both truth and legend, which would become inextricably linked with the East End. But crime will always be a risk, where the desperate or the immoral are in proximity to rich pickings, and the choice cargoes on the river certainly provided those.

Piracy, thievery and, consequently, the gallows became almost commonplace and, in 1798, the river police – now known as Thames Division, the oldest civilian police force in the world – was created specifically to deal with everything from petty pilfering to major theft on the water.

The incidence of crime on the Thames was exacerbated by the vulnerability of the cargoes, which were held on board ship in the middle of the river, sometimes for weeks on end, until they were unloaded on to lighters and then ferried over to the unsecured quays, all giving plenty of scope for the criminally inclined to help themselves. Eventually, the West India Company had enough; their Caribbean shipments were far too precious and, in 1802, they opened their own secure dock. With the novelty of the ease and security which this accorded, other companies soon followed suit and numerous docks appeared along the riverside. The blind, forbidding walls, rising massively above the sea of crowded streets, alleyways and courts, became a familiar part of the East End landscape, which would be changed only by the terrible destruction of the Second World War, and would finally disappear with the transformation of the docks into Docklands.

It wasn't exclusively the river which brought change and prosperity; having the wealthy city dwellers and merchants as their close neighbours, the poorer people of the hamlets had a ready-made market for the goods and services they could provide. But the story of the East End, as the working-class, slum-ridden, overcrowded, industrialized quarter of London, is as closely linked to the upheavals following the Reformation and the dissolution of the monasteries as it is to the river or to the development of trade and industry.

The power of the early Church and the wealth of the monastic estates that had thrived beyond the city walls had been barriers to any further eastward spread of the capital. The situation altered radically with Henry VIII's dissolution of the monasteries and nunneries in the 1530s, when his confiscation and selling off of Church lands both helped fill the crown's coffers and opened the way for changes in land use and ownership and, subsequently, for much opportunistic redevelopment outside the jurisdiction of the City authorities.

Happening at a time when the population of London had increased from around 50,000 to somewhere in the region of 200,000 people – partly caused by recovery after the famines and plagues that had so depleted earlier generations, but also by Henry's encouragement of selective European immigration as an aid to the development of industrial techniques and skills – the opportunity was pounced upon.

Sold off by the crown, the eastern approaches to the City underwent a revolution in land use. Urbanization and overcrowding of the area had begun, the negative effects of which, as always, being worst for the poorest inhabitants. The poor were already suffering from the disappearance of the monasteries and nunneries, as the alms and medical help traditionally provided by the religious orders also disappeared. Only St Katharine's by the Tower, an order long benefiting from royal protection, was permitted to survive and to continue with its charitable works.

Descriptions of this remarkable process of change are vividly chronicled in his *Survey of London* by John Stow, a man who spent all his life (1525–1605) in Aldgate. Although he approved of the increasing prosperity which he observed, he wrote about many of the changes with obvious apprehension.

From having boyhood memories of being sent for milk to Goodman's Field – Goodman being a Tudor dairy farmer, still remembered today in various building and place names around Whitechapel – and of walks through green pastures, Stow watched as the Tower Hamlets were transformed. By the end of his life, many of those fields had been supplanted by streets and houses.

The potential for expansion was still blocked to the west by the boundaries of the City, to the south by the river, and by non-monastic farms, nursery gardens and estates to the north, but could now proceed towards the east without hindrance. The road from Essex, leading across Bow Bridge and linking Whitechapel to Aldgate, had long been where town met country, but it was paved over in 1542, just two years after the final abbey fell to the crown; the drovers no longer steered their animals to slaughter through a country lane past fields and meadows but along a bustling High Street, past crowded coaching inns, thriving tradesmen and the elegant homes of wealthy merchants.

Alongside the burgeoning river- and ship-related enterprises, and the businesses set up to service the needs and demands of the wealthy, the nuisance trades, or stink industries, were flourishing. The prevailing winds were now giving the cockneys' neighbours to the more salubrious west the added advantage of remaining upwind of the stench of not only metalworks and slaughterhouses but increasing numbers of breweries, gunworks, tanneries, lime kilns, glue, soap and candle works, and the rest of the disagreeable or dangerous trades, whose reek and polluting fumes were now wafting downstream towards the estuary.

The subsequent pressure on housing, to hold this growing working population, was met, in the rapidly developing Whitechapel, by the building of what was described most disparagingly by Stow as no more than a shanty town. But still the area was home to a social mix of rich and poor, and just about every other social level in between, in a way that is hardly conceivable when the Victorian East End is conjured in the imagination.

Stow considered the details of these developments in the Tower Hamlets, observing how, during his lifetime, the rural was so quickly becoming urban. The rapidity of change would nowadays, perhaps, seem almost leisurely, but in those days must have seemed astonishing. In his 1908 introduction to the *Survey*, Charles Lethbridge Kingsford neatly sums up the impact of this moment in history by saying that the author was witnessing 'the passing of medievalism and the birth of the modern capital'.

Stow cites a petition to Queen Elizabeth which points to the overcrowded East End as not only a potential health hazard for its better-off neighbours but a threat to the queen herself. This led to a royal order for the limitation of building there, but the result was contradictory in that more people simply squeezed into less space, making the housing even more overcrowded and insanitary than ever.

Not only were housing conditions unhealthily unpleasant, the streets, waterways and workplaces were contaminated with waste and by-products of both people and their trades. Yet Samuel Pepys could still write, well into the seventeenth century, of enjoying visits to a pastoral east London, with friendly inns near the Lea, and of his pleasure at being the guest of his friend Sir William Rider at his mansion, Bethnal House, in Bethnal Green. It was to Rider's home that Pepys escaped with his most-valued possessions, including his diary, during the Great Fire of London in 1666.

It was not until the effects and demands of the Industrial Revolution that the spread of the slums would result in the East End coming to resemble nothing less than a squalid hell, where people did what they could, or had to, to get by. That would not be experienced in all its wretchedness for several generations, but the embryonic pattern that had first emerged centuries earlier was now set, and would last for centuries: finance would be the business of the City; government and the retailing of luxury goods would be centred in the west; and the manufacturing, processing and finishing trades, in all their unpleasantness and with all their concomitant dangers, would be sited in the industrial quarter of the east.

Towards the end of the sixteenth century, a lingering agricultural depression, affecting much of rural England, resulted in an influx of desperate farm workers flooding into London's East End, seeking employment. As well as these domestic newcomers, there were increasing numbers of immigrants from overseas. A survey carried out for Queen Elizabeth in 1571, when the population of the whole of London was estimated at just 80–90,000 people, put the numbers of foreigners living in Stepney alone at around 700.

The petitioners of the queen, concerned about the potential problems of overcrowding, had been right and, regardless of matters of safety and comfort, the proximity of so many people meant that diseases could more easily spiral into epidemic proportions.

By the second half of the seventeenth century, the situation was becoming critical and, when the Great Plague took hold, almost 100,000 Londoners died during the terrible winter of 1664–5, when even the extreme cold, which froze the Thames, did not kill the contagion. Plague hospitals – the dreaded pest houses – were built, including one in Stepney, but even these were soon filled.

Spring and early summer saw unusually high temperatures and the death rate soared. Those who were able to, abandoned London for what they hoped was the safety of the countryside. Servants left behind by their masters survived by looting, or found work driving the carts full of dead to the plague pits which had been dug beyond the city limits – just as they had been during the Black Death of the fourteenth century, and in Roman times before that.

If plague was discovered in a household, all present were locked inside for forty days, during which time they would either die or survive to eventually emerge from their enforced quarantine. With the exceptionally hot weather and the standards of seventeenth-century hygiene, it is hard to imagine how anyone survived.

Towards the end of 1665, the death rate finally dipped and, despite the appalling stench of putrefaction – the promise that all communal burial sites would be limed was never fulfilled – the situation was deemed sufficiently safe for the court to return to St James's.

The population of the East End, having mostly escaped the devastations of the Great Fire of 1666, began to recover and, by 1700, the residents of Stepney – the parish which now included Mile End Old and New Towns, Spitalfields, Poplar, Bethnal Green, Bow, Limehouse and Ratcliff – numbered in the region of 50,000 people.

Accommodation for the labouring classes was more scarce than ever. Marshland, previously considered uninhabitable, was drained and built upon, some of it, even in this period, with fine homes for wealthy merchants and ship owners, but housing for the increasing ranks of workers was the growth area.

There were little, if any, controls and no overall plan, as cheap, insanitary workers' housing, with no separation between industrial and residential use, was hurriedly erected as the demand grew and profits rose. The birth of what would eventually become known in the nineteenth century as the 'City of Dreadful Night' had happened.

From a population of less than 100,000 in the mid-sixteenth century, the suburbs east of the City had, in a little over 100 years, grown to approximately a quarter of a million, with many of the communities now of sufficient stature to warrant the building of their own neighbourhood churches. But there were still pockets of the East End relatively untouched by urban development. Even the very heart of the East End could, up until the eighteenth century, boast a fine nursery, noted for the excellence of its fruits, sited behind the lively Whitechapel High Street, on land bounded by what are now Old Montague Street, Brick Lane and Greatorex Street. There was also an impressive windmill and a ducking pond close to Brady Street, a facility which was apparently in 'much request for curing shrewish wives, drunkards and other obnoxious persons'; and the country path leading to the hospital of St Mary's in Spitalfields was still referred to as Hog Lane.

The capital continued to prosper, bolstered by the growth of English sea power and international commerce. Skilled craft workers, both local and foreign, were tempted to the capital by the new opportunities, with the busy port providing the point of entry for many. There were no restrictions on where the arrivals might live, but rules which operated in the City, with its strict guild system, meant the newcomers usually chose to settle outside the walls.

The Sephardic Jews elected to reside in Spitalfields, and also in the smart new developments around Goodman's Fields and Mansell Street in Whitechapel. Here they dwelt alongside the German community, one of the oldest immigrant groups in London, who had lived close to the Thames from the earliest times. The Germans had, supposedly, been expelled from the country by Elizabeth I, but during James I's reign immediately after there were still an estimated 4,000 Germans in London alone.

The descendants of the original Jewish settlers had been driven out, in their case successfully, by Edward I in 1290. They were, however, encouraged to return by Cromwell for the financial services they could provide. This invitation, contrasting with the intolerance they were experiencing in Spain and Portugal, saw many Sephardic Jews coming to England during the period of the Commonwealth.

The London community established their first place of worship since their thirteenth-century banishment close to the City boundary in a house in Cree Church Lane in December 1656, and their own cemetery – the Bethahaim Velho – behind what is now 243 Mile End Road in 1657. According to the 1695 census list, forty-one years after Cromwell's death there were approximately 600 Jews living in the east London parishes.

Soon after the arrival of the first Sephardim, Ashkenazi Jews, from central and eastern Europe, also began arriving in London. On the whole, they were less affluent and sophisticated than their Sephardic co-religionists and, rather than conducting financial business, they took up small-scale manufacturing and street trading, establishing a lively and growing community around Petticoat Lane, an area which became well known for the second-hand clothing trade, which they dominated.

By the end of the seventeenth century, the Ashkenazi community was of sufficient size to warrant its own place of worship, the Duke's Place Synagogue, and to have its own burial ground. But even this fast growth would seem negligible when compared with the two major moments of Jewish immigration in the nineteenth century.

*

Spitalfields did not attract only Jewish settlers; it was an area, along with Soho, favoured by the Huguenot silk weavers, who generally, at this time, prospered, although their fortunes were to fluctuate.

Silk weaving was established in the East End before their arrival, with both local and foreign craft workers involved in the trade, but it was with the arrival of the Huguenots that the district became renowned for the manufacture of fine silks and brocades.

These predominantly urban, French-speaking weavers were, like the Jewish newcomers, fleeing religious persecution, and, being Protestants, were attracted to London by Henry VIII's split from Rome.

The Huguenots assimilated comparatively quickly. Such was the extent of their intermarriage with the host community that many modern family-history researchers seeking their East End roots will find at least one Huguenot blood-line in their ancestry.

The French refugees continued to arrive – it was the Huguenots who introduced the word refugee into the English language. Some of them were well off, being master weavers with thriving businesses and grand lifestyles, but the exiles came from across the whole social spectrum. At the end of the seventeenth century, Mile End New Town was created – causing Mile End itself, a place with comparatively fine houses, to become known as Mile End Old Town – as a hamlet within Stepney to accommodate the poorer of the textile workers. The first of 650 homes were built around Greatorex Street.

Regardless of personal circumstances, the Spitalfields weavers became famed for their production of luxurious materials, elegant cravats and waistcoats, but the fashion for what were considered their superior talents made them unpopular with the established community of weavers, who resented the competition.

Huguenots did not confine themselves to the silk industry. They were renowned gold- and silversmiths, and excelled in areas as diverse as clock- and hat-making, bookbinding and wig-making, the manufacture of scientific instruments and other technological innovation. The flourishing economy of the seventeenth century, with its growing class of people able to afford and wanting high-quality goods and services, meant their skills were in great demand.

Not all were to excel as the Courtaulds, of the textile dynasty, had done, or the Dollonds, whose name is remembered in the Dollond and Aitchison optical business. Some who made less of an impression on their new country were eventually to suffer greatly.

As the weavers' skills became obsolete, in the face of advancing technology and competition from new factories in the north of England, there was a constantly growing pool of labour swollen by new immigrants, such as those from Ireland, all trying to survive in the now poverty-stricken East End, all prepared to work for lower wages. The once-sought-after weavers protested, their grievances spilling over into anger and eventual rioting, and they became, like so many immigrant groups before and after them during tough economic times, targets of threats and violence. The tragic result of one altercation was two men being sentenced to hang outside the Salmon and Ball pub in Bethnal Green.

But their influence on the East End had been great. Evidence of their transitory dominance can still be seen in their elegantly proportioned homes, designed to let in the maximum light for working on their handlooms, and one particular building, on the corner of Brick Lane and Fournier Street – itself a Huguenot name – is often cited as the physical embodiment of the waves of immigrants who have arrived in the East End, settled into a community and then left, making way for the next group.

Originally a Huguenot chapel, built by the French Protestants in 1743, the building was taken over in the 1790s by the London Society for Promoting Christianity amongst the Jews; ten years after that it was serving as a Methodist chapel, a use which continued for eighty years; then, in 1897, it was reconsecrated, this time as the Great Synagogue for the Machzike Hadath community of eastern European Jews, who had fled the pogroms and were now working in the sweated garment trades. In 1976 the building found yet another group of worshippers, this time in the local Bangladeshi community, who bought the building and restored it to become what is now known as the London Jamme Masjid, a religious focus in a lively neighbourhood of shops, restaurants and galleries.

It is not only buildings and names that were left by the Huguenots; there are continuing reminders of their passions and pastimes, such as their fondness for growing and displaying flowers and for keeping songbirds and pigeons. An article in *The Day of Rest, the Illustrated Journal of Sunday Reading* dated 15 August 1874 regretted that, with little interest coming from young people in learning how to use the weavers' traditional tools and methods:

London will remember her lost weavers only by the famous livestock market in Club Row – a market created by the love of all the French exiles for birds, dogs and pets of all kinds . . . [They] were all passionately fond of gardening, each having, if possible, a small garden – if only a patch of flowers – attached to his house. Another French attribute was noticeable, there being hardly one dwelling without its pigeon-house.

These traditions have lasted. George Bernard Shaw could write of the admired 'cockney art of carpet gardening', which he saw in the Victoria Park of his time, and today pigeon lofts, aviaries and colourful, neatly planted back gardens can still be seen around the housing estates which are now home to many east Londoners. But the majority of cockneys were to remain in the East End for a few more generations yet.

By the beginning of the eighteenth century, London, with its growing class of wealthy financiers and industrialists, was entering a period of massive economic expansion. Trade trebled in volume and the capital had become the busiest port in the world.

Housing developments for the rich in London's West End meant a demand in the luxury market for fashionable fittings, decorating and furnishings. There was some filtering down of wealth to specialist tradespeople and suppliers of the most exclusive goods, but the poorest experienced no such benefit and continued to suffer. As the population nearly doubled, rising from approximately 490,000 in 1700 to 950,000 in 1800, overcrowding and subsequent public health problems were now permanent features of their lives.

Some efforts were made to improve conditions, with measures such as better sanitation and the hard-surfacing of roads with cobbles, but these were directed towards the more affluent homes, districts and main thoroughfares. Conditions in the meaner areas continued to be of the most base quality: streets were stinking, congested and noisy, with the marshy areas closest to the river being the most unhealthy and unpleasant of all.

Travellers along the eastern route out of the City would have experienced the foul congestion of all the traffic servicing the trades and businesses, the herds of abattoir-bound beasts leaving their filth behind them, and all the other dirt and pollution in this overcrowded quarter. In the midst of all the commotion and chaos, they would have seen the Whitechapel hay market.

In existence until 1928, the hay market continued to operate as a relic of a time when the alleys and courts which peeled off the High Street were still serving their original purpose as the yards of coaching inns and taverns. Despite the area's many poor residents, they did a thriving trade on the lively thoroughfare, with its many shops and houses and, according to Dickens's Sam Weller, its ranks of oyster stalls that fed the poor:

'It's a wery remarkable circumstance that poverty and oysters go together ... [there is] an oyster stall to every half-dozen houses. Blessed if I don't think that ven a man's wery poor, he rushes out of his lodgings and eats oysters in desperation.'

Whitechapel was also, at this time, beginning to earn itself a reputation for being the home of not just growing numbers of poor but also of less than desirable elements of society, who could disappear in the myriad lanes and turnings which lay behind its High Street façade.

By the Victorian period, Whitechapel had become notorious: a thieves' kitchen, a refuge of whores and a place of shameful public exhibition of 'freaks' such as the unfortunate John Merrick, the Elephant Man, and the other hapless souls exhibited in cheap sideshows.

During this spreading urbanization, Bethnal Green was promoted from the status of hamlet to being a parish in its own right. It was still an area with three virtually separate identities, divided as it was between market gardeners, continuing with their almost rustic way of life; forbidding tenements, in which resided the poorest weavers and workers without the resources to live elsewhere; and even the occasional enclave of wealth, hints of the locality's former glories. But, as with much else that happened in the industrial history of the East End, once it started, the growth of Bethnal Green was quick and largely indiscriminate. By the end of the century it had taken on yet another identity, that of a district blighted not only by overcrowded slums and poverty but by a criminal fraternity as bad as those of the rookeries around Petticoat Lane and Houndsditch.

Further east still, Bow and Bromley, with their proximity to the Lea and the open countryside of Essex, preserved their village natures well into the nineteenth century, although neither was devoid of industry, with some of the most notable trades being cloth fulling and dyeing, brewing and distilling.

Across the border of the River Lea in Essex, the land in Newham was, in the eighteenth century, predominantly put to agricultural use and was renowned for its fine market gardens. Outsiders who found their way there were usually itinerant labourers – often poverty-stricken agricultural workers from Ireland or the outer reaches of the impoverished Essex countryside, displaced by the introduction of the new agricultural machinery – looking for stop-gap, seasonal employment at harvest time, or other casual work that would earn them enough for a bed for the night and something to satisfy their hunger.

Back upriver, the Thames-side, as opposed to Lea-side, districts were expanding as the import and export trade centred on the Port of London intensified.

Port business was originally carried out above the Tower, with the only dock being the one belonging to the East India Company at Blackwall, and that was used solely for building and repairs. Ships discharged their goods, sometimes directly, though most often via lighters, on to the so-called legal quays, but the escalating size and volume of traffic, and the lack of security on the river, made it necessary to create more adequate, and secure, facilities further downstream to the east.

Security problems had become so grave that the annual 'losses' to crime in the late eighteenth century were thought to amount to over half a million pounds. This is an almost unbelievable amount when translated into today's terms, but not so surprising when a conservative estimate suggests that upwards of a third of all workers on the river were operating as thieves or fencing stolen goods.

The West India, opened in 1802, was London's first trading dock.

It was soon expanded into the West India Import and Export Docks and the Millwall Docks, for the handling and processing of timber, sugar, fruits, rum and grains.

Next to open were the London Docks at Wapping in 1805. With their deep-water basins, secure walls and massive warehouses, a wide variety of cargo could be handled there, including wines and Guinness, dried fruits, drugs, spices and ivory.

St Katharine's Dock, the dock closest to the City, was opened in 1828, with the Royal Foundation of St Katharine's precinct being razed to the ground and the order moved out to Regent's Park. This was the order which, through its unique protection of the queens of England, had actually survived Henry VIII's dissolution of the monasteries, but it was powerless in the face of the march of trade and commerce. Much of the most valuable cargoes, including teas and essential oils, were handled at St Katharine's, being brought up by barge from the lower docks.

As these new enterprises flourished they were quickly followed by developments in the East India Dock and by the Royals group. With their associated warehouse complexes, roads and canals, they formed a chain along both banks of the river, from the Tower right down to Blackwall and beyond. Then, in 1886, downstream on the Essex marshes, twenty-six miles from Tower Bridge, the Tilbury Docks were opened, with little hint of what an important, even devastating, role they would play in the lives of the dockland community in the second half of the next century.

With their precious stores of spices, silks and other luxury goods, gleaned from the far reaches of the Empire, the docks were built with as much thought for security as the great Tower itself had been back in the time of the Conqueror, though it was now almost overshadowed by its parvenu neighbours.

The buildings were a symbol of the prosperity of the few; for the poor they were a presence of wealth that was literally so near yet so very far away.

In *London Labour and the London Poor*, Henry Mayhew describes the docks of the 1850s as being the 'real hell', where men with 'sweaty faces dyed blue from the cargoes of indigo' and others 'coughing and spluttering as they stacked the yellow bins of sulphur and lead-coloured copper-ore' all battled to earn a living. He writes of the dark vaults that were the warehouses, where men inhaled 'fumes of wine, the fungus smell of dry rot, and the stench of hides', and of the coal-whippers, those who heaved the fuel, black with the choking dust 'from the roots of their hair to the tips of their finger-nails'.

As one coal-whipper told Mayhew:

'I have known the coal-dust to be that thick in a ship's hold that I've been unable to see my mate, though he was only two feet from me.'

Even with such working conditions, people were still prepared to fight one another for the opportunity of even half a day's casual labour. Life was brutal and often short for these workers, but trade prospered as the new docks brought more business into the port and to the associated trades and industries which serviced it. The economic and physical influence of the docks impacted ever deeper on the lives of the people of the East End.

It is difficult now to envisage the presence of the great fleets of ships packed so closely that a person could walk right across the river, moving from ship to ship as if on a bridge; and to imagine a time when the river was so busy it might take up to two months before a ship could discharge her cargo.

There was an irony that the communities which had grown up at the water's edge were now being ripped apart by the coming of the docks, as homes, shops and workplaces were swept away by the new developments. Then, with the coming of the roads, canals and railways to service them, the topography of East London was transformed for ever – another foreshadowing of the future, when communities would disappear with the closure of the docks. But for now they were the very lifeblood of the East End, and the labour and services needed to keep trade going – from stevedore to carpenter, from rat-catcher to brothel-keeper, from pawnbroker to rope-maker – were provided by the cockneys in their riverside parishes.

These were to earn themselves the reputation of being the most unpleasant and licentious of all the neighbourhoods east of the City, as the previously isolated hamlets took on the new roles dictated by the pressures of speculation, trade and Empire.

*

The East End which, at the opening of the eighteenth century, had been a series of discrete, semi-rural settlements, separated by open spaces, where comfortably-off residents and visitors strolled through meadows, admiring the wild flowers, before stopping for a drink at a pleasant inn, had, at its close, been all but supplanted by a very different East End.

The labouring poor, with their daily grind of getting by in the best way they could in the overcrowded, vermin-ridden slums, packed into narrow, dung-slicked streets and foggy alleyways, all reeking of Dickensian deprivation, would leave far more of an impression on the popular imagination as defining images of the East End of London.

PART 2

Feeding the Imperial Powerhouse

Lines of imperial power have always flowed along rivers.
Simon Schama

3

With the financial and commercial dominance resulting from the Industrial Revolution, and with growing riches being accumulated from the expansion of Empire, London was experiencing a time of extraordinary boom. Urbanization was moving apace; growing numbers of immigrants were arriving from home and abroad; and, for some, there was unprecedented bounty.

Even at the beginning of the nineteenth century, some of the well-to-do individuals who were benefiting from these transitions were still living in the East End alongside the labouring classes, who had to either find some sort of work or rely on outdoor poor relief. But the social structure was changing and London was becoming the socially segregated place it largely remains today.

As the prosperous flourished on the tide of wealth washing in from the Empire, carried aboard the ships moored in the docks on the Thames, the poor suffered as they competed for the privilege of unloading the goods and raw materials ready for processing in the sweatshops and factories of the East End. The remaining ranks of the increasingly rich were now choosing to move out to join their peers in the wealthy enclaves further west, abandoning the East End to progressive exploitation, overcrowding and impoverishment.

With the pressure coming from rising numbers of domestic and foreign immigrants, most of whom gravitated towards the cheapest places to live, the East End was fast living up to its reputation as the 'City of Dreadful Night', described by James Thomson in his disturbing poem about the slums, and in the stark engravings of Gustave Doré. It was becoming a place fit only for paupers, criminals and the despondent. The American author Jack London, who wrote of this divergence of fortune, called those who suffered without benefiting from England's 'industrial supremacy' the 'ghetto folk'.

As well as this widening gap – both physical and financial – between rich and poor, industrialization and urbanization were having their own impact on traditional ways of living. Some changes were arguably for the better: mass-production meant that more people could afford the new, factory-made goods; and the political climate was such that centuries-old inequalities of opportunity, privilege and obligation were again being questioned – just as they had been at the time of the Peasants' Revolt. But, for the majority of the labouring classes, particularly the casuals, the negative effects of industrialization crushed any potential benefits underfoot. It was not solely the appalling living and working conditions – workers, whether urban or rural, had never exactly lived in fine style; it was the destruction of traditional communities, and the subsequent loss of family structures and customary patterns of life, which were to be of revolutionary significance. Freed from feudal-rooted tyrannies that had so ordered their lives, workers were now in thrall to the vagaries of the clock, and of the market, with its ever more powerful mechanism swallowing them up like so much anonymous fodder to be chewed on and discarded once the goodness had been consumed. As industrialization surged forwards, the very nature of work itself changed: having left homes where their families had been settled for generations, workers found themselves alone and competing with machinery, and not always successfully. As Thomas Carlyle wrote:

The shuttle drops from the fingers of the weaver, and falls into iron fingers that ply it faster.

The experience for many was of poor health, sickly children and insecurity – a brutal life. Edwin Chadwick, the health reformer, concluded in his 1842 report that the foul conditions in which people worked and lived produced

. . . a population short-lived, improvident, reckless and intemperate, and with habitual avidity for sensual gratification.

When nothing, except possibly hardship, was guaranteed for the poorer among the working classes, it is no wonder they sought some kind of gratification.

As manufacturing expanded, it was ever more dependent on factory-based production, and availability of work was, ironically, more unreliable than ever. Labour-intensive trades were unable to compete with the more cost-effective – in financial terms, at least – machine production, and larger workshops were being moved out to the provinces, where there were cheaper rents, space for expansion and lower fuel costs. These changes accelerated the decline of traditional East End trades such as leather-processing and heavy engineering, and added to the already grave problems being endured by workers such as the hand-loom weavers of the silk industry. But the change which probably had most impact on the area, because of the effect it had on its own workers, and also because of the ramifications for all the ancillary trades and services, was the virtual collapse in the 1860s of Thames ship-building.

The Poplar shipyards had witnessed a tremendous period of boom at the beginning of the decade, with those involved in the direct workforce rising from fewer than 15,000 in 1861 to almost 30,000 by 1865. But this good fortune was to prove transitory. The distance from essential coal and iron supplies meant that fixed costs were always high, and an economic crisis in 1866 saw the industry facing other problems. As a result, the first of the ship-building companies collapsed. This was to be the initial domino in a long line of others that would, by the beginning of the following year, result in 30,000 jobless in the immediate Poplar area alone, marking the start of the terminal decline of the London-based industry.

Those who were still employed found themselves vying with a greatly swollen pool of labour, as two other major East End occupations of the time – house and railway construction – were also caught by the downturn.

What employment there was was often casual and in noxious industries, with workers receiving inadequate wages in an environment which damaged their health and destroyed their spirit. But 1866 was to prove a bad time for reasons other than unemployment. That autumn, a cholera epidemic killed almost 4,000 East Enders and left many more sick and ailing. When the costs of treatment – such as it was – and of burial were added to the rocketing bread prices, the result of a disastrous harvest, the financial burden on people already close to pauperism was catastrophic. Then the winter of 1866–7 brought weather so severe that the remaining river trades were brought practically to a halt. Rising appeals for assistance saw the crisis spreading, as the financial pinch was felt by East End householders, who were liable, through the rates, to meet the costs of parish relief for the needy.

The Boards of Guardians, who ran the workhouses and decided on entitlement and the rate of relief, faced with these escalating demands, attempted to encourage any workhouse inmates who were reasonably able-bodied to take part in schemes to send them to the colonies; moving the problem elsewhere was a sure way of getting them 'off the parish'.

Men, women and children were shipped off, the majority to Canada, as cheap, unskilled labour. Most were never heard from again. The Guardians of East London were still not happy, however, as fewer than 1,000 individuals took up the places offered, leaving behind the vast majority still needing relief.

But there was one growth area in employment: as large-scale industry plummeted into serious decline, there was an opportunistic mopping up of those prepared to work in the sweated trades.

Sweating was a system of mass manufacture of cheap goods, which involved jobs being broken down into simple tasks, involving assembly or finishing of some kind, so that the cheapest, unskilled labour could be used. The Victorian invention of the sewing machine, the steam-powered sawmill and the band saw provided the means for middlemen – the sweaters – to supply their ill-paid workforce with supplies of garment and shoe parts, brush bristles and heads, card and paper for matchboxes and so on, which they would make up into finished products for the sweater to sell on to the wholesaler. This repetitive, labour-intensive production was carried out either in the workers' or in the sweaters' homes, typically in jam-packed, insanitary, ill-lit conditions, by a workforce which had little choice about whether the environment was acceptable.

Charities, philanthropists, social investigators and theorists, parliamentarians, popular novelists and thrill-seekers were all beginning to focus their attention on what was happening in east London. Drawn by stories of poverty and immorality, they looked into problems such as homelessness, but they also saw the place, with its inhabitants, as a problem in itself. In 1855, for instance, a Royal Commission, ostensibly concerned with housing and overcrowding, was most anxious about immorality among the poor, and its contribution to the ungovernable nature of the creatures evolving in the slums.

In *Culture and Anarchy* (1869), Matthew Arnold described the inhabitants of east London as 'those vast, miserable, unmanageable masses of sunken people', as if there was no helping them by effecting change, or no separating them as individual human beings.

There were observably disgraceful conditions in which people were expected to survive, but, for those observing, there was also the worrying presence of an insubordinate and unmanageable underclass – the 'roughs', the casual labouring poor, the itinerants – whose squalid lives were so alien and hideous that they might as well have been living in a foreign country as on the boundary of the financial centre of the greatest empire ever known. While the Victorian City prospered, people less than a mile away were working as pure finders – collecting buckets full of dog excrement from the streets to sell for use in the leather industry – and desperate girls and women were selling their bodies for pennies in the shadow of the massive blind walls of dock warehouses stuffed with riches from all over the world. It was said that so-called darkest Africa was more familiar to the middle and upper classes than were the East End slums on their doorsteps.

These people were to be pitied and dealt with, but were also to be feared. *They* were an immoral underclass living in hovel-infested courts, the breeding ground of savage criminals; and *they* were too close to *us*. The idea that they might turn nasty and actually spill out of their rookeries was terrifying. And the problem was spreading.

According to the 1851 census, getting on for half of the country's population was now urbanized – a unique event in the history of the world – and all too many of them were gravitating towards the already heaving East End.

If the fuse was not to be blown, something had to be done, and Andrew Mearns, in *The Bitter Cry of Outcast London*, published in 1883, was right when he suggested that until the housing crisis was dealt with, the good works of all the missions, churches and philanthropists put together were pointless. With multiple occupancy of rooms, sanitation was at best inadequate and at worst non-existent. To exacerbate the problem, many were ousted from what meagre places they did inhabit as whole areas were cleared to make way for extensions to the already massive brewery complexes, docks and railways, and for the roads to service them, the warehouses to hold the goods, offices to administer them and factories and their yards to process them.

If a person was unable to afford a bed, or could not find a place with one of the charities springing up throughout the East End, the options were stark. The casual ward of the workhouse was one choice, but a high price was exacted: humiliating questioning, sharing a communal bath and the requirement that a person undertook some pointless, back-breaking labour such as stone-breaking or turning a treadmill.

Common lodging houses, bad as they were, were cheap and certainly preferable to the workhouse or to 'carrying the banner' all night – walking the ill-lit, potentially violent streets, finding what shelter you could, while risking being charged as a vagrant or attacked by thieves too drunk to realize you had nothing. The very poorest and the unemployed, or unemployable, had no option but to live on the streets, scavenging what livelihood they could from the detritus of the surrounding slums, but the common lodging houses proliferated, patronized by those who could find the few pennies necessary. Any scrap of space was let to as many as could feasibly be fitted on to the bug-ridden straw and sacking-covered floorboards, and could share the communal bucket that served as their lavatory.

Many such lodgings were attached to pubs, providing a ready and willing market for the publican's wares, and earned themselves, not entirely unfairly, the reputation of being the haunt of criminals. At that end of the social continuum, crime was not so much deviant behaviour as a means of making a living through a time-served apprenticeship.

After the 1848 cholera epidemic had cut its way with such catastrophic consequences through the squalid lodging houses and overcrowded courts, leaving the tenants of newer, healthier accommodation comparatively unscathed, public opinion was focused on the conditions in which some people were living. The time was right for Lord Ashley to describe to his peers how he had witnessed five families sharing a single, sorry room – one in each corner and the fifth in the middle – and to put his Lodging House Bill through Parliament.

The Act introduced licensing by local authorities, dependent on inspections, to ensure the existence of at least basic sanitary facilities, segregation by gender and the 'respectability' of the person in charge. In practice, however, the licences were easily secured, needing just three signatures from local residents, and as, at that time, the authority which controlled the process was the police – who were more concerned with crime than sanitation – most of the lodgings continued to be run in a way that would maximize profits for their owners. These were individuals who, on the whole, were as unconcerned by notions of charity as the police were with the sleeping arrangements of London's poor.

With the arrival in the mid-1860s of what would be the final major epidemic of cholera, parliamentary action was taken on sanitation and housing, but this was done alongside an effort to abolish all outdoor relief, the intention being to teach the poor independence, and to separate the deserving from the indolent. In effect this resulted in little more than punishment of the already desperate.

More positively, attempts were being made by those who genuinely wanted to provide decent housing for those flocking to the East End. Model dwellings were erected by trusts, but, no matter that they were charitable, they still offered profits for investors and, when land prices rose, rents were raised to ensure those profits were healthy. Unfortunately, this made the new housing unaffordable for many of the target tenants.

Things other than rent rises proved a barrier. Trusts such as the Peabody, for example, while originally barring tenants who earned over thirty shillings, also excluded anyone earning less than twelve shillings, and those who did qualify were required to pay their rent in advance and to provide an employer's reference, both of which were, by definition, impossible for casual workers. They were also not allowed to do homework in case it should be in one of the offensive trades. As most casual work, from fur-pulling to glueing matchboxes, was offensive in one way or another, they were, if they wanted to continue working, ineligible for a tenancy and so were condemned to the foul conditions of the unregulated tenements and hovels run by private landlords and to the common lodging houses.

Other regulations required that tenants be vaccinated; that they would not keep dogs; that they would not decorate their rooms with paint, paper or pictures; that washing would not be hung outside to dry; and that they would prevent their children playing in the corridors or stairwells. The rules even extended to a curfew, with the main door being locked and the gas supply turned off at eleven p.m.

Being unable to hang out washing was bad enough – many made a living by taking in laundry – but probably the most restrictive of the regulations was the Peabody Trust's refusal to allow the sharing and subletting of rooms, practices which would have made the rents manageable.

So, although the model dwellings were an undoubted improvement, their success was limited to the better-off section of the labouring classes who had regular, comparatively well-paid employment. The rest were effectively excluded, and ironically, by clearing the slums, the developers were displacing more people than they were housing.

Lord Iveagh, a member of the Guinness family, decided to conduct his own investigation into housing conditions to see what was needed and what realistic rents would be, and set up the Guinness Trust with Lord Rowton. Rowton was shocked into action and Rowton Houses, the 'poor men's hotels', came into being. These were open to any man too poor to have a home of his own but who still wanted 'comfort and decency'.

When the fifth of these was opened on Fieldgate Street in August 1902, the *Municipal Journal* described it as

... a handsome structure ... situated in a very typical area of Whitechapel, and the lines of its elevation stand out conspicuously from the dirty and squalid rows of surrounding houses.

The low cost and freedom from petty, restrictive rules made the houses popular with both the very poorest and those in work who preferred the facilities offered by Rowton to the often much worse alternatives.

The social reformer and founder of the National Trust, Octavia Hill, thought the question of housing the working classes required a more educational approach. Financed by John Ruskin, Hill bought up slum housing and employed female rent collectors, including

Beatrice Webb, who were to help the poor learn better ways, and to manage their households and budget their income. Once 'improved', she believed they would aspire to larger, cleaner homes and would become increasingly self-sufficient, although she was concerned that certain low types should not be housed together in tenements because they were not fitted to living in such a manner and would cause all sorts of trouble.

To ensure profits and money for repairs, rent had to be paid regularly. The consequence of failing to do so was eviction, a lesson for the ne'er-do-wells and an example to others. Hill also insisted, when addressing a parliamentary committee on housing, that it was 'quite sufficient' for working people to have one shared water pipe on each floor rather than one in each individual dwelling.

Beatrice Webb was not made of such stern stuff and was appalled by the conditions she found when out collecting rents close to the Tower of London:

[along] the blank wall ran four open galleries, out of which led narrow passages, each passage to five rooms . . . Within these uniform, cell-like apartments there [were] not even a sink and water tap . . . on the landings between the galleries and the stairs were sinks and taps – three sinks and six taps to about sixty rooms – behind a wooden screen were placed sets of six closets on the trough system, sluiced every three hours [which was] used in common by [the] 600 or more inhabitants of the buildings.

Still demand for cheap accommodation continued to grow and poorly constructed, two-storey terraces were built throughout the East End, but never enough to relieve the pressure; the shortage meant that rents rose, and the common lodging houses continued to thrive.

Yet more charities and philanthropic societies were set up, legislation introduced and tenement blocks constructed, although many were only partly occupied. Even with supposedly reasonable rents, decent, if gloomy, facilities and their superiority over what was offered in most of the private sector, they were still out of the reach of all too many, and there was also a resistance to living in these early high-rise flats which still exists today. Those who were trying to help misunderstood the nature of what was required.

One scheme which flopped, because the character of the locals was not taken into account, was the market in the Columbia Square housing development. Built in Bethnal Green in the 1850s, it was one of the many generous projects undertaken by the philanthropist Baroness Burdett-Coutts. Unusually, the housing blocks were filled straight away, and even had a waiting list, but the adjacent, elaborately designed Columbia Market, opened in 1869 with the aim of providing healthy food at good prices for the local residents, was a total failure.

There was the usual need for homes in the area and there were enough people who could afford to become tenants, but a highly ornate indoor market found no place in local people's lives. One major hindrance to its success was the stipulation that it would not open on Sundays, an important shopping day for working people, particularly for the large Jewish population in the area; but also open-air street markets played an important role – and still do – in the traditional lives of East Londoners, as a place to buy inexpensive goods, as a place of employment for casual labourers and, probably most importantly, as a free, noisy, lively meeting place. It is little wonder that Columbia Market, with its impersonal formality and its solemn instructions for 'Soberness' and 'Vigilance' etched around its walls, failed.

There was a more worrying failure in the attempt to clear the slums. Often, when old housing stock was demolished, it was not the original tenants who moved into the new, replacement homes. With higher rents and strictly administered tenancies unsuited to their traditional way of living, they moved on, occupying a diminishing number of multiple-tenancy houses, not only with individual rooms now being let out and shared, but with beds and floor space rented on a rotation system that operated throughout the day and night on a 'hot bed' system.

And so the problems continued, made worse, if only temporarily, for those forced to leave their community by the clearances. Throughout the second half of the nineteenth century, the scandal of the slums was periodically brought to the public's attention, sometimes by the well-intentioned in their attempts to raise funds for their humanitarian work, and sometimes, such as during the autumn and winter of 1888, when Jack the Ripper was terrorizing Whitechapel, by sensationalist publicity surrounding crime and depravity.

A vision of this appalling world was brought into public awareness by Henry Mayhew in his *London Labour and the London Poor*. This began as a series of reports in the *Morning Chronicle*, in which the author disclosed the lives of those caught up in poverty, crime and deprivation, reproducing their stories in their own words.

As they read Mayhew's articles, the affluent in Victorian society became uneasy, but, as ever, hypocritical consumers of social investigation could disapprove in the comfort of their drawing rooms as they read of young girls working as prostitutes and of young boys committing desperate acts of violence, while being titillated by the gory details – all without the bother of having to consider that it is far easier to be 'moral' with a full belly.

Others refused to believe that the subjects of the pieces really had no choice. Charles Booth, who would become a champion of the impoverished, was originally as dubious as other cynics regarding how these people supposedly lived.

A prosperous ship-owner, Booth believed that the extent of poverty in the East End, as documented in 1885 in the studies of the Social Democratic Federation, was little more than wildly exaggerated Marxist propaganda, and he determined to prove the truth of the situation by conducting a survey of his own. The results were surprising: they showed that the Federation's conclusions were a complete underestimate of the problem, and that 35 per cent of East Enders were actually living below the poverty line. Unsurprisingly, the poorest workers of all were employed in the sweated trades, but at least they had work, however inadequate and badly paid, and that usually meant they could afford some sort of shelter, the all-important step up the ladder that saved you from the workhouse – the hated 'bastille'.

The new Poor Law of 1834 that had introduced this tough regime, as a replacement for outdoor relief for the able-bodied pauper, was as much about deterrence as relief of the needy. But the intention that the workhouses would be self-sufficient did not succeed and the burden on the ratepayers increased alarmingly, with the poorest districts, having the fewest ratepayers and the largest numbers to support, suffering excessively.

Much the same worries as are expressed in the tabloid newspapers of the late twentieth century were being voiced then: assistance without sacrifice would encourage the poor to become idle scavengers and kindness would be abused, so life should be made hard for the recipients of benefit or they would prefer it to finding honest work. The memories of people of my father's generation – born early this century and remembering an older family member being in the workhouse – make it quite clear that the system was never seen as an easy option. Being made to dress in harsh, heavy uniforms and do back-breaking, pointless tasks for the barest minimum of food, warmth and shelter, while separated by gender from your family, was hardly an attractive prospect.

Everything possible was done to reduce costs and workhouse hospitals would simply turn away sick people if they 'belonged' to a Poor Law Union in a different parish. Accusations of brutality were frequent and the more notorious incidents, such as the so-called Andover scandal of the 1840s, when the inmates were actually starved, resulted in small flurries of concern, but it is obvious from contemporary sources that little was done to improve conditions.

One advertisement, of 22 April 1864, for the position of assistant matron in Mile End Old Town Workhouse, Bancroft Road – a building which now forms part of the Royal London Hospital – stipulated a single woman or widow without a family, Protestant, with experience of cutting-out clothes, who, for just twenty-five pounds a year, also had to be

. . . a strict Disciplinarian . . . willing to devote her whole time to the performance of such duties as may devolve upon her.

Discipline was certainly strict. Misdemeanours resulted in punishments which seem totally out of proportion in their severity, but the Guardians were more concerned with protecting the pockets of the ratepayers than with the lot of the paupers in their care. Punishments were made public as a warning to others. On 17 November 1858, a poster was distributed proclaiming that Louisa Crankshaw and Mary Clarke, both aged eighteen, and Mary Brown, aged nineteen, had been sentenced to

. . . one month's imprisonment with hard labour for tearing their clothes in the Casual Ward of Mile End Workhouse.

Many posters broadcast stories of deserted families being left to the mercies of the workhouse. Such abandonment was illegal under the Vagrancy Act, which covered the 'Punishment of Idle and Disorderly Persons, Rogues and Vagabonds', and stipulated:

every person running away and leaving his wife, or his or her child or children . . . or whereby she or they, or any of them, shall become chargeable to any parish, township or place, shall be deemed a rogue and a vagabond [and] that it shall be lawful for any person whomsoever to apprehend any person who shall be found offending against this Act, and to deliver him or her to any Constable or other Peace Officer.

One found guilty of such behaviour was Henry Eason, who received three months' hard labour for leaving his family, a sentence which served as both a caution to others and a punishment for his 'crime'.

Considering the description of the dock labourer Charles Beaumont, alias Smith, of Commercial Road, issued by the Guardians after he deserted his wife, Mary, and their four 'lawful' children, he would probably also have been caught and punished before very long:

The said CHARLES BEAUMONT, when last seen, was dressed in a low crowned hat, dark jacket, brown waistcoat, corduroy trowsers [sic], and Blucher boots. He is about 4ft. 3in. high, dark hair, and full whiskers, pitted with small pox, and has a cast in the right eye; supposed to be working in the name of CHARLES SMITH at the St Katharine's or London Docks.

It was not only men who were charged with such behaviour; in the days before reliable, manageable contraception, women regularly left infants to be maintained by the Union, adding, according to the Guardians, a further 'heavy burden upon the rate-payers'.

The workhouse was not exclusively the last resort of the poor. An advertisement was posted in 1863 for a male attendant 'to take charge of the HARMLESS LUNATICS in the Male Imbecile Ward'. If the 'imbeciles' were physically fit, they might well have been set the exhausting task of breaking some of the '200 Tons of the best Guernsey Granite' for which tenders were requested by the same institution.

Paupers found at fault in their commitment to carrying out such tasks were swiftly repaid with a term of imprisonment. Even so, there were still those keen enough to enter the workhouse that they were prepared to risk the punishment. According to a report of 1853 in the *Evening News*:

A man who applied for admission to the St George's East casual ward was found to be wearing two pairs of trousers while a package containing 1s 5d was discovered tied round his leg. He has been sent to prison for a month for falsely declaring himself to be destitute.

Presumably the magistrate who sentenced him would have been a ratepayer and therefore not very sympathetic towards anyone falsely attempting to increase the 'heavy burden'. Considering the conditions within the workhouse, the man with the abundance of trousers must have been either desperate or more suited to the 'male imbecile ward'.

Regulations did, however, vary in their strictness: the 'pauper inmates' were usually allowed out once a month, sometimes even less, and then only if they were over sixty years of age – the older inmates not being of much use for the physical work they were obliged to undertake. Some Boards of Guardians allowed 'dissenters' and Roman Catholics to attend outside services on Sundays – which might explain why my grandparents could take my six-year-old father to visit his elderly, Catholic, great-aunt, Mog, on Sundays, and why she was allowed to stay at his childhood home on occasional weekends. Where they put her, however, is more of a mystery, with the nuclear family of five children and two parents living in just a front room, a kitchen and scullery, and with two upstairs bedrooms being let out to lodgers – the eight-strong Howard clan, with whom my father's family shared the one outside lavatory.

According to the memories of some of the more elderly contributors to the oral history, it is an ingrained dread of the workhouse and of relying 'on the parish' which accounts for their fear of accepting Social Security and help from Social Services, and of going into hospital; for them, accepting assistance is still associated with the last resort of the absolutely desperate and the dying.

And no wonder. In December 1913, well within popular memory, the *Bethnal Green News* carried the story of an inmate of the Bethnal Green Casual Ward, 'suffering somewhat from malnutrition', who was imprisoned for seven days after a doctor testified that he should have been able to have finished grinding the whole nine pecks of corn he had been set to crush on the workhouse mill in the allotted seven and a half hours, refuting the sick pauper's claim that he had been able to grind only one peck in five and a half hours, the work being too hard for him in his malnourished state.

With rents for decent housing too high for too many – even if they could satisfy the residence qualifications – and the streets or the workhouse hardly representing a reasonable choice, it is little surprise that so many found themselves living in the overcrowded, dangerously insanitary, multi-occupied slums of London's Victorian East End.

4

With the majority having to get by without private facilities, public baths and wash-houses played a vital role in the health and well-being of the citizens of the East End. One of the first to be opened was in Goulston Street, Whitechapel, in 1847, paid for with the aid of donations from a group of City businessmen concerned for the welfare of their less well-to-do neighbours.

Similar establishments were soon being built all over the East End and were surprisingly well equipped, with baths complete with soap, hot water and towels, and laundries with washing troughs, boilers, drying horses, irons and mangles. These were a boon, but they were not free, and the benefits of having clothes cleaned, dried, ironed and aired away from the cramped conditions of home were not the lot of the less well off. Rather than having the luxury of doing their laundry elsewhere, poorer women would take in the dirty linen of others, and would somehow manage to launder it in their already restricted rooms. It was grinding, steamy drudgery, done without the benefit of even the most basic labour-saving technology, but it was a means of getting by; the difference between having nothing and something, no matter how small.

An 1888 advertisement, issued by the Poplar Baths and Wash-houses, set out their regulations and asked customers to:

extend the benefits of the Public wash-houses as much as possible [and] earnestly request you will recommend your friends and neighbours to use them, instead of washing in the rooms they live in; *Time*, *Money*, *Labour* and *Trouble* will thereby be saved; Health will be promoted, and their families will avoid the discomfort of washing at home.

It concluded with two mottoes exalting cleanliness: 'Sickness is often brought on by having a Dirty Skin' and 'Dirty Clothes are like a Second Dirty Skin, and help to make the body sickly.'

Important as personal hygiene might be to a decent quality of life, the availability of water for drinking played a more significant part in the well-being of East Enders. The high likelihood that, in the more insanitary past, water was contaminated meant that beer, which had at least been processed, was used to slake the thirst. By the eighteenth century, however, gin had taken over as the favoured drink of the labouring classes, with more than half of all grain sold in the capital being distilled into alcohol. As the contemporary phrase had it, you could be 'drunk for a penny, and dead drunk for tuppence'. Investigations into the problems caused by this appetite for gin resulted in little more than a series of ineffective attempts to control its abuse, accompanied by a continuing rise in its consumption.

By the late 1820s, the situation was reaching crisis point and, in 1830, the government responded by scrapping the duty on beer and allowing ale houses to operate without a justice's licence. Such moves finally helped lure drinkers away from the seductive splendours of the opulently mirrored and tiled gin palaces to the more prosaic, but much cheaper, 'beer shops'.

London's lack of decent water was highlighted on the occasion of the Great Stink of 1858. This occurred after a misguided public health decision was taken to outlaw the use of all the cesspits sited under the capital's buildings. In itself, this was no bad thing, as they continually overflowed, spilling out on to the lower floors, but no provision was made for an adequate alternative and the Thames was suddenly serving as both London's primary water source and its main sewer. The river quickly became so polluted with effluent from homes and factories, slaughterhouses and chemical works, as to be almost unbearably ripe.

When the Houses of Parliament could no longer function without draping soaked cloths at the windows to try to alleviate the stench, a bill was passed ordering the cleaning up of the river, and the go-ahead was given to the engineer Joseph Bazalgette to begin work on his London-wide sewerage system. But these ambitious plans did little to improve the immediate lot of the cockney.

Standpipes and uncovered butts filled from water carts were the inadequate source of their unhygienic supply, coming predominantly from the East London Water Company, an organization which would cut off the already sporadic provision as soon as a tenement's landlord failed to pay their rates, regardless of the hardships it caused the tenants.

In 1894, after years of failing and intermittent supplies, the East End experienced such a dangerous water shortage that wealthier consciences were at last pricked. Letters were written, articles appeared in national and local newspapers, cartoons were drawn and even poetry composed. Some sections of the press were keen to show the consequences of the drought and what happened when any dribble of water that did get through the standpipes was stinking and full of insects – according to the *Daily News*, 'All sanitation came to an end' in East London in the summer of 1894 – but not everyone was as sympathetic to the East Enders' difficulties.

Punch carried a drawing of an East London Water Company official informing a filthy-looking bunch, standing in a grubby street by a barely trickling standpipe, that they shouldn't

... go a wastin' all this 'ere valuable water in washin' and waterin' your gardens ... or you'll get yourselves in trouble ...

And a slightly later piece, written in the autumn, appeared in the *East End News and Dock Directory* and was equally flip about the situation:

The East Londoner has so long been used to oppression in various forms, that the latest, the stoppage of his water supply, does not seem to worry him.

The suppliers' interests were, of course, commercial, and they were not inclined to act, even though they had, in 1892, assured the Royal Commission that the East London Water Company would supply the area with plentiful water for the next forty years. Following the cholera outbreaks which had had such devastating effects on the East End, this had been an important, if hollow, promise. There were suspicions that the company was selling water intended for Mile End Old Town to the expanding, wealthier suburbs of East and West Ham, but, whatever the cause of the shortages, people were dying and the death rates were rising fast. When the drought reached its worst, the company was finally forced to obtain water from other suppliers. This was 1898, four years after the problem had begun.

As a result of this fiasco, all of London's water provision was taken over by the Metropolitan Water Board so that an adequate supply would be assured for the whole population. The present-day return to privatized water supplies, almost exactly 100 years later, is worrying. If this harking back to 'Victorian values' sees history repeating itself, it will, of course, be the poorest who suffer yet again.

When water shortages were a regular occurrence, or at least a recent memory, drinking fountains and horse and cattle troughs were highly valued throughout east London, a prized public service supplied by philanthropists such as Baroness Burdett-Coutts.

At the turn of the century there were twenty-three fountains and nine troughs in Stepney alone, and when, in 1912, the drinking fountain outside the East India Dock gates was scheduled for removal as part of a road-widening scheme, it provoked such local anger that it had to be re-erected close by. But the provision of fresh water for the masses was sometimes motivated by morality rather than concerns about refreshment and hygiene. An undated Victorian poster announcing a meeting to discuss the construction of a public drinking fountain in Bow read as follows:

[It shall] commemorate the useful life of the late Mr Joseph Dawson, and promote the great cause of Temperance *so much neglected in this town and neighbourhood.*

In the Victorian East End, some drinking water was actually available from natural sources other than the polluted Thames, just as it had been from the earliest times and still continues to be so.

Up until the Second World War, Shadwell underground station was an unlikely venue for those wishing to 'take the waters'. A constantly flowing stream, emerging through a retaining wall, could be sampled in a cup supplied expressly for that purpose. It probably emanated from the same source as the mineral spring discovered in the mid-eighteenth century in nearby Sun Tavern Fields, a piece of land which would have been roughly bounded by today's Highway, King David's Lane, Glamis Road and Cable Street.

A pamphlet, written in 1749, by D. W. Linden, MD, tells of the value of the Sun Tavern Fields spa water, taken either internally or bathed in, citing it as an

... approved cure for almost every disorder incident to the human frame ... It has been found very serviceable as an antiscorbutic, and in all cutaneous disorders.

Either he is trying to blind his patients with science or they were maybe better educated in those days. He further praises the water's special properties:

... even [in] some leprous cases, it has proved effective in the cure of the itch, scabs, tetters, and the scald-head; and in the sarcy and grease in horses: and, as a powerful dryer, repellent, and somewhat escharotic, has cured sistula's, stubborn ulcers ... and sore eyes [and] in stopping inward bleedings.

Something for everyone there. Maybe he should have bottled it, as the Tower Hamlets local authority is talking of doing with the mineral water that was recently discovered coming from a spring in Mile End Park.

Despite water shortages, health risks, poverty and the squalid housing conditions in its eastern quarter, this area of London was still part of the great port, the gateway to the world, the heart of the Empire, and as such continued to be a magnet for people from all over Britain and much of the rest of the globe.

By the nineteenth century, the East End was becoming truly cosmopolitan, a beguiling, if often empty, honeypot around which disappointed bees would buzz. But newcomers such as the Jews were as likely to be escaping from tyranny as they were to be drawn by stories of the rich pickings to be had on the gold-paved streets, and they arrived in ever greater numbers.

Familial, social, geographic and economic factors determined where people settled; the presence of a friend or family member able to speak to a landlord, or to an employer, gave a newly arrived person a start in the area. Or it could be the existence of affordable accommodation close to the docks which attracted newcomers, like the young sailors – maybe from China, Somalia or the Yemen – looking for a bed for a few nights while their vessels were in port. Some of those seamen, tempted by opportunities better than those to be found with the shipping lines, or back home, 'jumped ship' and stayed, putting down tentative roots which, in some cases, resulted in the organic growth of a close-knit community, such as that in Limehouse which came to be known as Chinatown.

Originally employed on East India Company vessels, the Chinese were prepared to work for very low pay, but with little to spend and generally no English they were doubly badly off while on shore leave in the slums which surrounded the docks. Even so, until their ship made her return journey or they managed to secure a job with another line, the sailors had little choice but to be patient and to manage the best they could.

With alternative work sometimes presenting itself during the enforced shore leave, a Chinese settlement began to emerge, with new arrivals gravitating to the district where they either knew or had introductions to someone living there. Families stayed put for several generations, but, when they were in a position to do so, most moved out to the more affluent suburbs, as generations of immigrants before and after them had done and would do.

As a community, Chinatown was never much more than a few streets around Pennyfields, but as strange-looking shops and businesses were established, and more of the curiously garbed individuals arrived with their robes and pigtails, the area became a focus for all sorts of outlandish rumours and sensationalist reporting, involving everything from white-slavery rackets to the indiscriminate morals of those who supposedly ran vice dens. The experience of people living in the area was, no doubt, influenced by the common prejudicial stance taken against any outsiders, but the opium and gambling dens certainly existed. My own great-uncle Tom was, in the 1920s, a minder for Daddy Lee, the owner of one such club, which was frequented as much by locally born East Enders who wished to avail themselves of the exotic facilities as it was by the Chinese.

Another group of incomers left to their own devices by their employers were the Indian servants and nannies, the ayahs, who, from the eighteenth century, had accompanied British employers returning to England. On arrival, they were not always given the return fare they had been promised. If they could not secure another job with India-bound passengers, they had little option but to remain in London, the port where their ship had docked. By the 1870s, the problem had become so acute that an Ayahs' Home was established in Aldgate to give the abandoned women shelter.

The majority of those arriving from the subcontinent in this period, however, were men. From the eighteenth century, a few Indian sailors – known by the catch-all term of Lascars, which was assigned to any dark-skinned, Asian, Arab and even, sometimes, to Chinese sailors – were taken on by the East India Company, and their numbers grew throughout the nineteenth century because, like the Chinese, they would do hard, dirty work for lower rates than any British seamen. Despite action by the government throughout the nineteenth century, in the form of Merchant Shipping Acts, to stop foreigners jumping ship and settling by the docks, some still managed to do so, and other communities, such as that of the Somalis, took root.

Further east it was a slightly different story, as the Royal Docks did not open until 1855, but from that date foreigners certainly became a more familiar sight in what is now the London Borough of Newham, and, by 1896, they were present in sufficient numbers to merit the setting up of a dedicated mission in Canning Town for sailors from overseas. One group who planned to come – some to stay, others en route for the United States – with hopes of a safer and better life, were the Jews fleeing the pogroms and persecutions which followed the assassination of Tsar Alexander II.

It has been estimated that between 1881 and the beginning of the First World War nearly three million Jews fled eastern Europe, and that the Jewish population in London increased from the 1881 level of 45,000 to an approximate peak of 150,000, with their East End population spreading over two square miles of Jewish homes and businesses.

These nineteenth-century Jewish newcomers, the Ashkenazim, not only came in greater numbers but had, on the whole, very different social, economic and cultural backgrounds from their more sophisticated and financially successful Sephardic predecessors. But the existence of a Jewish infrastructure, coupled with cheap housing and the possibility of work in Jewish businesses, made the East End an attractive place to stay. This, however, was to change.

By the late 1880s, the pressures of the unprecedented population growth, deepening economic problems, growing unemployment and the additional burdens on an already inadequate housing stock saw increasingly vocal anti-Semitism, as more newcomers arrived from eastern Europe. Efforts were made – some more sympathetic and defensible than others – by their established, better-off co-religionists to help them assimilate into their new, host community, or to find somewhere to settle away from the overcrowded East End.

From the mid-nineteenth century, the German community also experienced a large and rapid increase. They too had been driven from their homeland by poverty, revolutionary political upheavals, failed harvests, encroaching urbanization and the pressures of a menacingly high population rise in their homeland. But it was economics, rather than the German establishment or local prejudice, that eventually saw the dispersal of their community.

Most of the newcomers settled in what was already known as Little Germany, an area skirted by the Whitechapel Road, Cannon Street Road, the Highway and Leman Street, making the community at that time one of the largest of all the immigrant groups in London.

There were intellectuals and professionals among the German immigrants and they did well for themselves in their new home, but, as with the Jewish arrivals, the majority of the more recent residents of Little Germany were people from agricultural communities who had few appropriate skills to offer and were ill-suited to cosmopolitan life. They took the worst of the casual jobs at the meanest rates of pay, many in skin-dyeing but mostly in the massive sugar bakeries – the dangerous, debilitatingly hot sugar-refining plants which loomed like cathedrals over the Victorian Whitechapel slums.

At the height of the community's strength, the German labouring classes could worship at a choice of German churches, study in German schools, buy goods in German shops, spend their childhood in a German orphanage, have their health needs catered for in their hospital in Dalston and spend their final years in their own old people's home.

As populous as it had once been, by the late 1870s, with the disintegration of the sugar-baking industry and the hike in rents, Little Germany had begun to shrink. Some residents returned to their homeland and some moved on, making their way, like their Jewish counterparts, to the United States of America, but others stayed in London, moving further east to the increasingly urbanized and financially secure suburbs of what is now Newham.

There they played an important role in the economic success of the area, becoming involved in the rapid industrialization which occurred towards the end of the nineteenth century. This, along with the creation of Beckton, was to totally change the face of the area.

Beckton had come into being when the Gas, Light and Coke Company set up a massive works by the side of the Thames, in what was then Essex, choosing the riverside site to make easier the unloading of coal barges arriving from the north-east of England. It took two years to complete the vast range of buildings which comprised the works and the purpose-built estate to house the company's employees.

Named after Simon Beck, the head of the company, Beckton produced its first gas for public consumption in November 1878 and was soon prospering. Through a series of mergers and acquisitions, it became the leading supplier of gas in the whole of London.

As well as finding work in Beckton, the newly resettled Germans opened bakeries and butcher shops, and organized the German bands which were a familiar sight to those who lived in the area up until just a generation or two ago. The German influence, in trades like chemical-processing and glass-manufacturing, was so great that West Ham council actually provided material in English and German for businessmen interested in setting up in the locality. But the presence of immigrants was not always seen as bringing an economic bonus to the neighbourhood.

In 1901 a German manufacturer who chose to 'import' 150 of his highly skilled countrymen as glassblowers upset members of the local labour force considerably. In addition to the usual suspicion of foreigners, there was now massive resentment that they were the ones being employed, that *they* were taking *our* jobs.

According to a report in the *East Ham Echo*, dissatisfaction with the employment of outsiders was still being voiced a year later, this time at a public meeting held ostensibly in protest at the employment of foreigners at the Beckton Gasworks. A Mr Tuckwood, who was both a London County Councillor and a member of the Royal Commission on the use of 'alien' labour, spoke

... at some length on the state of affairs as they existed at Stepney, Poplar and other places in the East-End of London, owing to the large and increasing influx of Russian, German and other foreigners ... A resolution calling upon the Government to introduce a Bill to stop the importation of aliens into the country was carried unanimously [at the end of the meeting].

The Aliens Act, aimed at preventing increasing numbers of immigrants coming from Europe – as well as being a populist move to win political seats – became law in 1905, but the problem of 'importing' workers still exists in the East End. I asked someone at a Docklands-based company about the numbers of locals employed by them and was told:

I couldn't take on locals in the office. They're too ignorant. Not educated. I tried interviewing one. She didn't even know what the Home Counties were.

The person had herself been born and brought up in east London, although she certainly did not count herself as one of *them*. It seems that it is always *one of us* who should be employed; an odd paradox, in this case, when you have started out as one of *them*.

The objections not only to foreign labour but to foreigners *per se* also continued. In January 1903 the *Evening News* reported on the 'British Brothers' League', a 'tiny band of East End patriots' who held regular meetings in Stepney, and whose object was

... to stem, if possible, the great flood of alien immigration that threatens to wash all remnants of previous English occupation out of East London.

As if there was such a thing as an East Ender without some sort of immigrant connections. This fear of the newcomer, the outsider, as has been seen, was neither a new nor a selective phenomenon.

Even Jack the Ripper, the perpetrator of the grisly Whitechapel murders in 1888, was said to be foreign, as, so the argument went, only one of *them* could do such a thing, not only murdering but actually butchering women in the streets of Whitechapel.

Prejudices against the evil foreigner were further inflamed by events that occurred during the winter of 1910–11, when members of a revolutionary cell committed a series of crimes which culminated in the deaths of several police officers, a full-scale siege involving the armed forces and the fire brigade, and the Home Secretary, Winston Churchill, arriving in person to take charge. The end of the siege saw the charred remains of the revolutionaries being carried from their burnt-out rooms, and the siege of Sidney Street, with its cast of dastardly but, most importantly, foreign anarchists went down in East End history.

Attacks on foreigners – verbal and physical – did not come only from the indigenous community. On 12 October 1806, *The News* carried a story about a riot which had broken out between a group of Lascars and a crowd of Chinese seamen at lodgings in Angel Gardens. The Lascars, known for their timidity, had retreated under attack into their building, but the Chinese faction had, according to the article, failed to understand that 'an Englishman's [*sic*] home was his castle' and had gone in after them. The row escalated and spilled back outside on to the Ratcliff Highway. After several violent clashes, the sides had swelled until the original twenty-five Chinese numbered over 300, and the now 150-strong Lascar camp had been joined by a supporting group of 'sailors and Irish labourers'. It was then that the authorities intervened, and more material was made available for the press to sensationalize.

There are many similar reports of trouble breaking out between sailors staying in lodgings by the docks throughout the nineteenth century; probably a lot to do with fit young men coming ashore after a long trip, the availability of alcohol and the absence of the restraining influence of wives and families.

The Irish, another of the immigrant groups who initially settled close to the docks, also suffered their share of prejudice. They comprised, at first, a small community of those who had left their homeland during Tudor times, dispossessed by the English plantations. Their numbers gradually increased throughout the seventeenth century and, by the eighteenth, there were Irish settlements in the riverside hamlets of Shadwell and Wapping, and in Whitechapel, particularly around Rosemary Lane – now Royal Mint Street – a rough, tough area housing the famous Rag Fair, a place where second-hand clothes and goods, often of dubious provenance, were bought and sold with no questions asked.

With continuing problems in Ireland – regarding ownership of land, rapid population growth, ongoing economic underdevelopment and then the horrors of the famine, the Irish were being 'pushed' from their homeland as much as they were being 'pulled' by the lure of London. When their community had expanded until it was one of the largest colonies of foreigners in east London, their presence became increasingly conspicuous, causing growing resentment among the locals, who referred to the roads around Rosemary Lane and Cable Street by the derisive nickname of Knock-vargis – a play on the name of Carrickfergus, the port where William III landed before the Battle of the Boyne.

The work the Irish undertook was mainly casual: in the docks, factories and sweatshops, and as navvies – the labourers who excavated the docks and constructed the railways and canal systems.

Many of the Irish arrivals were young, single men who sought their entertainment and company around the Thames-side ale houses and dockside taverns close to their lodgings, and they soon found themselves with a reputation for low living and drunken carousing which, even in the twentieth century, was being perpetuated in a shockingly careless way. The secretary and librarian of the Institute of Historical Research could speak about what he called, with an astonishing lack of analysis, the 'Irish invasion' at a lecture in Stepney, reported in the *East London Advertiser* in November 1930, claiming that Irish immigrants in the seventeenth and eighteenth centuries

... caused a social problem of great magnitude ... They were not very popular, and did not deserve to be. They had a lower standard of living than most men, and would work for a lower wage than Englishmen, and were riotous and extremely violent.

He went on to talk about the Spitalfields Riot of 1736, when poverty-stricken workers were pitted against one another by employers wanting to pay the lowest possible rates. When the Irish workers underbid the locals, rioting broke out; ironically, the Irish weren't labelled as drunken, lazy wastrels this time, but were accused of being hard workers prepared to labour for a pittance.

In fact, the accusation, repeated throughout the nineteenth century, that the Irish kept down wages was often true, but they did so, like other immigrant groups and low-paid workers before and after them, from desperation grown out of poverty and dispossession, which actually left them open to exploitation by unscrupulous employers.

With so much ill-feeling, combined with worsening poverty, the East End was ripe for anger to erupt into action.

5

If a history of labouring people, and their struggle for fair pay and conditions, was being written, the East End could provide enough material for several volumes, just using the big, headline events, ranging from the fourteenth-century Peasants' Revolt to the News International print-workers' dispute at Wapping in the 1980s. The livelihoods of those who depended on the vagaries of casual employment, particularly in the docks and in the sweatshops, were always tenuous, and it is no wonder that labour relations became more antagonistic as workers realized the power of organization.

There were strikes in many East End trades during the nineteenth century, but it was not until the success of the match-girls' strike at Bryant and May in 1888, when the fight for reasonable pay and conditions was won, that the beginnings of the so-called New Unionism could be detected. In the following year, two further landmark actions – by gas- and dock-workers – resulted in similar triumphs, which would prove to be turning points in the history of industrial relations.

The Gas Workers' and General Labourers' Union successfully negotiated the precedent of an eight-hour working day for its members, and the Great Dock Strike won the battle for the Dockers' Tanner.

Working in the docks had, until the 1980s, been a tradition in many East End families, and one of the people I interviewed told me about his father's links with the 1889 strike:

> My dad was on Tower Hill sitting on his dad's – my
> grandfather's – shoulders during a meeting at the time of the
> Dockers' Tanner strike. One of the leaders of the strikers
> reached up and gave my dad a half a crown. Ben Tillet it was,
> who gave it to him. Half a crown. I've still got it.

The fact that industrial unrest spread through late Victorian London is unsurprising: work was unreliable, lives diminished, and, according to Charles Booth's calculations, 35 per cent of Londoners were living in poverty. But rather than anybody questioning the social, political and economic environment which had spawned this overcrowded, industrialized, insanitary quarter of London, with its ever-ready pool of cheap, casual labour, the poor themselves were usually blamed for their own deprivation.

It was believed that a minority were deserving of help but that the rest were feckless, reckless or simply bad, happily opting for a life of crime. However, the terrible conditions which existed in the most deprived parts of the East End, such as the Old Nichol or around Rosemary Lane, left the inhabitants with few options.

While the more successful, skilled workers would have had sufficient means to bolster themselves against difficult times, the lowly casuals, who supported the manufacturing industries and the services which grew up alongside them, were badly hit by even subtle changes in demand for labour. Jobs disappeared overnight and workers, especially those with no community or extended family network on which to depend, would be left destitute.

A hotbed of criminality and hatred of foreigners – be they from the Essex marshes, where the night-soil barges dumped their stinking loads, or the more exotic-looking newcomers, such as those getting up to their evil business in Chinatown – was being seeded in the slums of east London.

The area had now lost its more affluent residents and what had once been the grander end of the housing stock was split into multiple dwellings, inhabited by an almost separate race of threatening creatures who took raucous pleasures in the pub, the penny gaff and the cheap tart, paid for with the fruits of their illegal dealings. But while small-time, petty thievery could make the difference between a penny loaf and a starving child, there were also violent criminals who preyed on the weaker members of their own communities; some exceptional events excited the attention of pamphleteers and national newspapers, including 'celebrity' cases that involved personalities who grew in the public imagination as they were presented as amusing, if shocking, diversions.

An early example of an East End criminal who gained celebrity through a brisk trade in pamphlets describing her activities was Mary Compton, the so-called 'baby farmer', whose neglect and abuse of the children she was supposed to be caring for on behalf of local parishes made her notorious. The literature tells the story of

the Bloody and most cruel midwife of Poplar who, in 1693, was, with a daughter and another accessory, tried for felony and murder, in destroying, starving to Death and famishing several poor infants and babes

complete with gory details of the tiny bodies found in the cellar, the guilty verdicts and the women's subsequent capital punishment.

In the same century, popular tales circulated about the capture of Judge Jeffreys, the hated hanging judge of the 'Bloody Assize', who was apprehended in a riverside pub at Wapping as he waited, in disguise, for the boat in which he planned to flee the country. There were many ghoulish versions of his story, but in all he ended his life in the nearby Tower of London.

Entertainment and titillation were derived not only from hearing or reading such narratives but also from actually witnessing the punishment of felons. For instance, 20,000 people attended the execution of Elizabeth Herring, a Wapping woman who murdered her husband with a dinner knife after first sharing a meal with him in a pub in King Street.

But ghastly reports of violent crimes remained popular; tales of prostitutes being killed by customers, their bodies robbed of everything including their clothes; of poor widows murdered as they sat innocently by their very own firesides; and of unsuspecting victims being coshed to death in shadowy alleyways for little more than the few coppers they had in their pockets.

One event which really captured the public imagination, nationally as well as locally, was the Ratcliff Highway murders of 1811, which had the added poignancy of being committed close to Christmas time. A shopkeeper, his wife, their baby and servants were all killed by an intruder – the infant while still in its cradle. This outrage was followed just days later by the murders, in the very same neighbourhood, of a publican and his complete household.

At the other end of the century, street gangs, the original hooligans, erupted on to the streets during the Bank Holiday of 1898, focusing the public's gaze on the horrors and seemingly random violence which existed in the world of the cockney Londoner. But it was a series of crimes which had occurred a decade earlier, the Whitechapel murders, committed by the mysterious figure of Jack the Ripper, that became for ever associated with the Victorian East End, and indeed continue to be documented, pored over and fictionalized more than 100 years on.

Even the first person to be murdered on a British train was apparently a victim of East End crime. On 6 July 1864, Thomas Briggs stepped on to a train on the new Fenchurch Street to Hackney Wick line; only one other person was on the train, Franz Müller, a young German tailor. At Bow station, when other passengers joined the train, all they found was a bag, a chain, a hat and lots of blood. Briggs's body was found later on the track between Bow and Hackney Wick.

By detective work that would not have shamed Sherlock Holmes, Chief Inspector Tanner of the Yard, with the assistance of Sergeant George Clarke, tracked Müller to New York via a series of obscure clues, which included noting the design of a watch chain and the provenance of the hat that had supposedly belonged to the victim. Müller was hanged for the crime later that year.

From the presentations of crime, in ballads, poems and as melo-dramatic tales, it is difficult to assess whether they were intended to touch social consciences or were simply as entertainment. The truth is probably somewhere in the middle, much as it is with the reporting of crime in today's print and electronic media. The self-righteous breast-beating that followed the murder of young Charles Fariere, for instance, would probably be just the same today.

Charles was a small Italian boy who spent his days begging on the streets of east London, with a little cage of white mice hanging from a strap around his neck to attract attention and maybe the odd copper from a generous passer-by. He was murdered by three men for his body, which they then sold to King's College medical school in the Strand for nine guineas, after being knocked down from twelve. In media terms, the story 'had it all': child abuse, pathos, corruption in the medical profession, the death sentence for two of the perpetrators and transportation for life for the other. High profits were made by the vendors of such tales.

But the majority of crimes committed were of a far less villainous or excessive nature, being more to do with getting by than with brutal murder, and if they kept it that way, and knew their place, the labouring classes were just fine – working for little more than slave wages, entertaining their 'betters' out slumming by performing in the boxing ring or the music hall, and offering more 'specialized' talents in brothels.

But life in the Victorian East End was not all misery, crime and prostitution. There were the almost bucolic pleasures to be had in the newly accessible Victoria Park, opened up to the riverside slum parishes by the construction of Burdett Road, and there was an energetic working-class popular culture that, while it might not have appealed to some of London's more self-satisfied residents, was vibrant and affordable.

Traditions and enthusiasms, inherited from the Huguenots, of songbird- and pigeon-keeping and a love of bright, flowering plants which cheered up even a gloomy, shared lodging, thrived throughout the area. The packed Columbia Road sold everything from single wallflowers to full-sized shrubs; the bustling bird market in Sclater Street displayed cage after cage of home-bred canaries, and gold-finches and other songbirds trapped in the Essex countryside; and pigeon lofts, with both racers and tumblers, sprang up throughout the slums, with the young squabs being bought, sold and exchanged in pubs and markets throughout east London.

Markets were – and are – an important centre of social life, a place to meet friends and to appreciate the free entertainment provided by the irreverent banter of the stall-holders. According to Mayhew, there were 30,000 men, women and children working as coster-mongers in the middle of the last century – their name deriving from the sellers of costard apples, a variety known since the thir-teenth century and one of the first fruits to be sold by London street traders. Added to the official costers were the large numbers of casual poor who would try their hand at selling oranges, when they were in glut, or cheap ribbons and knick-knacks, or anything else that might find a buyer. Whatever the actual figures, it is clear that market life was booming in Victorian London, with cheap food, second-hand clothes and the occasional treat being snapped up by eager customers, or lifted by the light-fingered who were either un-willing or unable to pay.

Saturday was the busiest day, with markets staying open late into the night. Full of brightly lit stalls, the more humble barrows and even makeshift pitches with goods displayed on a scrap of cloth, the markets would spread out over many streets, and they all had their pubs, as did practically every little turning.

With one on just about every corner, pubs were another hub of social life in a neighbourhood, and there were also street entertainers with barrel organs and model tableaux to be enjoyed; outings to be saved for and looked forward to, with maybe a day trip on the Bank Holiday that had been introduced in 1871; boxing booths with bare-knuckle prize fights that could provide an evening's amusement for as little as a penny; and ratting contests between terriers that were free, with the added draw of an opportunity for some illicit gambling. Then there were the more costly, though still-affordable delights of the music halls, and, cheaper though no less fun, were the penny gaffs.

The gaffs were favourite places of entertainment, particularly with the younger members of what Victorian society considered to be the rougher element. These were set up on a temporary, usually unofficial, basis, in empty shops or small warehouses, by a theatrical troupe or impresario, in much the same way as so-called 'Cheap Jacks' nowadays open Everything-a-Pound shops in premises awaiting new lease-holders. The shows were flamboyant and melodramatic, with saucy songs, bloodthirsty playlets and, if patrons were lucky, a bonus in the form of a 'freak' or wax show to further thrill them. The audiences were as rowdy and raucous as the performers, and, so it was widely believed, were of a generally criminal inclination, which was only exacerbated by the inflammatory dramas they were witnessing on the impromptu stage before them. In fact, much the same fears and arguments were being advanced about the undesirability of the penny gaffs as have been voiced by parents and social commentators in the late twentieth century regarding 'video nasties'. A more acceptable pastime, but one which was also to degenerate somewhat in the eyes of the middle classes, was the tradition of the Fairlop Boat Fair.

The boat, not actually a seagoing craft but a contraption mounted on wheels and drawn by horses, was used to transport the workers of Daniel Day, a generous ships' block- and pump-maker of Wapping, on their annual treat: a day's outing to his weekend retreat at Fairlop in Essex. The practice began in the early eighteenth century, when Day announced that he would meet the cost of the trip and a dinner to be held at his house, but he stipulated that all those who wanted to go to the fair had to make the journey from the workshop in Wapping to his place in Fairlop by boat, a completely landlocked journey.

Day's hope was that this intriguing requirement, met by his provision of the strange vehicle, would popularize the idea of an annual beano with not only his own workforce but also other benevolent employers.

The fair, celebrated on the first Friday in July to commemorate the anniversary of Day's purchase of his country haven, became such a popular event that crowds lined the route to cheer the revellers and their eccentric transportation on their way.

When Daniel Day died in 1767 the fair continued, and even when the land on which it was held was cleared in 1853 under the Enclosures Act it still took place, close to the original spot in a field opposite the Old Maypole Inn. When that site was no longer available, it was moved again to a space near the Bald Hind Hotel at Chigwell. But wherever it was sited, the fair always began in the same, time-honoured way, with everyone assembling at Blackwall Cross – the junction of Poplar High Street and Robin Hood Lane – and then processing to the setting-off point in Grundy Street.

By the 1820s the fair had grown into a full-blown event, with commercial stalls and entertainment booths offering a whole week of distractions, and drawing far more Londoners than those originally intended to benefit from the fresh Essex air. They arrived in lines of brightly decorated vehicles, all following the boat, which was still drawn by the traditional six horses complete with smartly turned-out postilion. With the hugely increased numbers and the proximity of a pub, the proceedings became quite lively and, as the fair had no official charter, attempts were made to put a stop to what had become a considerably more unrestrained event than the original day's outing had been.

One effort to abolish it altogether was made in 1840 at the Ilford Petty Sessions, but all this succeeded in doing was reducing it from a week to a single day. But there was no holding back East Enders intent on having a good time and the fair soon returned to its inflated, week-long self. There were also police attempts, recorded in 1846, to dismantle the illegal booths and stalls, but they too failed when faced with so many objectors. It was only in 1853, with the deforestation of Hainault and the closing off of the site to the public, that the fair was actually stopped. But not for long.

By 1899 it was back, this time at the Maypole, and it had expanded even further, now including a mechanical fairground with swings and roundabouts, as well as all the other attractions. The idea of an annual beano had become a traditional part of the East End philosophy that 'we made our own fun', whether it was a charabanc outing to the Derby, a day's train trip to Southend or a brake ride to Hoddesdon Weir.

There was nothing peculiar to the Fairlop Boat Fair which frightened the establishment; bawdy behaviour and unlicensed goings-on have always caused concern among those not involved, or who do not get the joke, or do not themselves appreciate a particular pastime. And they probably always will. As late as the 1940s, a survey carried out by the London Diocesan Church of England Temperance Society, and the Churches' Committee on Gambling, blamed funfairs for being the direct cause of delinquency among the young.

But there was one particular leisure pursuit associated with east London that might have held more appeal for those who would have banned the fair. These were the Whitebait Dinners held in the Thames-side inns famed for their delicious fish.

The custom of giving Whitebait Dinners was started in the eighteenth century by an engineer, Captain Perry, who, during his work repairing the river embankment at Dagenham, had bought a waterside home called Breach House. A lake in its marshy Thames-side grounds became a select fishing club to which the Captain invited his friends, who afterwards shared a meal with him. When Sir Robert Preston of the East India Company took over Breach House, he continued the tradition of the suppers, inviting guests, including William Pitt the Younger and various of his Tory colleagues, to his 'fishing cottage'. The trip to Dagenham was not always possible for the Prime Minister, so the host, Sir Robert, moved the event to the Artichoke, a tavern at Blackwall noted for its whitebait. Even though salmon was easily caught on that stretch of the river, it was the quality of the much smaller fish that was widely praised, with newspapers carrying lengthy reports recommending them as a delicacy.

The event continued after the deaths of both Pitt and Preston himself, but the guests were now exclusively members of the Cabinet and the once Dagenham-based angling trips followed by a meal were now distinguished by the title of the Ministerial Fish Dinner.

Whitebait suppers were, of course, on offer to 'ordinary' members of the public, but by the mid-nineteenth century the Brunswick Hotel's reputation for the excellence of its food attracted so many members of 'high society' – from the Duke of Cambridge to the American philanthropist George Peabody – that it was no longer only newspapers which were praising the experience of eating at the riverside taverns of Blackwall. Thomas Love Peacock actually composed a poem in its honour.

A bill for dinner at the Artichoke in the 1840s comprising four fish dinners, followed by fruit, washed down with a bottle of sherry, two bottles of port and a brandy, and including a two-shilling tip for the waiter, boat hire there, coach hire back and a boat to the wharf, came to the grand total of two pounds six shillings and sixpence.

Less expensive and more active pursuits were more widely enjoyed in the East End. In the 1870s roller-skating, imported from the United States, immediately became a craze. Within a year of its arrival on British shores, there were fifty rinks in London alone, with a theatre in Shoreditch, the Royal Standard, being gutted and especially refitted as a skating arena. Ice-skating was also embraced and a massive centre in the Cambridge Heath Road, the Victoria, was packed out with an eager public.

Spectator sports were also popular, with many of the London football clubs having their origins in this period, the Football Association having been set up in the 1860s to oversee the regulation and development of the game. Millwall, for example, started life as a works team from Morton's jam factory – a place were seasonally unemployed match-girls could find summer jobs – and West Ham evolved from a team known as the Thames Ironworks, while Tottenham Hotspur were the football-playing element of a rather older cricket club.

But even innocent pleasures enjoyed by the locals, such as having a few drinks in the pub with your pals, gambling on a street corner on the flip of a coin, having a boisterous night out at a penny gaff or hollering yourself hoarse at a football match, could all be viewed very differently by outsiders, and especially by those who sought to improve the East Enders and steer them from their wicked ways.

6

In the introduction to his *Working-class Stories of the 1890s* P. J. Keating noted that it is 'difficult to exaggerate the degree of interest in the East End shown by settlers, philanthropists, religious missionaries, journalists, Salvationists and sociologists during the [1880s]'.

Necessary as it was for someone to do something about conditions in the slums, the motives, attitudes and intentions of these reformers, crusaders and radicals might at times seem questionable, and aspects of their work could certainly be condemned with modern-day hindsight. But they must be seen in their historical context, and even if some were patronizing, paternalistic do-gooders, at least they were doing something to relieve the deprivation of the most poor and neglected.

Thomas Barnardo was one advocate of change who was actually criticized by his contemporaries and for rather more than being patronizing. Recently arrived in England to study at the London Hospital in Whitechapel, the young Irish doctor was shocked by the deprivation he witnessed, and went on to dedicate his life to rescuing children and providing homes for them, declaring that no destitute child would ever be denied admission to his shelter. No other group in the East End had a greater need for welfare provision, however rudimentary, than the youngest and most vulnerable who found themselves living on the streets.

From his early, humble efforts, Barnardo's homes were to become internationally renowned, but, at the time, there were those who questioned both his reasons and his methods. There were allegations of financial improprieties, suggestions that the photographs of desperate children, with which his cause was publicized, were faked to increase donations, and, worst of all, accusations of cruelty to the youngsters in his care. Although nothing was proved, contemporary doubts regarding the doctor remained, but his work spoke for itself.

Like Barnardo, William Booth, founder of the Salvation Army, understood the need for publicity to promote his beliefs, although he was not so much condemned by his contemporaries as mocked and taunted by them. But there were occasions when the ridicule turned to violence, when mobs turned on him, enraged by his tub-thumping brand of religion, as he carried out his crusade to help the poor and to save their souls with his banner-waving, tambourine-rattling, military style of revivalism.

But when Booth wrote *In Darkest England*, the book horrified the country with its portrayal of the squalor and poverty in Victorian London, and he went on to gain much admiration for his fearless campaigns against child prostitution and the exploitation of sweated labour.

One reformer who seems to have puzzled rather than angered people was Frederick Charrington, who, because of his anti-drink and anti-vice beliefs, gave up all his rights to the massive family brewery fortune and committed his life to working in the East End. Charrington was proud of all the brothels he managed to close, using legislation which rewarded those who identified the so-called case houses to the authorities, but his obsession with the notion of evil led him to be suspected as being the person responsible for the Whitechapel murders; not of being Jack the Ripper himself, but of hiring someone to do the horrific killings to drive out the prostitutes. There has even been a suggestion that Charrington's anti-brothel offensive was a cynical move to empty out properties which he could then buy, in an area where land was at such a premium. This, however, is now one of the least popular theories about the murderer's identity, along with the idea that the Ripper was a midwife – a profession that would have provided a perfect cover for a bloodied appearance – extracting revenge following her remorse at carrying out abortions for the prostitutes.

Regardless of the actual identity of Jack, the Whitechapel murders certainly turned the spotlight firmly on to the East End, shedding little light but a great deal of heat, which generated a whole new wave of interest from charities, missions and the simply curious. One of the lasting legacies of this Victorian drive for improvement has been the university settlements.

It is most likely that the idea of establishing settlements originated with Edward Denison, the son of a bishop, when he moved to the Mile End Road in 1864. He was, like most nineteenth-century, middle-class newcomers to the East End, dismayed by what he saw. Believing that charity was not the solution, Denison wanted to show the impoverished masses a better way of life by encouraging educated individuals to establish a residential community amidst the slums where, through example, they would instil their manners and culture in their less-well-off neighbours.

His theory attracted much attention, although he himself did little to put it into practice. That was left to the Reverend Samuel Barnett, who was to set up what is probably the best known of the East End settlements, Toynbee Hall in Commercial Street.

Barnett moved from a West End parish in 1872 to become vicar of the socially and economically very different St Jude's in Whitechapel, his bishop having warned him that his new home was

the worst parish in the diocese, inhabited mainly by a criminal population, and which (he feared) has been much corrupted by doles.

Unlike those privileged souls who lived just a few miles away from the privations of the East End, and who were appalled and shocked by the lives of the poor but did nothing, Barnett, who was now in the middle of it, reacted very differently. He went to Oxford and spoke on 'Settlements of University Men in Great Towns' to an invited group, emphasizing that people should not be saying that something must be done but asking, 'What can I do?'

What Barnett did was persuade some of his friends to help him establish a settlement which would carry out the vision of 'active citizenship' which he shared with Arnold Toynbee, a history tutor from Oxford who had died tragically young and for whom the settlement was named. This involved creating a place where 'settlers', university teachers and students, could live and work for a specific period, and where they would, according to his stated intention, both learn from their research and investigations and teach their new, temporary community.

Toynbee Hall, a rather grand structure, affecting the style of an Oxbridge college, was opened at the end of 1884. A similar group from Oxford had already opened a more formally religious settlement in east London, Oxford House, in October 1884, but it was Barnett's Toynbee Hall which came to be known as the 'Mother of Settlements' and was a model for the many similar foundations that were to be created not only in east London but throughout the world.

Barnett's settlement concentrated on what he considered to be instructive and improving activities. He was instrumental, for instance, in setting up the Whitechapel Art Gallery and the library, but he and his wife were also involved in practical matters. They campaigned for universal pensions and the improvement of poor relief, and were advocates of educational reform; they were also responsible for the establishment of the East London Dwelling Company, which originally provided basic accommodation for working men, but eventually opened up to accommodate families.

An East Ender born in 1903 remembered living in one of the Dwellings as a boy:

> These buildings were old ... but were built solid, owned by the East London Dwelling Company. The rooms: one front, two bedrooms and a scullery with a toilet out on the landing. The scullery was distempered in red. There was a black iron sink, cold water, of course, and a large coal box. The landing had stone stairs and was lit by gas jets. There was no hall as such, you just walked into the living room.

Barnett and his wife, Henrietta, continued to be energetic workers in their new parish, being concerned as much with the social as the spiritual needs of his flock. Events, societies and clubs were organized, including the Children's Country Holidays Fund, an annual art exhibition and the Association for Befriending Young Servants; and, importantly, they encouraged influential people to visit the area to see, at first hand, the many problems which so desperately needed addressing.

Barnett was undoubtedly well meaning in that he recognized that the East End was not simply an amorphous mass but was made up of different types of people with different needs, and also that an integrated approach to change was a better way of dealing with social problems than imposing piecemeal schemes here and there, but he still believed that his middle-class friends and colleagues should come in to act as leaders amongst the local people, standing, for instance, in local elections, as he considered them more suited to such tasks because 'the change for good' required 'men of culture'.

The work at Toynbee Hall provoked argument and raised questions about why there were conversaziones, lectures on Sir Walter Scott and on chemistry, and orchestra recitals. What use were lectures on aesthetics and debating societies organized by a group of youngsters – the undergraduates who made up the community?

There were other concerns on two, contradictory, counts about what was going on at Toynbee Hall: some considered the attitudes of those at the settlement condescending, while others suspected that the locals would start getting ideas above their station. Unsurprisingly, there was less controversy regarding the provision of classes in shorthand, arithmetic and book-keeping – such pursuits did not cause the working classes to get above themselves, but actually made them useful.

But Toynbee Hall survived the criticism, and still does to this day, working with and for the community. Important progress has come about as a result of research carried out there, with the influence of living and working among the slums on the young William Beveridge contributing to the most significant of all social reforms during the entire twentieth century in Britain.

However, critics such as George Lansbury, the Labour MP for Poplar, still accused the settlers of spending time in the communities as a means of furthering their own ambitions and then leaving the East End to sort out its own problems once their stay had served its purpose. This might have been true of some, but much good work was done and great personal sacrifices were made by others, among whom, Clara Grant, the 'Farthing Bundles Lady' of the Fern Street Settlement, stands tall.

From girlhood, Clara Grant, who was born in 1867, had wanted two things: to teach and to live in London. Something of a revolutionary in that she abhorred traditional Victorian educational methods of rigid rote learning, in 1900 she became headteacher at Devons Road School in Bow Common.

The area was poverty-stricken. When, in 1905, the Poplar Distress Committee took a local census of the unemployed and casual labourers, the area around the school had the worst figures in the whole borough. It became clear to Grant that these children needed more than education; they needed the basic necessities of life.

In that same year, Grant opened a new school in nearby Fern Street and, in 1907, she established a settlement there, with a view to underpinning the children's families until conditions were sufficiently improved for the settlement workers, who were to live in three houses in the street, to 'render themselves unnecessary'.

She did not believe in giving hand-outs. Some form of payment, however small, would be expected for any assistance, thus allowing people to retain their dignity. Discovering that many of the children's mothers earned a pittance sweating, Grant set up a Work Fund and paid them a decent wage for producing clothes which were then sold through the settlement, with any profits being used to buy more cloth for them to work. The families were also invited to join the Boot Club, which sold subsidized children's footwear. If a family could not afford even a proportion of the price, then they were allowed to pay in kind, through work of some type. Similarly, Coal, Spectacle, Cradle and even Fireguard Clubs were set up to provide part-funded household necessities – the latter following the death by burning of a local child. Hygiene and sewing classes were offered, and breakfasts and nominally priced midday and evening meals were provided at the school, as was health care at what was the first school clinic in London. The Maternity Bag loan scheme, with all the essentials for new babies, was a poignant service offered by the settlement in response to the desperation of a woman who had so little that, after having two babies die and 'laying them out' to be buried in their nightgowns, she was left without sufficient nightclothes for her surviving children.

With all the good work that Clara Grant did in the area, she was still known for her questioning of the social-engineering aspects of some settlement schemes, but her belief in welfare with dignity meant that she continued to be spoken of with great fondness by those who benefited from the continuation of her work and by those who remember her for the Farthing Bundles. This was a tradition which grew from the piles of odds and ends – toys, picture cards, shells, boxes, scraps of material, whistles, beads and suchlike – that were donated to the settlement along with items for the regular clothing sales. The ever-resourceful Clara Grant decided to make them up into little newspaper-wrapped bundles and sell them to local children

1. The Whitechapel hay market, 1899. A legacy from the eighteenth century which continued until 1928.

2. The Waller family outside their butcher's shop in Watney Street, *c.* 1910, with a display guaranteed to horrify today's 'food police'.

3. Evans's dairy in Poplar High Street, *c.* 1928, offering a typically wide range of provisions with some almost forgotten brand names.

. A view of the 'LaBo', the La Bohème cinema, *c.* 1931, at the junction of Mile End Road and Burdett Road, viewed from Grove Road, where I lived (at number 109) as a child.

. Abraham Cohen's barbers, Ellen Street, Stepney, *c.* 1930. Small businesses such as Mr Cohen's once provided an important focus for local communities.

6. George Gardens, Bethnal Green, 1903. A terrace of houses with the 'luxury' of having somewhere to hang out the washing.

7. Drying racks in the Sophia Street laundry, 1931. With few of today's labour-saving devices, public wash houses were a boon.

8. Victorian dustmen. Refuse collection using a tip-up cart in Old Montague Street, *c.* 1895.

9. The drudgery of ill-paid homework, *c.* 1900. Mrs Robinson of Bethnal Green stuffs a palliasse with straw; for each completed mattress she was paid the equivalent of 5p.

10. Child victims of poverty in the East End. Members of a family of nine photographed in July 1912.

11. My father, Tom (circled), aged five, in 1924, with the rest of Mrs Chalkley's form at Alton Street School, Poplar.

2. Making their own fun. Children enjoying a game of leap-frog, 1905.

3. Using the tin bath as a makeshift paddling pool in the backyard of 109 Grove Road. I am in the middle, with my brother Tony on my right and one of his friends, *c.* 1954.

14. Celebrating peace by 'slipping the slip' at the English Fair, Poplar recreation ground, 1919.

for a farthing. It was an immediate success, a source of treasure trove for poor children otherwise starved of such simple pleasures.

Children came literally in their thousands, the demand for the parcels growing so fast that boys and girls had to be offered alternate weeks, and then, in 1913, the Bundle Arch was introduced. This was a little wooden structure bearing the legend

Enter now, ye children small,
None can come who are too tall

under which the child had to pass without resort to stooping.

My mother told me how magical those few scraps and bits and bobs seemed in the 1920s, when she was a child, and how she and her friends would buy their bundle and then run around the corner to swap coats and hats to try their luck at getting another turn through the arch.

Clara Grant, who died in 1949, would be saddened but, after her long experience in the East End, probably not surprised to learn that her work there is still not finished. Being situated in one of the most deprived parts of the whole country, Fern Street Settlement and its community-based work, including luncheon clubs, affordable sales, classes, company, care and, as always, the dignity of all involved, continues to this day.

Grant was a campaigner, but not in the directly political sense of another crusader for change in the East End, the suffragette Sylvia Pankhurst.

While studying at the Royal College of Art, Sylvia Pankhurst was given the job of decorating Pankhurst Hall, a new Independent Labour Party building named after her socialist father. It was when the club opened that Sylvia, her sisters and their mother, Emmeline, were mortified to discover that the place Sylvia had enhanced, that was given their family name and was supposedly for a forward-thinking political organization, was to be open only to men. The experience spurred them on to create the Women's Social and Political Union, and Sylvia was to undergo prison, hunger, thirst and sleep strikes, and the horrors of forced feeding and the cruelties of the Cat and Mouse Act.

But she was ejected from the WSPU in early 1914, when it became clear that her strongly socialist views were not compatible with the Union's approach to the cause of women's enfranchisement. Sylvia set up the East London Federation of the Suffragettes, targeting the work she thought most important: meeting the needs of working women by taking practical measures which could improve their lot in life, so that desperate mothers, showing starvation in their 'patient eyes', need never come to her again with their malnourished children.

In March 1914, she began producing and editing *The Women's Dreadnought*, which posited the objectives of the Federation:

To Secure the Parliamentary Vote for every Woman over 21, and to promote the Social and Industrial Welfare of Women.

She worked tirelessly to achieve those aims. The 20,000 weekly copies were sold at a halfpenny for the first four days after publication, with the remainder being given away free around the East End.

With its opposition to war and to the exploitation of women as cheap labour, *The Women's Dreadnought* carried many contributions from local women, with Sylvia making a point of not 'tidying up' their voices in the articles.

She still faced opposition from those in power, however, and Bow, Bromley and Poplar refused to allow her to use their halls, so the East London Federation opened its own at 400 Old Ford Road, attached to Sylvia's house, and made use of the traditional East End outdoor venue for rallies, Victoria Park.

In 1917, Sylvia and the East London Federation renamed their paper *The Workers' Dreadnought*, but they carried on their vigorous struggle to improve the social conditions of women. They fought for improved government relief, child centres and cost-price restaurants; they pushed for decent provision for mothers who had been left in reduced circumstances after their husbands were conscripted, set up milk-distribution centres, health clinics, cost-price kitchens, and the toy factory and crèche in Norman Grove, Bow, where the East End women who made toys for West End stores ran the factory for themselves and were all paid equally.

The Equal Franchise Bill was finally passed on 7 May 1928, after its seventh reading, and gave women the right to vote on an equal basis to men. But despite the efforts and energy of the likes of Sylvia Pankhurst, it is still a wonder that women ever got that far when the National League for Opposing Women's Suffrage had waged such a campaign, with their leaflets being available at just four shillings per 1,000 to ensure maximum distribution. They claimed the view put forward in their pamphlets was one of 'Patriotism and Common Sense' and urged readers of their literature:

Don't make yourselves and your country the *laughing stock of the world*, but keep political power where it ought to be – in the hands of men.

One leaflet, *c*. 1912, headed '*THINK BEFORE VOTING. A Happy Home is worth more than all the Suffragettes can get you*', made this point about the East London campaigns:

Mr Lansbury and some of the Suffragettes may be very sincere, and talk very cleverly, but if they get their way many a now happy household will be ruined. At present a woman may differ from her husband about politics, but does not necessarily quarrel over it. But if she had to vote, and differed from him, and insisted on voting for the opposite side, you can imagine the result!

With or without the vote, and with or without the good or bad intentions of intervening outsiders, life for East Enders was hardly easy, but despite the hardships, the poverty and the making-do, there was a cockney spirit, a humour and a vibrancy in the community which are still remembered with great fondness by those who lived there. From the turn of the century to the time of the slum clearances of the 1950s and 1960s, there was a Golden Age recalled and cherished by the many people I spoke to, and in the next part of the book this will be described in the words and memories of the East Enders themselves.

PART 3

The Golden Age

They was lovely times. They shouldn't be forgotten.

This section looks at the East End from the turn of the century to the slum clearances of the 1950s and 1960s, a period which would see many changes in both the social and the physical fabric of the area, changes forced upon it through a combination of officialdom at last dealing with the nineteenth-century legacy of overcrowding and industrialization, the traumas and destruction of two world wars and then – the major change – the dissipation of old communities and the evolution of the ones which replaced them.

It is a period of change and, more significantly, a period of increasingly *rapid* change, with any evidence of the 'old days' swiftly disappearing as the electronic age pushed its insistent way forward, generating different concerns, desires, interests and ways of living. Even the language and accent of east London have changed. My father's generation of East Enders – he was born in 1919 – do not speak the dull, uniform, flat-vowelled Estuary English which I – born in 1951 – speak. He will still use what is essentially Victorian idiom – phrases such as 'daddler mooey' and 'fard'n face' – and can speak the true cockney back-slang of the rookery and the street market, rather than the self-conscious, artificially created 'porkie-pies' type slang of the television mockney.

Links with an even earlier period were made by older respondents I spoke with. Some still remembered the Whitechapel hay market, which, although abolished in 1928, was part of a Whitechapel still retaining rural connections that harked back to the market's origins in pre-industrial 1708.

This is the East End of living memory, a world when 'we was all one' and that was, maybe because of the more leisurely pace of life, seemingly never-changing, but then took sudden, drastic and often painful lurches into modernity. Changes came with opportunities such as those offered by Butler's 1944 Education Act, which made the younger generation more economically and socially mobile, so that moving away was an achievable possibility; but they also came with the destruction of war, making a move out of the East End an imperative for many.

Regardless of a few practical improvements, the living conditions at this time were not dramatically better than those of the earlier generations – we, like many others, had no bathroom until we moved away to a new housing estate in the late 1950s – yet this period, from the turn of the century to the beginnings of the sweeping post-war slum-clearance schemes, is generally looked back on with great fondness and with not a little regret at its passing. These are the memories of East Enders recalling that time, stories of a Golden Age that is no more, remembering how it used to be.

7

When I think of the East End, I think of all the warmth.
Within a radius of two or three streets you had your own
little community. Like a village, it was.

There are many histories that can be written, many versions and
many ways of recalling the past, but a common ingredient in all
the memories which people shared with me, as they looked back
and thought about how they remembered the East End, was a
fondness – and a real sense of loss – for the time when 'we was all
one'. A time when you knew all your neighbours; when you sat
outside your street door on a kitchen chair during long summer
nights, chatting and laughing, and when you helped each other, if
you had problems, without a second thought. When the person next
door was more than an individual who just happened to be living
close by.

A striking example of how things have changed, in our perception
of what we might expect from our local community, was seen in the
response to my questions about the *problems of childcare*. Women
either needed me to explain what I was talking about or they laughed:
what need was there for such formalized arrangements when you
were part of a larger whole which looked out for one another,
regardless of whether they were family, friends or simply your next-
door neighbour? It wasn't an issue. If a woman worked, and many
did – had to – there was always someone to keep an eye out for the
kids. That's the way it worked.

And yet, as with many memories of the 'good old days', this
affection for the presence of a close-knit community is probably as
much a result of hindsight as a contemporary appreciation. When
families were living in such close proximity, there was little opportunity for peace and quiet, and even less for privacy. But the existence
of what we would now call a supportive network seems to have
compensated for the lack of more material comforts.

Even if you didn't have any money, you always had other
people. You had people, whether it was family or friends.
When I look back I remember security and friends, a sort of
love.

No matter how they described their experiences, people
remembered – and missed – that shared interest in their community's
welfare, a strength that 'could get you through' even the hardest of
times.

You know, I sometimes wonder how we managed. It was a
struggle making things stretch through to the next wage
packet – *if* you were lucky enough to have your old man in
work – but we muddled through together somehow. Today,
people get all worked up if the washing machine or the telly
goes on the blink, but we couldn't have imagined having so
many things in the first place, let alone getting worked up
about them being broke. But we had one another. And you
can't beat that. You were all in the same boat then, see, you
had bugger all, and you didn't care what the neighbours had,
cos they had nothing – same as you. But if one of you needed
help, they were there. You had friends. You could depend on
one another, if you see what I mean.

We lived in rows of terraced houses with just upstairs and
downstairs, and a few with basements [airys or areas],
wedged close together . . . We were much less private than we
are today, but it built in us a feeling of comfortable
community.

This sense of community really came into its own during times
of crisis, as will be seen in Chapter 16, when people remember living
in the East End during wartime, but peacetime also had its share of
difficulties.

Crises, problems and emergencies were tackled with resilience and
good humour, and there seemed no concept, at least in those who
spoke to me, of only looking out for yourself. You were part of a
self-supporting group, made up of people who looked out for one

another, who *had* to look out for one another, in order for everyone
to get by. Regardless of whether it was a matter of eking out the stew
you had managed to knock up from a few scraps and a bit of barley
to feed a few extra mouths or you were responding to something
which required a little more heroism or initiative, there was a perceived generosity and a lack of selfishness which many felt are no
longer with us.

It was 6 January 1926, just after midnight. We'd all gone to
bed, but my uncle was still out. He used to go to his young
lady's, which was over the swing bridge at Tidal Basin. You
used to have to walk everywhere in them days. When he was
returning home, he noticed as he was going over the bridge
that the water was coming over. So he ran home, which was
quite a long way, all down the North Woolwich Road,
knocking on as many doors as he could. 'Get everything you
can upstairs, the Thames is overflowing!'

When my uncle got home, 'Come on,' he said to us, 'it's
coming down the street, it'll be in soon!' [He and] my two
elder brothers put their trousers right up to their thighs, as
the water was gushing down the street, and [rescued] these
sleepers of wood that were coming down from Alexander's
Wharf, and roped them together to make a raft to help
people who couldn't get upstairs or couldn't get across to a
neighbour. My mum said to my eldest brother, 'If you can
manage to get down into your grandfather's kitchen, there's
four loaves of bread on the table. Try and get them if you
can.' It would be hours before it receded again.

Grandfather's kitchen was two steps down, so, of course,
the water was deeper down there. But he got the bread. As he
handed it over to us on the stairs, he said, 'I won't be a
minute, I'm going back for something else.' He'd seen this
thing bobbing about in the water. Plomp, plomp, plomp. So
he goes and gets it, and it's a Christmas pudding! Mother
always made extra to keep one for Easter!

[The people] opposite couldn't get up their stairs, so they
waded through the water to come over to us. My brothers
opened the windows to let them in! They was soaked! [And]

it wasn't only from the river, it was from the dock. We had to find dry clothes for them [and], of course, we couldn't sleep. The stench, it was vile. The doctor was coming for my dad, and my brothers got him on the plank raft.

'What a good idea,' he said.

Less exciting than rafting in a flood maybe but still valued were the acts of generosity, sometimes very simple, sometimes more dramatic, that people recalled as being an essential part of their everyday lives in a world which might have been less sophisticated but was remembered as being 'better'.

There was a neighbourliness and a readiness to help those in need, from the simple cup of sugar to helping a family who had lost their home because of a fire. Many times I have seen a family being turned out of their home when getting behind with the rent. But neighbours never let them suffer for long. With temporary shelter found for them somewhere in the street, their bits and pieces of furniture looked after until they found another home, they got through.

But the existence of such an intimate community could have its drawbacks and, before the post-war slum clearances, life in the East End was lived in a much more public way. Not only were the living arrangements such that it was difficult for people *not* to know one another's business, but more time was spent outside the home in the street. Such a way of life ensured you had company, allowed you to keep an eye on what the children were up to and let neighbours police the behaviour of any strangers who 'turned up on their manor'. There were plenty of other reasons for spending time out of doors.

[*Laughing*]. It wasn't exactly pleasant indoors, was it? You didn't have big, comfortable three-pieces like you have now to lounge about on and watch the telly, and you was all living on top of one another in a couple of rooms, so you was better off outside, enjoying the company and not having to worry about the bugs!

*

It was how you passed a few pleasant hours. You'd have a talk and a laugh. Better than sitting indoors by yourself while the old man was up the pub and the kids were out mucking about in the street.

In the 1920s it was a wonderful experience living in the East End – you lived outside. Because of the cramped living conditions in the very small houses, and the lack of home amusements, we were all out in the streets, including the children, till late at night. The children were never outrageously misbehaved because the local policemen knew where we all lived.

This woman explained how, if you were in trouble of some kind, there was no question of keeping your problems to yourself, as the person you turned to for help would often be your neighbour.

You'd rally round if someone needed you. If someone was unwell you'd mind her kids, make sure she had a bit of grub, see to her washing for her, that sort of thing. You knew what was going on in people's homes. It wasn't like you were nosing or nothing, it was just that there was more of a together feeling. We was, like, you know, sort of all one. It was a good thing. Take my old aunt, she used to do everything for people down our turning. She'd deliver their babies and lay out anyone who'd died. She'd even cut your hair, and, how can I say, she'd *help you out* as well – if you was in the family way again and couldn't afford to have another one. And it *was* helping you out in them days, when you *couldn't* have another mouth to feed, cos you could hardly feed the ones you already had. People might think today that everyone knew your business, but that's how it was. You didn't have a lot of choice. Not round our way, you didn't. You had to stick together. And it wasn't a bad thing either.

The decency of a community really could make the difference between a family 'getting by' and not. A woman told me about a family who had moved into her street when she was a little girl. With them being recent arrivals, the neighbours had no idea that they were going without food to the point when they were literally starving. In desperation they had eaten something bad that one of the family's many children had found somewhere, probably in the gutter after the local market had been packed away. The family, particularly the mother, became desperately ill. As soon as their new neighbours found out what had happened, they were taken under the community's wing. She told me how the women in the street had rallied round and, despite their own poverty, provided food, organized a collection to pay for the doctor, and new and loyal friends had been made. The family were no longer alone, but were part of their new community.

This person recalled a similar decency, which, in her case, was extended to her own family.

> They soon learned what problems my father had with my mum, and they simply surrounded him and did what they could to support him. I had dresses made for me by one person who was a dressmaker, and two elderly twins, who ran the Sunday School, regularly invited us to lunch or tea, where we had lovely home-made food. They saved their rations and made us meat pies, wonderful cakes and jam. It was like an extended family, without which we could not have survived.

Although there were instances when money was borrowed from the neighbours, it was most often practical help that was offered, as there wasn't usually any spare cash to share round:

> One time, Mum lent the family over the road a pair of Dad's shoes. There was a wonderful feeling of belonging in that street. People would never close their door on you.

Whatever the help, it was appreciated:

> People were very close. There was a sense of shame if you did something out of order, something bad, but there was no shame in being poor. We were all poor, you see. So, if you

had to go next door and ask for something to help you out
till the end of the week, it was accepted. You might borrow
a saucepan of stew or half a loaf. You'd go home with
it wrapped in a tea-cloth or in your apron. And you'd
appreciate it, having something like that. And who knows,
it might be their chap who was out of work next week.

People being so 'close' would probably feel claustrophobic to us
today, with our more private, increasingly solitary lives, but, as people
were usually living in shared, overcrowded housing, the proximity
of others and the consequent lack of privacy were taken for granted.
It was a lifestyle which provided good opportunities for sharing
news.

The postman was friendly, knew you all and would tell you,
'You have a letter' from such and such a place or a postcard.
He would tell you what it said.

And the shared supervision of children was another bonus.

If I can explain it like this: in them times, the community
policed itself. They looked out for one another, so, in your
own little community, you made sure that nothing too bad
happened. [*Laughing*] And it was harder for kids to play the
hop. If one of your 'aunties' [female neighbours] saw you
hanging about when you should have been at school, they
wouldn't look the other way. 'What you doing here?' they'd
say. 'Why ain't you at school? I'll tell your mother of you.
Now go on, off you go!'

My youngest was a bit on the slow side, but he still played
out in the street with the other kids. You could let them do
that back then. There'd always be a few mums sitting on the
step or on the window sill having a natter, so there'd always
be someone to keep an eye on him, if I was indoors getting
on with my jobs. They wouldn't let the others take too many
liberties with him or nothing.

*

Being part of a tight-knit community did not have to be intrusive; you could still set boundaries between yourself and the neighbours.

There were those who were forever popping in and out of each other's houses. It suited some, but we weren't all like that. We were still friendly, very, but I didn't like people coming over my step and knowing my business. I'd have someone in for a friendly cup of tea, of course, but not all the time. Not like some.

Although the boundaries were not always very formal, there were still expectations about taking part in the life of the neighbourhood.

People didn't shut their front doors because it was usually shared accommodation, so you had to have the front door open. But the front door was also left open because your neighbour would say, 'I'll come round and have a cup of tea with you at four o'clock.' So you'd leave it open so you wouldn't have to bother to go and open it. You'd be expecting them. And the children, they could just [run in and out]. I think if you didn't ask your neighbours for help, they used to think you were being standoffish.

Not all local characters were popular within their communities. Just as now, there were people who were considered less suitable than others to be around children, but there was also a tolerance of such people which today's sometimes overly anxious parents might find alarming.

There was this one bloke, he talked a bit posh, but he was dooky [dirty] and he shuffled about in these old clothes. I don't know how he come to be living round there. Anyway, he had all these books and always had sweets and he would talk to all the kids. Our mums warned us he was a bit funny and that we had to watch him. I don't think he'd ever have dared touch us. He knew our mums would have killed him if he did, never mind what our dads would have done to him.

But I don't think there was ever any thought that we'd get him out of the street or drive him away.

There were some peculiar people around, though they were really harmless, just unusual. 'Lavender Liz', who lived at the top of the street, and 'Dirty Wally', who went round wearing a straw boater and an old baize tablecloth like a skirt.

But it wasn't all sympathetic tolerance, and antisocial behaviour could easily spark off a quarrel among the more excitable members of the community.

Some people, to save the expense [of the sweep], would set fire to the chimney, a dangerous thing to do, and the whole street would be covered in soot and the washing ruined. [That] was the cause of many rows, and while there was this neighbourliness in most streets, there was the odd family feud between next-door neighbours. [Although] we mostly lived in harmony, each street had its noisy family, its dirty one, dodgy and sometimes downright dishonest ones. But everyone knew everyone else and mostly made allowances.

Or it might even provoke a full-blown fight.

Us kids would be having a street battle – our turning against one round the corner – it was our entertainment. [*Laughing*] We'd have sticks and stones as weapons, and dustbin lids as shields. And one of the kids would get a wallop off one of you that was a bit too hard, and he'd go running off home, and, before you knew it, his mother would be round after your mother, shouting the odds and threatening all sorts. Then the old girls'd roll up their sleeves and away they'd go! Fight like cats, they would. Mean it and all. That was as entertaining for us kids as having the fight among ourselves. But you'd have to be careful, you had to time it right, or you'd wind up getting a wallop from your mum when she'd finished. So you had to have it away on your toes, a bit slippery like, afterwards. Hide till it had all died down, or till

your mum was too busy fretting over one of your brothers
for something he'd been up to. It was funny when you think
about it. [*Laughing*] They'd be fighting over one of us getting
hurt, and one of us doing the hurting, protecting their kids,
you see, but then you'd both cop a fourpenny one from
your mum as well! It always blew over though. Even after a
proper fight, they'd be talking to one another like nothing
happened a couple of days later, or even having a cup of tea
together.

There were, however, some individuals who were not welcome in
the community at all, never mind into the back kitchen for a cuppa.
The woman speaking next came to east London from a rather more
demure community in Sussex with her policeman husband. She is
describing the period immediately after the war, when the bomb
sites, decay and dereliction on her husband's beat had attracted a
new group of residents – those who traded in vice and crime. Cable
Street had a thriving, if downmarket, red-light district, with all-night
cafés patronized by pimps who sat drinking coffee, while their 'girls'
did the business with the passing trade, many of them long-distance
lorry drivers working the docks and markets, whose vehicles lined
the narrow streets nearby. While the cafés were the meeting places,
the alleys and railway arches acted as the brothels.

His station was in Leman Street – an extremely tough area,
where all the toms, as they were called, were. I can remember
going to meet him or see him in the afternoon, when he was
on late turn. We used to meet at the corner of one of the
streets off the Whitechapel Road where there was a bombed-
out church. I used to be petrified if I got there before
him, because there weren't only the prostitutes, there were
all the meths drinkers sitting around in the churchyard.

It was even harder for those who were expected to live in the
middle of it all.

It was never much of a place round there, not exactly what
you'd call posh, and we might not have had much, but we

was respectable families. To see them trollops hanging
around the place, it was disgusting. Not right.

But the East End could be tougher still for outsiders, and more
so for those who came from further afield than the policeman's wife.
During the First World War, there was mounting hostility against
Germans, and retailers with German names, whose families had lived
in their communities for two, maybe three generations, had to do
their best to deflect the anger; having 'The owner is a British subject'
inscribed on the lintel above a shop doorway was not unusual. But
it still wasn't enough to prevent animosity from spilling over into
action, and there were several incidents of local shopkeepers having
their businesses smashed up and looted by their neighbours.

I'm not making excuses, but there was bad feeling. We were
at war, you see. And even though I was little more than a
baby myself, I still knew that we all hated the Germans. Got it
from my older brothers and my mum and dad, but I suspect
I was too young to know what a German really was.

It wasn't only the effects of wartime and of anti-German propaganda that could cause trouble within a community. Between the
wars, a letter in the *East End News* from someone who signed himself
'J. B. of Bow E3' talked of 'coloured pests' who are 'swarming into
this country' and are touching food on market stalls with their 'paws'.
And, in 1920, the *Evening News* ran a piece on 'the Lure of the Yellow
Man' holding a 'fatal fascination for English girls' who would commit
'moral suicide' if they visited Pennyfields, which is 'peopled almost
exclusively by Chinese, Japanese and coloured men' and is 'the
distributing centre for opium and cocaine'. The newspaper actually
suggested that there should be 'a cordon round this area of London
and [people should] forbid any white women from frequenting it'.

There has probably never been a time when prejudice of one kind
or another did not exist – the act of prejudging is something we are
all guilty of at some time – but different cultures have, on the
whole, managed to rub along together in the East End more or less
successfully over the years. There is a prejudice, however, regarding
the supposedly dubious nature of the cockney which I experienced,

and which embarrassed the unthinking perpetrator far more than it did me.

I was visiting a farm as part of my research for a book on hop-picking when it was explained to me – as a historian from a respectable university – that hand-picking of the hops had finished at the farm when a flash flood destroyed the huts, which had proved an ideal opportunity for bringing in machine-harvesting. The woman who was telling me this said what a relief it had been to be rid of all the 'cockney scum' who had come annually for hopping. When I said that I used to go hopping as a child, she immediately replied – red-faced – that we cockneys were, in fact, the 'salt of the earth'.

Even people who have chosen to work in the East End can have 'robust' views on cockneys, as this respondent discovered when she was looking for employment.

> I didn't grow up in the East End, it was really a job opportunity which brought me here [getting solicitor's articles]. I had thirteen interviews. It just coincided that the last one was in the East End and they were the ones who offered me the job. One of the partners told me they offered it to me because my CV showed I had worked for about a year in a psychiatric unit, so they thought I could deal with their sort of loony clients.

How people spoke about their feelings towards any new arrivals who came into their community varied, of course, according to their direct experience, but, when talking about their feelings regarding present-day immigrant groups, there were frequent, similar comments along the lines of:

> The Jews, now *they* were OK. They mixed in. They were more like us. They mixed in. Not like the ones today.

Such memories are not, however, supported by contemporary evidence, which shows the concerted efforts of the Jewish establishment as they did their best to pressurize the Ashkenazi refugees to blend in with their host community. A person who is himself from an immigrant family had the following thoughts.

The Jewish immigrants who lived around here – at the time
of my parents' youth, I mean – were more prepared, or
maybe *encouraged*, to integrate, I think, even if they did keep
their own customs in the home and in their worship. But
current groups of immigrants, people from my sort of
background say, too many of them want a separate
community. They're imposing a way of life on the area rather
than becoming part of it. I don't know if it's right or wrong. I
get confused, can see both sides. I appreciate some of the old
values, but I think keeping yourself too separate can make
you a target for prejudice, even violence or hatred. It's
difficult. Very difficult.

The argument for integration with a new community or for
celebrating diversity is, undeniably, a complex one, but good hearts
can cross barriers. Here, 'Nurse Hebrew' speaks of the importance
to her of getting to know people from different backgrounds rather
than just observing their difference.

I trained at the London Hospital between 1932 and 1936. The
first three years were pure slog and I don't even like to
think about them. The fourth year, however, gave me the
experience of a lifetime. I became 'Nurse Hebrew' – the
ward was called Hebrew and so was I! – in charge of a male
medical ward run on orthodox Jewish lines. There were four
Jewish wards, male and female, medical and surgical, on the
top floor. My year as Nurse Hebrew was the best of all my
training. The patients were wonderful to me; one boy of
eighteen years offered to take me to Brighton when he was
discharged! They loaded me with chocolates [and] one of my
patients – a very poor, elderly man – got his wife to make
me a bookmarker. I still treasure it. To me, therefore,
Whitechapel meant Jews. Door after door had a *mezuzah*
[a small box holding a parchment scroll inscribed with
the Shema, a prayer from Deuteronomy, found on every
doorpost in orthodox Jewish homes except the bathroom].
On walking from the hospital to the nearest Woolworths at
Aldgate one seldom met non-Jewish people. On Sunday there

was a street market run by the local Jewish population, where
I learned to haggle! But there were obviously some non-
Jewish people around, [particularly considering] the large
attendance at the nearby Great Assembly Hall – reduced to
rubble by Hitler – on Sunday afternoons for the service and
the free tea. Possibly the reason for the large attendance! But,
to me, Whitechapel and the Jews and the London Hospital
will always be connected. I was Nurse Hebrew and I got to
know – and love – my patients and their relatives.

The reason for suspicion within a community was considered by
this woman to be based, first, on difference between cultures and
then, when it became more hostile, on envy.

It was when the Jews began buying the best houses and so on
that people began being resentful of their success.

Other people were more intrigued by the foreigners in their midst.
My father, Tom, who was born in 1919, remembers as a boy seeing
groups of what were then called Lascars – Asian sailors – doing
business with the 'old girls' who stood with their bundles of second-
hand clothes in Chrisp Street – always known locally as Chris Street
– selling occasional odds and ends to passers-by. With the Lascars
the women had hit the jackpot, as the sailors would buy everything
they had, then walk off in a line, one behind the other, carrying their
spoils, or balancing them on one of the second-hand bikes they were
always eager to buy.

I was fascinated by their little hands. They seemed so small
compared to the great big forks the men had in my family.
I'd watch them as they'd be going along the street, back to
the docks, with six trilby hats stacked on their heads, a couple
of suits thrown over each arm, and piles and piles of shirts
and jerseys. 'Who wants this for a penny?' the old girls would
say, pointing to their bundles, and the Lascars, they'd buy it
all up and carry it back to their ships that were going back to
India. They had their own lavatories, you know, at the docks.
Ones you had to squat over. Much more hygienic when you

think of it than ours were. And they used to carry these little cans of water, to wash themselves. They had to have the right kind of facilities.

For some the difference between cultures was of interest because of the potential it provided for a welcome source of childhood income. For instance, the fact that orthodox Jews were forbidden to carry out any kind of 'work' during the sabbath gave employment to the so-called Sabbath Goys.

> In the 1920s and early 1930s, we never thought about people being immigrants. All we thought was that the Jewish families would pay us a few coppers to do jobs for them on their Sabbath. We didn't understand why. It was a way of getting money to get something more to eat. We'd fight to do it. We never thought they shouldn't be here. They were just people. But us kids did wonder why they couldn't turn their own gaslights on and that.

Differences within the community could also be a potential source of confusion.

> My mum *always* thought my husband was Jewish, because he was dark and had big brown eyes, and he was smartly dressed and used to speak Jewish. I went into hospital in Stepney Green [the Jewish Hospital] and when I was in the ward there, of a Friday they used to get one of the Jewish people to break off a bit of *chollah* loaf and drink a drop of wine for the Sabbath. They'd come over to me because the rabbi there liked my husband, and used to speak to me in Jewish. He always picked me out.
> My mother would be there and she'd say, 'I don't care whether you married a Jew or not, but he *is* Jewish, isn't he?'
> 'Mum,' I said, 'he's from quite a strict English family. How can you say they're Jewish?'

'English' as an alternative to 'Jewish' was a distinction often made by people I spoke to who were in their seventies or older, people who could still remember first-generation Jewish immigrants speaking in foreign accents, so they had not been classed by them as 'English'.

The complications surrounding the ambiguous pedigree of the possibly Jewish son-in-law multiplied.

> I only had one child then, he was about four. The Jewish people that lived upstairs used to burn candles of a Friday. And my son always used to say, 'Light candles!'
>
> I used to say, 'We're not Jewish, we don't burn candles on Friday.'
>
> But my husband would say, 'It if pleases him, burn candles.'
>
> One day, I said to my mother, 'I'm frying some fish tonight. Bring Aunt P. round and I'll do us some fish and chips.'
>
> I fried the fish and my husband liked this *chrane*, beetroot and horseradish mixed in a jar, that you could buy. So I got the fish on the table, this jar of relish, and I got these candles burning – it's Friday.
>
> And my mother and her sister waltz in.
>
> 'Look,' said my mother, 'he's Jewish. The candles are burning and that red stuff's got all Jewish writing on it.'
>
> I'd already got the chicken on the stove, stewing for the next day, so I went over and scooped up all the *lokshen* [thin noodles used in Jewish cookery, especially with chicken soup]. 'We put vermicelli *in* our stew,' I said. 'Jewish people cook their *lokshen* separate.'
>
> My mum was watching all this and she said, 'I don't know why you don't say he's Jewish. That's given the secret away, that has.'

It wasn't just the 'English' who reacted to the presence of foreigners.

> My only real experience of racism as a child was when a family of Mediterranean people – they may have been Greek – threw their shoes at us as we walked home from school. One assumes that ethnic minorities would be more tolerant.

Nothing of the sort, we are all intolerant. It seems to me the original sin is intolerance and prejudice.

And it is that prejudice which fuels the belief that the majority of people from ethnic minority groups are scroungers who come to live off our benefit system and rake in huge amounts of money. I spoke to someone who is herself from an immigrant background who works in Newham.

There probably *are* examples where [a family] has nine, ten, eleven children, and with yourself, or your partner, or a child who is entitled to disability living allowance, and your entitlement to attendance allowance [then] there will be people entitled to several hundreds of pounds a week. But if you divide that by the number of people it is meant to feed and clothe, and all the rest of it, it is not unreasonable. But it must be extremely difficult for people not to have these reactions. Especially if people appear to be different in clothing, in accent, in colour, in religion. It is a natural reaction to blame other people when they themselves are badly off. And many people here *are* badly off.

Despite there always seeming to have been some wariness between different cultures, the anxiety within the community as a whole, which results in the world outside the home being seen as a threatening and dangerous place for the elderly and for children, appears to be a more recent phenomenon.

After school you didn't come indoors at all. I suppose we put our things in, but then you were out again. Out playing with all the kids. No one seemed to worry about you, because nothing happened to you. You never felt there was someone round the corner waiting to take you away. You did have it around, I suppose, but you knew everyone in your community. You knew you were safe.

People who spoke to me certainly remembered the East End as being one big playground. In the next chapter, they share their recollections of a childhood world – unregulated and alarmingly dangerous by today's standards – of tarmac and lamp-posts, barges and canals, larks and mischief, games and pranks.

8

We'd be out from first thing till it got pitch dark.

Children in east London spent much of their spare time outside amusing themselves: raking the streets and playing games with their friends, making do with few toys and little purpose-built equipment, using, instead, their imagination and surprising inventiveness to create things to entertain them. It is amazing the uses to which old wheels can be put – everything, apparently, from making hoops and carts to constructing canal-dragging equipment.

As can be seen in these stories and memories of childhood, the phrase 'we made our own fun in them days' is a cliché which actually reflects the truth.

> We made our own games then. Didn't cost nothing. Fashion a cricket bat out of something or other and play cricket in the middle of the road, using a manhole cover for a wicket. The only thing you had to watch was the windows, cos the streets were very narrow. Or we'd draw three lines across the street and make that a tennis court. We had an old ball and used our hands for bats. The game I really enjoyed – there were so many it's hard to choose – was called Release. There were probably about a dozen of you split into two teams. You'd spin up or whatever [toss a coin to decide] and six would run and the other six would try and catch them. You'd mark out a space on the pavement to use as a gaol. If you were caught you'd get put there; stand there until everyone was caught on your side, then you'd change over and chase them. That used to be good, because if you used your loaf you could hang about round corners and dodge them. You'd wait till they had about four of your mates imprisoned on the pavement, then while they were distracted, looking for you, you'd run across to the pavement gaol and shout out, 'Release!' And the ones who'd been captured would run off in all directions, all

over the place. You'd run miles. Tire yourself out. It was great.

Mostly we just played out. Marbles in the gutter, hopscotch on the pavement, football in the road.

We had group games like cricket, with a home-made bat and three sticks for a wicket. These were physical, rough and tumble games which sometimes resulted in a severe reprimand when you got home. There was not a lot of money for new clothes and we were threatened with not being allowed out because we would have nothing left to wear.

The toy I played with most was a hoop, which was a bicycle-wheel rim with all the spokes taken out. I would get a stick which fitted the hoop and just run all over the place.

My childhood was happy. We were not surrounded by a lot of children with wonderful toys making us envious [and] there were no big stores filled with unobtainable goodies. The only shop we knew with anything like *wonderful* things was Woolworths. [Instead] we made our own amusement. We had marbles, some clay and others more valuable, called glarnies, made of glass, which we put a value on depending on size. One enterprising invention with marbles was [to] get a shoebox and cut small, arched holes along one edge that would allow a marble to pass through; mark a series of numbers over each one, up to ten, then put the box upside down on the pavement. [The object] was to get your marbles through the arches, from several feet away. Those that didn't get through were taken by the owner of the box. The size of the arch with ten above it was just about legal. We also used to gamble with cigarette cards. Each lad would have four or five, and you would flick them in turn along the ground towards the wall. When finished flicking, the nearest to the wall took the lot.

Games had rules and a vocabulary, and there were rhymes to

pronounce you 'out': 'Eeny-meany-miny-moe', 'One potato, two potato, three potato, four'. And crossed fingers and 'fainlights' gave you protection.

A game, described below, which would raise a few eyebrows if children were caught playing it nowadays seems to have been played in all innocence in the 1920s. When I asked the respondents about whether they really were more naïve during their own childhoods than youngsters would appear to be today, the general view was that although people lived on top of one another, children were apart from the adults, leading almost separate lives, with their own childish and childlike concerns. It wasn't only that children were expected to be 'seen and not heard' but that grown-ups had little to do with, and often knew even less about, the carryings-on of the kids during both their school and their leisure time. It was this partial segregation that resulted in children being able to avoid more mature matters and sophisticated issues for far longer than those who are now exposed to an almost constant diet of adult concerns, worries and behaviours through the mass electronic and print media. Television, as will be seen in later chapters, was often cited as being a major source of change for the worse in all kinds of situations.

One street game was called Undercover. There was a crowd of girls and a crowd of boys. Some of one lot would get under a load of old coats, while the other lot were hiding. Then they used to come back and guess who was under the coats just by touching.

A very popular pastime that was both creative and money-earning involved setting up grottoes. There was a general agreement on what they should be like, but the particulars varied according to what was available and how artistic you were.

You'd upturn an old crate or a box and cover it with a cloth. Then you'd lay out all your treasures on it. Postcards, stones, beads, anything you could find. You'd have to shield it with your arm so no one could get a look unless they paid to see it. Ha'penny a look they'd charge. And the kids'd pay it if they could. There wasn't all the stuff kids have now to amuse themselves. It was something special.

We always had a grotto. It was usually on someone's step so you could build it up. You'd get a farthing sheet of coloured tissue paper. You'd put the paper all over the step and you'd get a board or a stool. Then you'd get anything like shells or beads or anything colourful or shiny – we used to save old beads and make butterflies with them on fuse wire, tiny beads – and you'd set it all out. We used to ask for money to see the grotto. Then we'd share it out amongst us and go and buy sweets or something to eat with it.

When you'd made your grotto – it could have anything on it from old postcards to a bunch of weeds in a jam jar, anything a bit attractive – you'd shield it, with your arm round it, so no one got a free look. If they didn't pay their ha'penny, then they didn't get a look. I'm not sure why they were called grottoes, but the idea probably came from the shrines that the mums from the Catholic families used to set up by their street doorstep when it was the day of the local Catholic church's parade. Whatever the reason for them being called grottoes, they brought in a nice few coppers for us for sweets, like doing Penny for the Guy.

Going out 'guying' was done by most children in the weeks leading up to Bonfire Night. There was no adult apprehension about whether such behaviour would be construed as begging, or about what the little devils would get up to once they had collected their spoils – buying a few loose fags in the corner shop or a pocketful of bangers to throw at passers-by was practically a traditional rite of passage.

The effort put into the enterprise varied from the production of half-hearted affairs with heads made from brown-paper bags and a few scribbled crayon features to the rather more creative undertaking of this young man and his friends, who based their 'guy' on a popular wireless programme, guessing, rightly, that it would go down well with potential penny-givers.

One Guy Fawkes day they dressed me up as an Arthur Askey character, Nausea Bagwash, sat me in a pushchair and wheeled me round collecting money for the guy – which was me. I was dressed in an old bagwash sack, with holes cut for my arms; they put make-up on me, and a scarf tied round my head. This got a lot of laughs, and it also got us money for our fireworks.

There was work other than collecting pennies to be done before the big night and children would haunt local markets, timberyards and waste ground for old boxes, scrap timber or anything else they could set light to. Organizing the fire was a serious business.

There was hardly any traffic down our little side turning, so we'd start building up the fire a good few days before Guy Fawkes. Like a great big wigwam sort of a shape we'd build. You could get all sorts of odds, stuff that would burn well, and from all the little firms round there. [*Laughing*] Sometimes we even used to ask if we could take it! That'll do, stick that on the barrow!

As with the annual preparations for Bonfire Night, games and pastimes often ran in what were called seasons, what we would now call fads or crazes.

I remember we had what were known as seasons for games. There were cigarette card seasons, marble and glarney seasons, peg top seasons, and, in the autumn, the conker season, with horse chestnut battles, quickly followed by collecting for Guy Fawkes and Firework Night, with the street fires on 5 November.

At voting times, there was a regular kids' activity – you'd have a rolled-up newspaper tied up all over with string. That was your weapon. And you'd go round to another street and find another crowd of kids. 'Who do you vote for?' If they didn't vote the same as you, you whacked them!

*

There was a game that, now I look back on it, was bloody marvellous. It was a game of skill called Diablo. You had two sticks, with a piece of string tied to the end of each one and a huge sort of cotton-reel affair – probably got them out of a factory. Someone would put the cotton reel on the sticks, while the other one held them, then they'd move the sticks up and down until the reel was spinning. Then they'd throw it up in the air! And I mean *throw* it. Right up and down. And, nine times out of ten, they would catch the reel right back on that string. It was bloody marvellous how they did it. Marvellous.

Tin-can stilts. I loved them. One kid would come out with a pair – empty cocoa tins, with a hole on each side near the bottom to put string through; turn the can upside-down to stand on it, and hold the strings in your hands and just walk up and down, clanking and clonking and falling off! One kid would come out with them and you'd all want them. You'd pester your mother: 'Got any empty tins, Mum?' They had to be strong ones, like cocoa or treacle tins, or they'd just collapse. We all had to have them. It was terrible if you had to wait a day or so for what was in the tin to be used up.

We followed all the games in season. There was hopscotch – I wasn't much good at it, but I loved to chalk the grid on the pavement. Marbles. Good mums made little bags to keep the collection in, but mine never did, and I made do with paper bags and pockets. The marbles themselves gave me a great deal of joy. They came in all sizes and were bought at Woolworths. They were all made by hand and every one was different. Each glass sphere was a tiny world, and the streaks and colours were beautiful. We also played with whips and tops. One of my uncles made me a top, which I thought was craftsmanship beyond belief, and I was so proud of it. We skipped to songs, often made up about the war and its principal characters. I was good at skipping and enjoyed it. We also played Jacks – five stones, gobs – with five cheap clay stones tossed in the air and caught on the back of our hands.

The game could go on for hours. The boys played conkers in season. They soaked them in brine or vinegar and baked them to improve their longevity. Any horse chestnut tree was savaged by small boys throwing pieces of wood up to make the conkers rain down. I collected conkers too, not to play with, that was only for boys, but because I was moved to find such beautiful treasures inside the prickly skin. They were polished, silky to touch, a wonderful rich colour, and sometimes marbled with a grain. They always shrivelled and went dull eventually, but there would always be next year.

Seasons could also encompass special treats.

Suddenly in the market it would be pomegranate time. The stall-holders would have so many they'd sell them off cheap before they went rotten. Every kid in the street would be spitting out the bitter yellow pith and pips and have all red juice running down their chins.

One widespread pastime, which was never out of season, was making a nuisance of yourself with the neighbours.

There was Knock Down Ginger. We used to get hold of a piece of string and tie it on a knocker and trail it across the road and stand around the corner holding the end. You'd just pull it and the knocker would bang on the door. The lady or man of the house would come out and, especially if he was a bit old and couldn't see properly, he'd be looking all up and down the street. You'd do that about four or five times, and, in the finish, they used to go potty, used to do their nut. They used to shake their fist: 'I know what you're doing!' And snatch the string off the knocker!

We had a bit of a variation on Knock Down Ginger. The streets were very narrow and you could tie a string from one door to one across the street. Leave the string a little bit slack, then knock on the doors and leg it round the corner and wait for them both to try and open their doors and start going barmy when they couldn't. That really used to amuse us, that did.

Aggravating your family could be just as entertaining as causing mischief for the neighbours.

There were lots of daddy-long-legs under the windowsills in the backyard and [my brother] hated spiders, but I wasn't frightened and would pick them up by the legs and taunt him with them. One morning, as we were getting dressed, I told [him] that I had seen a spider in his trousers just as he was putting them on. Of course, it wasn't true, but he created such a fuss, and I was in trouble for upsetting him *and* telling lies.

It was a wonder that some amusements, such as the ones described next, did not end in tragedy, or at least in a few more bruises than they did.

We played quite a dangerous game of jumping on the back of a lorry when one stopped at the traffic lights. We would ride along [until] we felt it was picking up too much speed and then we would jump off. Sometimes we would hold on to the back and be pulled along by our roller-skates. Luckily we all managed to survive and, what's more, not get caught. Amazing!

We would make a pop-gun from a short length of a tree branch. The pith was bored out and another piece of stick was made to fit into the bore hole, then an acorn was rammed into one end. As the stick was pushed in, the pressure sent the acorn shooting out. They could have been quite dangerous, because the acorn went at quite a speed.

There was a lot of debris from the bombing around our area left over from the war. We all had great fun playing on and around them. My friends and I used to rummage round looking for treasure. Of course, there was nothing but rubble.

When I look back on it now, I suppose it was quite dangerous.

We were fascinated with lighting fires – anything that we shouldn't have been doing, see – and poking around for rubbish on the bomb sites and in the half-demolished houses. Sometimes a floorboard would give way and it would frighten the life out of you!

Even team games were boisterous to the point of being dangerous.

High Jimmy Knacker involved two teams of five or six boys. One team would have one of you being the pillar – you leaned back against the wall to steady yourself – then someone would bend over in front of you, in a sort of leap-frog position, and wedge their head hard into your stomach and grip you round the waist. The others from your team would get behind him in the same position. Then the first one of the other team would come running from the other side of the street and spring forward to get as far along the line as possible – so he was sitting on the back of the one with his head in the pillar's belly! If he was a bit feeble he'd only get so far along and there was no room left for the others to get a good strong position – that being the idea, how many could get on and stay there, and try and make the ones underneath collapse. If the kids underneath caved in and fell down, you'd shout, 'Weak horses!' But if you'd got all the other team sitting on your backs, you'd all holler out, 'High Jimmy Knacker! One, two, three! High Jimmy Knacker! High Bobbereee!'

There were some games which were rather less violent, and were seen as almost exclusively feminine.

The girls used to get a length of rope – wherever they got it from, Gawd above knows – it used to stretch right across the street. They would get four or five girls all skipping together.

One would go in and start it. And they'd go round and round, and call out, 'Come on, Mary!' And the next one would dive in. Kate would have a go and then Liza. It used to be great. We'd stand there, the boys shouting, 'Go on, girls, show us your knickers!' And that would be it. They'd run and chase us all over the place.

I was born after the war, but my mum taught me a skipping song that we all used to sing, even if we didn't have a clue what it meant:

> *Underneath the spreading chestnut tree,*
> *Neville Chamberlain said to me,*
> *If you want to get your gas mask free,*
> *Join the blooming ARP.*

We all sang it. Like 'Salt, Vinegar, Mustard, Pepper'. You know the one. Sometimes the songs we sang would go with sort of dancing games. *They* didn't always make sense either. You'd dance round a circle of other girls, singing:

> *In and out the dusty bluebells,*
> *In and out the dusty bluebells,*
> *In and out the dusty bluebells,*
> *Fo-l-low the master.*

Then, when the rhyme stopped, you'd tap the girl you'd stopped by, and sing:

> *Pat a little doggy on the shoulder,*
> *Pat a little doggy on the shoulder,*
> *Pat a little doggy on the shoulder,*
> *You shall be my master.*

Then she'd join in behind you and you'd both dance round singing the first bit. This would go on until there were just two girls left in the circle, and you'd dance under an arch they'd made with their arms – like with Oranges and Lemons.

Then, when there was just one left – this isn't very nice [*laughing*] you'd kind of pat the one who was left a bit vigorously!

Girls played five stones – gobs – and would mark out an outline for games of hopscotch, using a piece of old roofing slate for a marker. You'd just look round and find a bit of slate that had fallen off a roof.

As the girls skipped they would chant ditties. I remember 'Salt, Mustard, Vinegar, Pepper'. Another one that started, 'All last night and the night before'. Then there was 'Oranges and Lemons' – the Bell Bows song – as well as 'Handy-pandy, Sugar Candy'.

Skipping encapsulated one of the most important features of any type of childhood amusement: it cost nothing, or very little, to take part in and enjoy.

We used to play with old cans. Line them up on the wall, and you had to knock them down. You made do. You never had anything bought for you.

My favourite game by far was a rope tied around the top of the lamp-post and just swinging round and round, or climbing to the top without falling off.

Some activities took the children much further afield than their immediate neighbourhood. Life was very different for youngsters unhindered by parents' anxiety about what they were up to every moment of the day, and children could also take the opportunity to exercise their resourcefulness to earn a few extra pennies.

There was part of the Hackney Marshes that was used by the council as a rubbish tip, but it was also our adventure playground. It was about four miles away, but to us with our one skate or home-made cart – a box on four pram wheels – we would spend all day searching among the rubbish and

using the mounds of smouldering waste in our games, and
still have energy left to race each other home. Our parents
never worried too much about what we were doing, and only
started to be concerned if we didn't turn up for meals.

The most popular toy was a cart we built from planks of
wood and pram wheels on which we used to travel for miles.
Most Saturday mornings we used to visit [the] market and
collect old wooden boxes, which we chopped up and sold as
firewood. Many miles were also travelled hanging on to the
back of horse-drawn vans. Many a time we were forced to
abandon our 'transport' on hearing the shout from some
unfriendly individual, 'Whip behind, guv'nor', at which the
driver would flip his whip to get rid of us, his unwanted
cargo.

As there wasn't much money about we had to try and earn
some ourselves to get pocket money, so with all the horses
about we would go and collect the manure and sell it to
anyone who had a garden. One day [my brother] was going
out with his mates [with a] handmade cart collecting manure
and he had to take me, so when I got tired [he] sat me on top
of the pile, while he pulled it along. [We also] made bundles
of firewood and sold them. We had to go round the streets
getting the wood to chop up. Some of it was old fish boxes –
I reckon some of the fires smelled a bit choice. We also kept
our eyes open for when the roads were being repaired,
because the original surfaces were made up of tarry blocks,
which were wooden blocks soaked in tar. If we got a load of
these we could either sell them or take them home for our
own fire.

It was not only money they were after. Cigarette cards were a
valuable commodity that could be collected, swapped and even used
as currency in gambling games.

We would go to the Salmon and Ball on a weekday evening
to catch the men coming home from work. We waited at the

bus stop and, as the people got off, we would say, 'Got any cigarette cards, mister?' There were lots of diffcrent series to collect: film and radio stars, footballers and cricketers. Each different brand had its own collections. Some of the more expensive brands had silk cards in their packs and today would be worth quite a bit of money.

Because the grown-ups were all card players, we were well versed in games of chance from an early age, and many hours during dull winter days were spent using cigarette cards as collateral. There were thousands of cigarette cards around. I remember having boxes filled with cards in different states of condition, from dog-eared to mint.

We would go and stand outside a cigarette shop and ask the man leaving with his pack of cigarettes if we could have the picture card inside. Most young men would give it to you; older ones kept them for their own children.

Even something as apparently worthless as a used bus ticket or a pile of cherry stones was much sought after by children who were expected to amuse themselves and whose parents would have been puzzled by children hanging around the house complaining they were 'bored' or had 'nothing to do'.

We collected old bus tickets. There would be some way of adding up numbers on them, and we would claim we had a 'lucky' ticket. They weren't even ours, just rubbish we'd scrounge or pick up off the ground near the bus stops. Probably because we had so little of our own, everything was precious, nothing was wasted. You could make a game out of nothing – hanging around bus stops and collecting old tickets! And asking strangers for them!

We would play cards and use cherry 'ogs [stones] as money. I don't think we even washed them!

We would also try and get the different kinds of maps from

the conductors on the bus, tube and Green Line. I don't know why, but it was something else to collect.

The Thames, the Lea and the canals were dangerous magnets for London children, who could get up to all sorts of mischief in the water and mud.

Our Georgie was a real devil. He had no fear. He'd dive in off Stink House Bridge for ha'pennies people threw in, and go swimming off the waterman's stairs in Wapping. Didn't care how dirty the river was.

We used to go down to the river Saturday nights and watch the pleasure boats come up the Thames. All lit up. Dancing, there used to be. We used to sit there watching them, thinking, 'Ain't it lovely to be old? We could do that then.' We used to go down to the river at other times and watch the steamers coming up to the Pool of London. The old tug pulling them up river, belching thick black smoke out of the funnel. And we used to stand there looking. We knew what most of them was carrying – you'd be used to it over the years, growing up there – especially at Christmas time. One boat used to come loaded with tomatoes. And we used to wait outside the dock gate for the vans. It was mostly horses and vans then, there wasn't that many motors or lorries. We used to wait for these vans to come out of the gate and they'd be loaded sky high with tomatoes. They was only light, wasn't they, but we never used to think that. We used to say, 'Look, the poor horse has got to pull them up the hill.' But it didn't make no difference to what we did. We still used to run along behind and hang on the tailboard, put our hands through the paper covering the boxes or trays and get a few tomatoes. Put them in our shirts and drop off again. Someone would shout, 'Get away from there!' and the old carman would look round and out would come his whip. And over it would come. If you was cute, you'd duck underneath while the carman pulled away from you and you'd have it away with a shirt full of tomatoes. You'd either take them home or, if it got around

you had them, you'd share them with your mates. Sit down
and have a good feed of tomatoes.

The East End actually had its own beach on the river, at the Tower
of London, created from 1,500 tons of sand along 800 feet of the
shingle foreshore. King George V gave his approval for the supervised
beach, following a campaign to protect cockney children who, sometimes fatally, used the Thames as their playground.

The King officially opened the beach in July 1934, declaring that
young Londoners should be given, when the tides allowed, 'free
access for ever'. From the beginning it was packed, and not only
with children; whole families turned up to make good use of deck
chairs, buckets and spades, and even to enjoy Punch and Judy shows.

Being right by Tower Bridge, the beach revellers, on their man-
made playground, could watch the passing pleasure steamers taking
other Londoners to the 'real' seaside at Southend. But the sand by
the Thames was just as good.

As well as the beach, the children of east London could enjoy
open spaces and entertainments in the various parks, and, as the
man speaking next explains, some 'rural things' could be appreciated
well into the 1930s.

We may have lived in the East End but there was still some
rural things around us. Horses were stabled [nearby] and
there was a forge where they were taken to be reshod. We
would watch as the smithy hammered the red-hot shoes to
size and shape, and I can still smell the odour as it was
pressed on the horse's hoof. There was also a dairy which
kept its own cow in the yard so that it got fresh milk.
Pasteurized? Never needed it! [But] for open green fields we
had to go to one of the parks. I suppose the nearest to where
we lived was the Bethnal Green Gardens, which were next to
the museum in Cambridge Heath Road, or there was the
'Barmy Park' outside the library a bit further along. Then
there was Meath Gardens in Green Street, [now called]
Roman Road, where we could go in the season to collect
'Hairy Jack' caterpillars in jars.

Young cockneys could find opportunities for making a bit of mischief even in the gloriously pastoral surroundings of Victoria Park.

> As kids, we would stand on the bridge that spanned the lake in Victoria Park and, of course *accidentally*, spit on the rowers in their double sculls or the lads showing off in their single sculls. Only sixpence an hour!

> When the holidays came for us kids, Vicky Park was the target. Off in their thousands went the young ones, in groups up to a dozen; laughing, crying, shouting and hollering kids with their bottles of tap water made tasty by bunging in a spoonful of cheap lemonade or sherbet powder, or even the exotic taste of liquorice powder. For kids visiting the park, one penny's worth of sweets would do a fine job.

But they could also be surprisingly mature. Here one of the 'Little Mothers', girls who minded their younger siblings, describes her outings to the park.

> We lived a few yards from the entrance to Lloyd's Park. By the time I was five, and [my brother] was six months old, I would be in the park all day with him during the school holidays. He had an old-fashioned pram with a well beneath it. We could take out the stiff cover, when he was older, and he could sit up with his feet in the well. From the time he was six months old, I would be sent off with him in his pram to the park. In the well would go two made-up bottles of National Dried Milk for him – the milk fat floated in globules on the top when you mixed it – and a bottle of tap water and a round of jam sandwiches wrapped in newspaper for me. In the park I watched the ducks, played on the swings, allowed other girls to take turns with my live baby doll – rocking the pram and pushing him. There was always summer holiday fun arranged: Punch and Judy, Pierrot shows, concerts and road-safety shows.

Boys, as was then the accepted way, had a more carefree time of it.

> We would go along Hackney Road, then across Cambridge
> Heath Road into Bishop's Way, which led to the main park
> entrance, [then] over the canal bridge, stopping to see if there
> were any barges being towed along by horses, then turn left
> to the pens where they kept the guinea pigs, rabbits and
> wallabies, then have a look at all the different birds in the
> aviary, and, just round the corner from there, the playground
> with swings, slides, sandpit and other things to ride on. After
> playing there for a while, we would go a bit further round on
> to the island with the Chinese pagoda and have a look at that
> before going on to see the deer. A bit further round was the
> jetty to the big lake and if we had enough money we could go
> for a ride in the big motor boat, which took you all round
> the islands in the lake.

Both boys and girls would play out until it was, by today's standards, astonishingly late.

> We'd go out after school and Mum would just say, 'Come in
> when it's dark.' In the summer that could be gone ten
> o'clock, but it was safer then, of course. You had no worries
> about your kids being on the streets playing.

> Off we'd go after our tea and we wouldn't come back until it
> was pitch dark. We were gone for hours on end.

> It didn't seem to worry us that we were out and about at
> night. We'd hang around in a group, sitting on the kerb,
> usually by the lamp-post. Someone might have some chips if
> you were lucky. All wrapped up in soggy newspaper with the
> vinegar dripping out. 'Go on, give us a chip!' you'd go. And if
> it was cold we'd throw all the coats over our legs.

Although sometimes the dark could seem threatening to susceptible young imaginations.

There was a great deal of excitement when a house up
towards Claredale Street was supposed to be haunted. The
police had come round and closed the street from Old
Bethnal Green Road up to Claredale Street, and stories were
going round that a policeman was thrown down the stairs by
some unseen spirit, and someone from the Home Office was
supposed to be investigating the phenomenon. It was some
time after this that [my brother] went on an errand one dark
evening for Dad for cigarettes. He came running back yelling
his head off about a horse's head in the doorway. Well, Dad
went up the street to see what had frightened him and found
that in an arched transom over a door two triangular panes
of glass had been replaced with wood, giving the appearance
of a pair of horse's ears, so that mystery was solved, but if I
ever had to go up there in the dark, I would run like the devil
so nothing could get me.

You'd always have one of the bigger kids giving you the
willies, telling you stories about the Grey Lady. I don't know
who she was, but I was scared stiff of her!

I can remember being equally scared hearing about Flannel Foot.
He was a cunning cat burglar who, according to a girl who lived
round the corner, padded his feet with cloths so you couldn't hear
him breaking into your house. I would lie awake, too terrified to
sleep, in case he picked our house to burgle.
  Scared off the street by such tales or just being ready for your tea,
when it was eventually time to go home, getting in wasn't always an
easy business.

To open our street door, there was a piece of string attached
on the inside to the latch, and the string then went out
through a hole in the door, or was suspended so that it could
be reached though the letter box, then you just pulled the
string to open the door. [But] if the door was locked, I was
too small to reach the knocker, so I would hold on to the
door knob and walk my feet up the wall until I was upside-
down and I could lift the knocker with my feet.

*

I'd been out playing and I must have come home earlier than
my mum expected. But it was all right, I just went along the
road to the corner baker's shop and went in there. They let
me go down into the kitchen, where they were getting stuff
ready for the next morning. It all smelled lovely. And your
mum wouldn't be worried, she'd know you were safe.

Once indoors, there were some entertainments for the children,
although they often required a little resourcefulness for them to
succeed as amusements.

We didn't have an over-abundance of toys, so we had to look
after and repair what we could. We had some lead – yes, real
lead – soldiers, and a lead bear whose head had come off and
was stuck on again with a matchstick. We also had to use our
imagination quite a bit to make or improve our playthings.
One evening [my brother] and I were playing down in the
kitchen, Mum was out somewhere and Dad was looking after
us. [My brother] was cutting out a farmyard from newspaper
and standing all the animals up. I blew them down by
jumping over them. He says I jumped on the scissors, I say he
stabbed them up into my foot, but I remember Dad went
potty, as he usually did in a crisis.

Some of my happiest memories of childhood are of [Aunt
Marie] getting home from work and teaching me to cut out
paper doilies and playing Fly Away Peter.

We didn't like being stuck indoors in the wet weather, as our
flat was small, but we would always find things to do. We had
board games, and sometimes would do drawing or colouring.
We used to collect hundreds of different buttons, which we
kept in an old tin box. We played a game with them by
throwing several of them on the table, then, licking the
thumb to make it moist, we would try and pick up as many
of the opponent's buttons as we could without rewetting our
thumb. The one that could pick up the most in one go would
win the game and all the buttons on the table. My parents

would save their cigarette packets and we would make a little
house or a handbag out of them or anything that caught our
imagination. A teacher at school made Buckingham Palace
out of hundreds of cigarette packets, which was very
impressive.

A real indoor treat was going to the cinema – the 'flicks', the
'pictures', the 'bug house'.

I loved the Saturday morning flicks. If you were lucky and
had a few coppers to spend that you'd earned running
errands, you could pay to get into the pictures, buy a lump
of honeycomb, a few ends of sweet rock, and even a little
celluloid fish that told your fortune, *and* see the serials!

We always went to [children's] Saturday morning pictures.
Prior to the film starting there would be some form of
entertainment. At one time there was a man showing us what
he could do with a yo-yo; another time we had a woman
showing us different animal shapes that could be made out of
balloons. If there was nothing special on, then a pianist
would perform until the film started.

On Saturdays we were given our pocket money; this only
happened if Dad had a good week. We would go to the
Excelsior Cinema to the 'Tuppenny Rush', as it was called.
On the way we would go to Meads, a shop in a ground-floor
flat with a wooden box over the windowsill to serve as the
counter. We would get two 'Ha'penny Bags', which contained
a mixture of broken biscuits and sweets that had become
unwrapped; we thought these were great value. We mostly
saw serials on these cinema visits. I don't ever remember
seeing a full-length film. The other kids would flick milk-
bottle tops up through the light rays so they looked like
shooting stars. The usher would walk round the side balcony
calling, 'Watch it! Watch it!' Though whether he meant
'Watch the film' or 'Watch out', I don't know. They were
mostly cowboys or science fiction, with such stars as Ken

Maynard, Buck Jones, Roy Rogers, Rin Tin Tin, 'The
Lightning Warrior', or *Buck Rogers in Space*. On the way
home we would pretend to be riding a horse, galloping along,
slapping ourselves on the backside.

If the projector broke down you should have heard the 'cheye
eyeking'. Riots practically used to break out, with all the kids
pelting stuff and hollering. And, when the film started again,
you'd get this commentary, all the kids offering advice to the
hero up on the screen: 'Look out, he's got a gun!' The serials
always ended with a cliffhanger. But you *knew* the goody was
going to be all right, and he'd live to save everyone again next
week, but you still got really caught up in it. And you could
tell what sort of a story we'd all seen by how we were acting
when we came out. Whether you were from space, a soldier
or a cowboy, or whatever – or even a horse! We'd make
someone be the baddy and all pile in on him on the way
home.

Despite claims, and a genuinely held belief, that 'it was safer then'
for children to go out and about, there were instances when it
certainly wasn't, although the seriousness of the threat to their
well-being varied considerably, as the following memories show.

It seems incredible now, when children are perceived as being
in danger whenever they are out alone, that my mum let me
go to the park from the time I was four and a half years old.
There was little room to play in the garden, which was all
taken up with the air-raid shelter. I would roam the park,
attaching myself to bigger girls. On one occasion I wanted to
get on a swing, which was like a bench and took six or eight
children. There wasn't room for me, so I decided to hang on
the end. This was fine and exciting while my feet touched the
ground. As the swing went higher, so I went up with it, and
[I felt] a great sense of exhilaration. But my little arms would
not support my weight and I let go, falling on to the concrete
below. A gaggle of girls took me home in someone's
pushchair. I had a bump on my forehead as large as a hen's

egg that was all the colours of a rainbow. A wet flannel was put on it and the doctor called. He gave us something in a dark-blue ribbed bottle labelled *poison* to put on it. I was very afraid I might accidentally drink the poison or that the baby would.

One day I went with some other kids who were going dragging down the Regent's Canal. Dragging was done by wrapping a sack round an old bicycle-wheel rim after the spokes had been removed so that it was in effect a large sieve, then it was tied to a piece of strong string and thrown in the water and dragged out, hopefully with some tiddlers caught in the sack. The time passed and I was enjoying myself, even though I had lost a shoe in the water and my socks were soaking wet. By the time we decided to go home it was getting late. Mum had called the police to look for her 'missing' child and, when I turned up, I got a good hiding and sent to bed.

I was six [and we were living] in Leyton, near to the Hollow Ponds. One day, I was playing by the edge of the water and a man came up and talked to me. I had stepped in the water and had got my stockings wet. They were horrible thick, black woolly ones, held up by elastic garters. It was a sunny day and he suggested I took them off and hung them on the bushes to dry. He insisted on helping me. As he did so he put his fingers in my knickers and touched me in a way which made me squirm and feel very uncomfortable. When the stockings were finally dry he 'helped' me put them on and touched me again in the same way. All the while, my mind was working overtime in an effort to get rid of him. I instinctively knew it was wrong, what he was doing, but I felt I could not tell anyone, especially not my parents. I lived very near and was afraid to run off in case he should follow me. The terror I felt is still so vivid. I remember I invented an address in case he should ask me where I lived. It was 9 Happy Villas. When I did finally get home I began to have nightmares about it.

*

There was this one time when a man was hanging around by the school. He was like a sort of tramp. One afternoon, I was sitting in the cloakroom with my friend – we were meant to have gone home, but it was freezing out and we were sitting on the hot pipes chatting. Well, he only came into the cloakroom – little juniors, we were – and his what's-it was hanging out. He was disgusting. He asked us if we'd touch him. We were petrified. We'd been warned that there were 'nasty' men about but had had no real idea what that meant. We knew then all right. We scrambled under the rows of pegs and ran for our life. Lucky there were two of us. The daft thing is, we told all our mates, even sort of bragged about it, full of ourselves, you know. But neither of us told an adult. It was too dirty, if you understand what I mean. It wasn't the sort of thing you talked about with adults then. Not a teacher, not even your mum. Mind you, if I had told my mum, she'd have been after his bits with a bread knife. She was very protective.

I was playing with a friend on a bomb site and a man came up to us. He was furtive, looking intensely at his fingers. He asked us if he could show us his prick. I had never heard the word [used in that way] and didn't realize that he meant his penis. I thought he had a splinter in the thumb he was staring at so intensely. I was ready to go and get a needle to get his 'prick' – or splinter – out. Just then my dad came for us and the man scarpered. When I found out what the man meant, I thought we should tell the police – we *couldn't* tell our parents – and I thought out a description we could give to the police. I could give it now, I remember it so well. But we couldn't go to the police station without an adult and we were too scared to tell anyone, so the incident just passed by.

Even without the threat of playground accidents and threatening strangers, not all childhood memories are happy.

My uncle bought me a beautiful porcelain doll from wherever he was serving in the war. It had translucent skin, long lashes, tiny fingernails, real hair, and was, to me, an absolute idea of beauty. I was rarely allowed to play with it in case I broke it, so it was kept in a box in my bedroom, where I peeped at it with love. One day, when I had not possessed it very long, my aunts and uncles all came to our house, maybe it was my brother's first birthday. The doll was brought out for them all to admire. My mum allowed me to dress it in my brother's christening robe, which fitted it perfectly. It lay on the table with the long silk train reaching nearly to the floor. In that week [my brother] had begun to walk. Taking one or two steps, he would suddenly sit down or grab at a chair or table to support himself. On this day, everyone was laughing at him, clapping and encouraging him as he tottered forward. He reached the corner of the table, walked along one side of it, tottered, grabbed at the christening robe to support himself, sat down abruptly and there was my precious doll – no one else in our street had one anything like it – in tiny, sharp shards on the floor. My aunties told me endlessly, 'He couldn't help it', 'He didn't mean it', but none of that helped. I knew no one would ever buy me a doll like that again. [But] years later, when I was twelve and desperately unhappy in a children's home, when my dad asked me what I wanted for Christmas, I said I wanted a doll. It was to be a secret – girls of twelve didn't play with dolls, that would be too babyish. But he took me seriously, didn't ridicule me, recognized I needed something of my own as I was so lonely there.

When a childhood treat as rare as an outing was so anticipated, the actual event could prove to be very disappointing.

We didn't have holidays. The most I can remember was a day's outing, when Nanny was taking me out on a trip to the seaside to Southend. We got there and walked down the front and I wanted to go in paddling straight away, but Nanny said we had to go and have our dinner first, which we did. But when we went back to the beach, the tide had gone out and all there was was a long stretch of mud as far as I could see. I cried my eyes out.

*

For some children there was a more regular disappointment: the agony of having to go to school every day.

The East End has had a tradition of schools being supported by guilds and companies, primarily as a way of ensuring a literate workforce, and there have also been charitable and religious foundations, and other private patrons concerned with the education of the children of the labouring classes. From 1833, there were the beginnings of a formalized financial commitment to an embryonic state system which would provide schooling for the poor; then, with the 1870 introduction of free, universal elementary education, the opportunity for basic learning was put in place, and with it the London School Board.

Despite such provision, literacy remains a problem for children from disadvantaged backgrounds. When a child is needed to contribute to the family budget, or to mind the other children while their parents are working – as my own mother had to – education comes further down the list than it does in more financially privileged families.

For those who did attend school, the experience of being educated left varying impressions.

> I consider the education we, the children of Bethnal Green in the 1920s, received was sound, well balanced and expertly imparted by the teachers. Discipline and obedience were maintained from an early age and the method of teaching known as the Three Rs has been proven by my achievements and those of schoolfriends in later life. The times tables was most effective. Some critics of the system called it brainwashing. [But] I have always been thankful, after seventy years, I do not need a calculator to tell me what seven times nine adds up to, and know immediately if I have been given the right change after a purchase. Spelling bees, handwriting and composition exercises, with good old lines for impressing a wrong-doing. A hundred lines could do more good for learning right from wrong.

> The thing that can take me right back to nursery school – I went just after the war, when there were still nursery schools

all over the East End, set up so that the women could do war
work – is the smell of Bakelite. We used to sit with our little
overalls on at tables of four for our lunch – we used to call it
dinner – and with a beaker of water each. It was the smell of
that beaker I remember. I'm back there in that nursery when
I recall that smell.

I've never slept that well, even as a child, but every
afternoon we'd be expected to have a nap. The blanket on
your little cot had a little appliquéd badge – a house or a tree
or a lamb – that matched the one on your coat peg and the
badge on your overall. I would lie on my cot, fed up, staring
up at the glass and cast-iron roof, high overhead, wishing it
was time to get up and play again. I hated being there doing
nothing. I'm still the same, but there was no accounting for
difference in those days. It was nap time and that was that.
And as for not liking what you were given to eat! Forget that.
You ate it, no questions.

The classrooms were heated by coal in a big black stove; on
this a crate of milk would stand ready for us to drink
mid-morning. The school was lit by gaslight and the teacher
would light the lamps with a long wick as it started to get
dark.

Why did they always keep the milk near the radiator? Warm
milk! Yuch!

In rows we'd sit, behind lift-up-lid desks, with a china
ink-pot set in the top and a ridge for your dippy-in pen.
You'd learn things by rote. Repeating them over and over
again, and God help you if you got it wrong. I suppose you
learned your tables and the counties of England and stuff, but
you had no idea *why* you were learning it, what use it would
be. You wouldn't dare ask.

Discipline was a grim and unyielding business, with punishment
being brutal yet accepted as part of education.

From what I can remember, most of the teachers did not like children. I remember going to school one day when I was about seven years old and a boy had been caught with a pet mouse in his pocket. The headmaster had just seen the boy as I arrived. He callously took it off the boy and whipped it several times on the ground until there was blood everywhere and the poor creature was dead. I was always far too frightened to speak up if I didn't understand something for fear of ridicule [from the teachers]. When it was play time or home time a boy or girl would be given the job of ringing the bell. This I always wanted to do, but never did.

No disruptive activities of any kind were allowed while lessons were in progress. No talking, not paying attention and certainly no familiarity with the teacher. The cane was a thing that we had a fear of, administered across the palm of each hand and in front of the class. It was a physical and psychological hurt, because you had to get the cane and punishment book from the headmaster's study.

[In 1937] I started in the same class that [my brother] had been in two years earlier. The teacher was a bald-headed, cross-eyed Welshman. I hated him because he frightened the life out of me, he was so stern, and especially after I saw him give the cane to [a boy]. There were bits of cane flying past my ears as he brought the cane down each time [on the boy] and when we saw the great weals he had raised.

[When] I went back to school my new teacher would grab you by the hair and push you back over the desk and tell you off very quietly. He was another sadist.

We had this teacher – he'd be called a psychopath today – he used to throw the blackboard rubber, heavy wood with a metal hook on the end, directly at your head. You only had to displease him in some little way and you'd get a swipe round the ear. Not gentle, a real crack. He was the type who seemed to take pleasure in humiliating you. He'd read out things you'd written in a stupid, sneering voice. How can children respect someone who humiliates them? The only control he had over us was by fear. You couldn't ask him if you didn't understand something. You understood first time or you were thick. What a way to educate children.

But some recalled the rewards that there were to be had from attending school.

My schooling prepared me nicely at the age of fourteen, in 1930, to go out among the grown-ups and work, earn money, but still have respect for the older person. Business must have benefited by our indoctrinated obedience and respect for authority. Likewise, the government should have recognized, when war came along, that it was this discipline and regimentation that enabled myself and thousands of my generation to be drafted into the armed forces with a built-in respect for discipline and an ability to take orders.

Prize-giving day – what an incentive that was, with all the school present and you being called up to receive your nice shining new book or box of paints, things our parents could not afford to buy us.

However, the rewards were not always quite what children might have hoped for after doing their best.

I was thrilled. I was about six and I'd done really well at school and I was told I was going to get a prize on this special day, when these important people were going to come to the school, and I had to go up to the stage, curtsy and say, 'Thank you.' Well, I went up on the stage and I did as I was told and I was given this whole *pile* of books. I was so pleased. Books weren't things many people had at home in the East End. But when I came off stage, one of the teachers explained that the prize was *given* to me for what I had done, but they were to be kept for all the class. She took them off me and put them in the cupboard. God, I felt cheated.

*

I was allowed to sing a solo at our infants Christmas concert
– in the nativity play – as a treat for doing well. A treat? I
went through agonies singing that carol.

Some of the misunderstandings probably arose from the teachers
not being part of the local community and coming from quite
different backgrounds from that of the children. This difference
worked better for some children than for others.

I was a scholarship girl and they [the teachers] were more
interested in trying to make me 'speak proper' than in
showing me how to develop my brain or my character. I
hated every minute of it.

Looking back [I was born in 1915] I realize we had very good
schools. I was supposed to go to the convent in East India
Dock Road, but I refused to go in the door when I saw a nun.
[Later] I passed to go to the Central School. We had every
facility there: French, algebra, geometry, maths, English,
shorthand and typing, and good strict teachers. There was
even a flat where we went every week to learn housekeeping
and cooking. We had drill and netball [and] were trained to
earn a living in the outside world.

So many of us could not spell as well as we should, because
of our cockney way of speaking.

We were very fortunate, our local elementary was superb.
From [there] we took exams for entry to the Central or the
secondary school. That was in 1932, the first year that the
secondary, which until then had only had 'paid for' pupils,
allowed scholarship girls to enter their portals. We called it
the Roedean of Bow. In fact, it was Coborn School for Girls.
The standard of education was just superb. It helped round
off my cockney accent, which hasn't totally gone, of course.

There were things remembered about schooldays which would
appear archaic and even a bit strange if they were encountered today.

My mum took me to school on the first day, showed me where I had to go, then that was that, I took myself off every morning by myself. Parents weren't expected to go inside the school gates, that would have been interfering, and East End mums and dads used to be of the opinion that the teacher always knew best, and their own children's education was nothing to do with them.

[While we were evacuated] me and another boy were supposed to be helping another boy to learn to read, but every time he made a mistake we would hit him with a ruler on his head or his hands. We were vicious little sods and must have made his life hell. Whenever [the teacher] left the room, he would leave one of us in charge of the class, and one day, when he went out, everyone started messing about and someone shouted, 'Let's pretend a fire bomb has come down the chimney.' At that, one of the boys started peeing on the fire, but, as luck would have it, [the teacher] came back and caught him. I can't remember who the boy was, but I do remember he got a right caning for it.

History was a very serious subject in order to give pride to and for the country. We had special teachers for this type of lesson, with songs to learn for Empire Day and national songs.

My best friend was a Sikh, she was from the first Indian family in our school, and her birthday was on Empire Day. It was strange, I suppose, her joining in celebrations for the Empire. But that was what we did in those days. Without ever questioning what or why. It was just another celebration, like wearing light or dark blue on boat race day. We knew as little about Oxford or Cambridge as we did about the rights and wrongs of imperialism. And if we had known we wouldn't have questioned any of it. You didn't question anything at school, not if you valued the skin on the palms of your hand.

*

Some things about the more disciplined schooldays were recalled as working well.

Absenteeism [was] taken very seriously by the authorities. No child could be allowed out of school without a note from its parent. A rigid roll call each morning and after lunch would be taken and any child absent would warrant a call from the school board inspector. The truant man was known by everyone in the street. Parents were anxious [regarding] their respectability, even though they were poor. There was no arguing with authority [and] you could be sure of another chastisement from Dad or Mum.

You were scared of the school board man, if he caught you in the street. You didn't have to wait for the police to come up to you and say, 'What are you doing home from school?' If you saw the school board man, you bolted.

From the window of our flat, I could see the school I was to attend. September seemed an age to wait, I was so keen to go. Finally, the great day came. I remember the classroom vividly. There were small tables and chairs, coloured friezes on the walls, charts with numbers and dots, large charts with small-case letters to copy. It was an old school, with high windows. Then there was Miss Brown! I knew at once that my teacher was a film star. I had never been to the pictures or seen a film, but I knew what a film star should look like. My Uncle Dave had married a glamorous younger woman who, my mother always said, was like a film star. Miss Brown was as glamorous as anyone I'd seen before. She had large breasts, a tiny waist, slim pencil skirt, high heels and a shining fall of brown hair worn over one eye. What's more, this vision of loveliness was kind and encouraging, and I was instantly her slave. Even in the infants there were jobs to do in the classroom and I asked to be chosen to help give out the milk and change the weather board. Milk came in little squat bottles with cardboard lids. The lids had a central circle that could be pressed out and a straw inserted. Resources were short in wartime, so everything was saved to be used in the classroom. We learned to make woolly pom-poms by winding wool round the washed milk-bottle lids, cutting it and tying it up. Miss Brown thought of countless things to do with straws: plaiting and painting, blowing ink, printing. I had always drawn at home [but] Miss Brown encouraged in me a passion for drawing that later led me into becoming an art teacher.

The school authorities catered for more than the intellectual and creative sides of their pupils' lives; the health and hygiene of young Londoners were also accepted as being their concern.

I loved the malt we all got given every day, but I didn't like the cod liver oil so much. Do you know, we all had our spoon of malt off the same spoon! All the mothers would be up the school complaining if they tried to do that now.

There were regular visits by trained nurses to inspect for cleanliness and general appearance. To the children she was known as Nitty Norah, with her steel comb and bowl of disinfectant, to combat lice in the hair.

You could tell the kids who had nits. The nit nurse would shave all their hair off and paint this red sort of coloured stuff all over their head. We used to really take the mick out of them. [*Laughing*] Kids are horrible little monsters at times!

I think, as far as possible, the school officials kept an eye on the general well-being of the children. [By means such as] the free milk which was given daily. We all took advantage of this, getting a third of a pint at morning break. Most of the children at school were poorly dressed, clothes being a low priority in a poverty area such as Bethnal Green. I saw many children's funerals when I was at school, large families and much unemployment. Because of the poverty, schools had to supply every item. There was no expecting the parent to provide pens, pencils and exercise books, all had to be provided, including hundreds of educational books, one for each child.

But school was still school.

The only thing I liked about school, the *only* thing, was the malt. I couldn't get enough of that, but I could get more than enough of school. I couldn't wait to get home of an afternoon. It was like being let out of prison.

When he speaks about being so eager 'to get home', the man above was actually talking about being eager for liberation from the discipline and rigours of the school day, and for the freedom of the streets. Much as he probably loved his family, he would not have been exactly eager to go home, as such. Overcrowding and slum housing were almost as much of a problem in the East End of living memory as they had been back in the dark Dickensian days of the nineteenth century. But, as I was told:

It wasn't much, only a few rooms, and a shared cooker out on the landing, but it was our home.

And many others felt the same.

9

Our backyard had a few chickens; the pigeon loft; a rabbit run – they were to eat, like the chickens, but we still gave them names; my old pram – I was the youngest, but I don't suppose Mum wanted to risk getting rid of it, just in case; the tin bath, hanging from a nail on the wall; the outside lav; the dog's kennel; my little trike and my brother's home-made cart; and a lean-to scullery with a stock of fuel for the copper – which was also in there – along with the mangle, the scrubbing board, the chickens' and pigeon food. And hanging up outside the back door was the meat safe. All in that little yard.

At the beginning of the century, living conditions, for the majority of working people in east London, were very basic indeed. Overcrowded housing had been a problem ever since the area had first started to become urbanized and, with growing industrialization, the East End would become associated in popular imagination with soot-covered, terraced houses lining streets of dung-slicked cobbles, and with thick, choking fogs in which the criminal and the dangerous could stalk their unwary prey. That image was not far short of the actual experience of those who lived in the area up until the slum clearances of the 1950s and 1960s.

The lack of regulation and the ad-hoc nature of development only added to the problems of the people who had to pay rent for the privilege of living in those slums. But the poor and the needy were, as ever, attracted to a place that held the possibility of work, and they had to be housed. It was the availability, rather than the condition, of the housing – often cheap, insanitary lodgings – that was the major concern for tenants and landlords alike.

This description of a family home is given by a man born at the end of 1903.

[Our street] comprised a school and rows of houses of the

two-up and two-down variety, no bathrooms [and] a trip to
the toilet in winter was no pleasure as it was outside in the
yard.

There were very few gardens then, just yards. Our house
had the usual passage done in brown walls and with no
lighting, bare boards and stair treads. No gas or electricity,
only paraffin lamps which had to be cleaned before use.

My mother used to work on uniform overcoats and many
a coat has kept us warm in winter as we only had wood fires.
I remember my mother used to put a hot poker into her pint
of beer on the trivet of the fireplace.

Even for those born in the 1930s and 1940s, conditions remained
stark.

[Our] terraced house consisted of, on the ground floor, two
large rooms, one of which was our living room and the other
was the 'front room', but at times both of them doubled as
bedrooms. Down the passage to the back of the house there
was a small kitchen and behind that was the scullery. The
kitchen had a coal range with an oven at the side; there was
just enough room in the kitchen to hold a table and a couple
of chairs. The scullery had a copper built in just behind the
door from the kitchen and this was used for the weekly
washing. There was also a small butler sink with a cold tap
above it. Next to this was the gas cooker, which sometimes
got wet because above it was the back of the tiles and rafters
for the roof and the rain would blow in underneath. There
was no hot water in any part of the house. Doors from both
the kitchen and the scullery led out into the backyard, where
there was another cold tap. Out there was the toilet and a
coal store, which we didn't use for coal but more as a junk
store, because the coal was kept in an indoor cupboard under
the stairs. Also in the yard was a big cast-iron mangle with
wooden rollers and the tin bath which hung on the wall. At
one time there was a cane kept there, which we would get
threatened with, but we were never hit with it. One day I
wound the cane into the cogs of a mangle and then tried to

pull it out and of course it was all zigzagged where it had
been in the cogs.

Upstairs there were two big bedrooms and at the top of the
stairs a small boxroom which was also used as a bedroom.
The front bedroom was let out sometimes, once as a
bed-sitting room to two old ladies who both worked in a
pickle factory and consequently both permanently smelled of
pickles; another time [it was let] to Bill and Daisy M.

While the front room was let out, Mum and Dad had the
upstairs back bedroom, my two sisters were in the boxroom,
and we three boys all slept together in a big iron-framed
double bed in the downstairs back room while we lived in the
kitchen and the front room was kept as 'best'.

There was no electricity in the house, so all the cooking
was done on either the gas cooker, gas rings or the coal fires
which were in most rooms. All the lighting was by gas as well,
so we had to keep a supply of pennies handy for the meter
and gas mantles, [which] were constantly getting broken as
you went to light the light. There didn't seem to be any inner
brick walls, they were all either lathe and plaster or wood
panelling, so the house wasn't very soundproof.

It makes me laugh, the amount of us who lived in our house,
two full families, with grandparents, the odd aunt or uncle,
all the kids and the parents. All sharing beds, and sleeping
top to toe, and they talk about morals nowadays!

The house was a total slum, already condemned by the
council. I have very vivid memories of lying in bed listening
to the rats scuttling about in the roof. One of the delights of
summer was the bug-hunt, when my nan and I would strip
the beds and search for bedbugs and proceed to drown them.
We had simple pleasures in my day! The house was three
storeys high, with two rooms on each floor and a cellar. On
the ground floor my nan and uncle lived, he sleeping in the
front room and all the living being done in the back room. I
realize now it was very dirty, but then I knew nothing else. A
visit to the 'cleansing station' to be deloused was a pretty

regular occurrence for me. My nan did all the cooking over an open range, and, as all the family worked or lived very close, everyone came there for lunch. I still remember the newspaper tablecloth and eight or nine of us sitting down every day. On the second floor lived a prostitute and her baby. My nan had befriended her while working as a lavatory attendant [at the station, where the prostitute worked]. My nan's bedroom was at the front and contained a piano which [my uncle] had bought with some workman's compensation he received for an accident at work. Unbelievably, the accident had caused him to lose three fingers – some pianist he! My mum, dad, brother and I lived in the two rooms on the top floor. The four of us shared the front room as a bedroom, my brother and I sleeping in a single bed until I was eight and he was twelve. The cooker was on the landing outside, but as we all ate downstairs that was fairly academic. There was no running water upstairs at all, so all supplies had to be carried up three flights. The only toilet was in the backyard and at night everyone used a communal bucket in the bedroom. Enough said, I think . . .

It was bitterly cold. We used to stuff clothing rolled up like sausages at the door and newspapers into the ledges of the windows. We had no fire or anything. I hate to think of it now, how we used paraffin stoves in there. It used to smell to high heaven.

By contemporary standards, the conditions in which these East Enders were expected to live were appalling, but because they had nothing to compare them with, they accepted that this was simply the way things were – it was how you lived and you got on with it. There is even a view, such as that voiced below, that life might actually have been better then; not the conditions, but the social environment in which people were made more resilient, more self-sufficient, than those accustomed to a life of welfare dependency.

It must sound as if we had a dreadful childhood, but you must always remember that we knew no different. When X came out [of prison] he had nowhere to live, so my dad took him in. I remember him living with us but God knows where he slept, there were already four of us sleeping in one room. I also remember Aunt L. spending her leaves from the ATS with us. Where did we all fit in? N. also lived with us for a time. It was when the state did not provide for you if your family possibly could, or even, as in our case, if they couldn't. But it was a better way.

My childhood was a very happy one, one I think back on with warmth and pride. In Canning Town the people were poor by today's standards but rich in love, loyalty, trust and friendship. The houses were mainly used for two families. We had three rooms and a scullery downstairs, and the loo. There were six of us. Mum and Dad, two brothers, my sister and myself. Mum and Dad slept on a couch, bed-chair-type thing, in the front room; my brothers in the one and only bedroom, and my sister and I in a bed-cabinet in the kitchen-cum-living room. We had an old black lead range, no hot water, but a copper in the scullery for the washing.

As people spoke about their childhood homes, back in the 'good old days', they did so with a warm, rosy glow that probably has far more to do with being young and without the cares of adulthood than it does with their acceptance of the conditions of the East End's housing stock. They also spoke fondly of the ease with which you could get somewhere to live, because either you came from the area or you knew someone who did.

When you were getting married, your mum, or an aunt, or someone, would speak to the landlord. They'd ask if he had a place going that would do you. And you'd take a room or two in a house. Not that special maybe, but it would be near the family. Only a room or two, but in the neighbourhood where you came from. *Your* neighbourhood.

Perhaps the arrangements weren't ideal, but, with a bit of help, you could at least find somewhere of your own that was affordable

and in the area where you wanted to be, no matter how primitive it
might now seem.

> We got the flat through [someone we knew] talking to the
> landlord. He knew there would be a couple of rooms there.
> The only thing was, the landlord had to come in past our
> kitchen, up three stairs into his room, where he'd got all his
> tailoring equipment, and next door to that was our bedroom.
> So we had no privacy. And the thing that was against his
> ruling in our rent book was: no pets, no children. And, of
> course, my husband found a stray cat one day and brought it
> home. He knew how much we both liked cats. The dear little
> cat got a bit bigger and then I got a bit bigger! When the
> landlord used to come in every Friday for his rent, I'd be sat
> there with the table hiding the cat *and* my lump.
>
> We had no washing or toilet facilities, but had to go
> downstairs and out through the back door, which belonged
> to a husband and wife on the ground floor. Out in the back
> garden was the toilet. When we wanted a bath we had to walk
> down to the public baths at Stepney Green. Not very nice in
> the winter months, especially when I was expecting my first
> baby. But all the families around the square were very nice to
> us, even though some paid frequent visits to the police
> station.

> Not such a cosy memory was having to use the outside toilet.
> In the winter months it would get extremely cold. We didn't
> have toilet paper. We had cut-up squares of newspaper tied
> to a piece of string hanging on a nail on the wall. As two
> families shared the toilet the paper wouldn't last very long, so
> we would be constantly cutting up squares to use.

No matter how poor or lacking in facilities that housing was, it
still had to be paid for, and no matter how low the rent, it wasn't
always easy to find.

> One thing the old lady always used to tell us: 'Don't matter
> what else you do, boy, always pay your rent, or you're out.'

And she was bloody right, wasn't she? She never missed the
rent, no matter what happened. She'd be there with her old
starched apron on, with her curlers or pins in her hair – or in
a bun she'd have it – waiting there with her rent book. 'Hello,
Mr so-and-so.' She'd see him fill it in. She'd look and see he
had. 'Thank you.' And away he'd go. He'd had his three bob
or his half a crown, and he was satisfied, and we was all right
for another week. [*Laughing*] Bloody house wasn't worth half
a crown, when you come to think of it. Mind you, they never
charged us nothing for the mice.

Sometimes something as little as that half a crown could prove
impossible.

Doing a moonlight wasn't that unusual. Pack all the stuff in
the pram and on a barrow you'd borrowed off someone, and
you'd have it away on your toes. No one liked the landlord in
them days. They'd keep an eye out for you if they knew what
you was up to.

[Mum] took part of a house with a married sister in Forest
Gate. We thought we was right posh. There were six of us
still at home at that time and I don't know what happened,
but we were soon on the move again. Probably owed the
rent.

Even 'doing a moonlight' or 'having it away on your toes' was not
always possible.

Only time I ever saw any real, nasty violence in our turning
was when the landlord sent the bailiffs round to kick this
family out on the street. You should have seen the women
going for them blokes. But they never stopped them, not in
the end.

We had two rooms in one of them big houses in Bancroft
Road, with a stove in one of the rooms. I used to clean all
that house – top to bottom. All the steps, all the paintwork

outside – so the woman would let me have cheap rent. I nearly killed myself doing it, but he [her husband] didn't hardly have any work then.

The landlord of our houses was hated. He would turn up in a flash car, any car was flash looking back then, wearing his Crombie coat – apparently what the nobs wore – and prance down the street with his minder, and us kids would run a mile. I remember Mum having a terrific row with him about the state of the outside of our house and him replying, 'If you don't like it – move!'

This ambivalence about the 'good old days' wasn't related only to not having money for the rent or the state of the outside paintwork.

I remember the friendliness, but I'm not sure that I miss the old days; we lived in a terraced house with no bathroom and had to go to the public baths, which we did once-weekly. There were three boys and five girls in our family and the only place to wash in the house was in the kitchen. We had to have rotas for use of the sink, and it *was* a sink, not a basin. And no central heating, you just hoped your underclothing was dry enough to put on.

There was, however, always someone poorer than you in the East End, and a neighbourhood which was considered rougher, even less desirable than your own.

We had a road near us which was out of bounds to us as Mum said the children there had fleas and weren't clean. I used to walk down there without Mum knowing and felt so sorry for the people there. The majority had no shoes and wore really raggy clothes. The houses were without windows and had sacking nailed up instead. There were always kids fighting and women shouting. I learned later that they were people who had been evicted from elsewhere and were put in the bomb-damaged houses at very low rent.

Regardless of how bad the conditions were in those rented rooms, there was a reluctance to living in flats, even before the advent of the high-rise blocks of the 1960s.

> I dreaded the thought of having to go in those flats. I preferred to stay where we were in the sparse, overcrowded, part-furnished rooms, with its shared toilet, than to have gone there. Living in flats in that area was no life for children. There was a survey done while we lived there by a schoolteacher and they got children to write a little bit about their family background. He could tell those that lived in the flats by how restricted they were from those that lived in rooms in houses like we did, where you could come and go out of a front door and sit on the step and talk to your neighbours and run around. I was so relieved that we didn't have to go to the flats.

With the lack of private facilities, local authority provision for bathing and laundering was welcomed, and the recent closing down of many of the public baths and wash-houses has been met with emotional, though sadly often unsuccessful, opposition.

> We managed to get old bicycles and once a week we would have a ten-minute ride to the public bathhouse for our weekly clean-up. We had a number given to us as we went in and paid our money. When the number was called, we were shown into a small cubicle. The bath was filled by the man with levers outside. If it was too cold you would have to call out, 'More hot in Number 6, please!' then call out again once it was hot enough.

Despite the lack of bathrooms, bathing at home was not unusual. The tin bath would be fetched in from the yard and filled with hot water boiled on the stove or in the copper. The younger members of the family, being the lowest in the pecking order, would be the last to go in the bath and were left with rapidly cooling water made filthy by a whole week's worth of dirt washed off parents, brothers and sisters, and any other family members who happened to be lodging with them at the time.

There were other problems with bathing at home, especially in the winter.

> It was all very nice having the tin bath in front of the fire, but your back used to freeze. The places were so draughty. No central heating of course. In the mornings you'd have ice inside the windows. Ice. *Inside.* We all had chilblains. My nan reckoned that if you stuck your feet in the po the wee would cure them. I must say, I never tried it myself. Others would rub on an onion.
>
> Back to the bath – you'd have to take your turn. All right if you was first in. Lovely, nice and clean and warm. But in big families like our'n, and a lot of them was big families up until the war, you'd come a long way down the list. The water'd be all grey and scummy. Horrible. And the bath would have to be emptied. I'm glad it wasn't my job. Poor old Mum again. They worked like donkeys, the old girls in them days.

It wasn't only the absence of decent bathing facilities that resulted in hard manual work; most domestic chores were either physically hard or relentless, or both. The continual battle against vermin was just one of the many unpleasant tasks which took time and effort.

> If it wasn't the nit comb to sort your hair out, it was the Flit spray to get rid of the bedbugs. Never-ending.

> If they found you had nits at school they dowsed you with Lysol, and then [back home] Mum used to have us on our knees, with a sheet of newspaper on her lap, and she'd get out the old nit comb.

> With the crowded conditions and lack of hygiene, there was always the threat of infestation with fleas, bedbugs and black beetles, mice and rats from the sewers. I saw my father painting the bedsprings with spirits of salts to deter them.

*

In the summer the bugs used to crawl out of the walls and we killed them by squashing them on the walls. Their eggs got into the wooden sides of the bedsprings and they multiplied in two hours. It was not unusual to see a bug on someone sitting indoors. [You could see] fleabites too on the necks of some children. Many people sat outside their street doors on summer evenings just because the bugs disturbed their sleep. The only way to get rid of them was to burn their eggs and, believe me, that took some doing.

'Put a penny in the gas, quick, it's going out!' You couldn't let it go out, otherwise there'd be bleeding mice running about all over the place. At night, you'd put the lights out and the bleeding house used to come alive! Still, fact was, we didn't live far from the stables, see, and I didn't mind the mice so much, but I didn't like the big fellers [the stable rats] flying about the house.

At a time when domestic work was carried out without the labour-saving devices which are now practically taken for granted, children, even the very young, were expected to do their share of the chores. They did so, more or less, willingly.

I used to stay at home and clean the house – anything rather than go to school – but I used to hate shaking them coconut mats, because you got smothered in dust. And they was a ton weight and I was only a little thing. We didn't have no vacuum cleaners, nothing like that. Not until Mum bought us a beater and then you could put them on the line and whack them. We did graduate from floorboards and that, on to mats and lino, but you still had to scrub everywhere.

It was hard graft, but Mum expected us kids to do our bit. It was the only way she could keep things nice, the way she liked them.

And there was a real pride taken in keeping those youngsters, as well as your home, as 'nice' as you could. Having little money and few material possessions did not stop mothers wanting to give a good impression regarding their conscientious approach to domestic duties. Being respectable was important and cleanliness was closely associated with self-respect.

> My mum would go *barmy* if you went anywhere near her clean step. It was a matter of pride, like sending us out in clean clothes. Even if they were raggy and old, they were spotless . . . Well, when we went out they were. I'm not so sure about when we came back in from playing out.

> The passage [had] shiny lino and coconut mats in lovers' knots.

> Nanny and Grandad C. lived with their ever-increasing family – eleven of them altogether – in the downstairs part of the very small terraced artisan's house in Custom House. Upstairs lived Mr and Mrs N. – eleven of them too – and everyone shared the spotless scrubbed-pine lavatory seat out in the backyard.

> When Dad was painting the front door, he used to make an artificial grain in the paint by putting on a light coloured undercoat then a dark coat on top of that and, while the second coat was still wet, he had a metal comb and this was drawn over the surface, twisting it to scrape the top coat away and looking like proper wood graining.

> In the spring, Grandad would whitewash the backyard wall and the outside lav, and put a few plants in a tub by the back door. Used to look all lovely and clean and fresh.

> You didn't have to be lousy just cos you were poor. Soap don't cost much. But I'm not saying it was easy keeping yourself or your place nice. It was hard work, but you didn't lead off about it or nothing, you got on with it.

Doing the laundry presented its own problems. Week in, week

out, the same back-breaking, hand-chapping, sopping-wet job had to be done, regardless of weather or time of year; although in those pre-man-made fibre, pre-washing-machine days clothes were not changed nearly as often as they are now. Laundering anything was too much of a demanding, lengthy rigmarole for clothes to be tossed into a laundry basket after just a few hours' wear.

The scullery was distempered or whitewashed and was the scene of much activity on Mondays, which was washing day. There was a large copper in the corner with a small iron door at the bottom which led to the fireplace underneath. This was no machine wash of about an hour! Oh no! It was a whole day's washing. First you had to light the fire with wood chips or a bundle of firewood, which cost a farthing. Then, of course, there was no hot water, just cold. When the washing was under way, the steam would cover the scullery and the women would sweat after scrubbing the clothes up and down the washboard and wringing them in the mangle, then they hung the sheets and so on out on the line in the yard to dry again. No tumble-dryers. If it was a rainy day the washing was hung in the kitchen to dry, where you had to dodge the stockings, towels and underwear.

She only had the rubbing board and sink or bath for the washing. And she was pregnant every year or eighteen months. We had a copper in the scullery, where you lit the fire. Any old thing went on that fire. Any old shoes if they was beyond repair. My dad used to try and repair them until he couldn't do any more. I used to be scared of that copper; as a little child I always thought it had no bottom to it. When she used to fill it up and put the clothes in, I always had that fear that there was no end to the water. The old copper stick and the mangle, with the huge wooden rollers and great big wheel, were out the back. One of us kids had to turn it and we were so small you needed two hands to get it round. One to catch the washing at the other side. Mind your fingers! All year. Freezing cold.

*

I used to go on this errand for my nan. With an old pushchair, I'd go round to the wood place under the arches, to collect a load of offcuts for her to light the copper. I can remember the smell now, like pine resin, of all the wood being cut and all the sawdust everywhere. A whole load I'd get her, so's she could boil up for her washing.

Not all coppers were used just for heating water.

I remember my brother hissing at me, 'Quick, get the lid off.' I did as I was told – he was bigger and older than me – and with that he opened his jacket and pulled out two pigeons that he'd nicked from somewhere. He shoved them in the copper and slammed the lid back down. He winked and said, 'Mum'll be pleased with them.' She used to make pies, you see, and when he 'found' a few birds he had to hide them till she was ready to pluck and draw them for cooking. [*Laughing*] Everyone had pigeon lofts round there and they might have been *lost* by their owner.

Memories of damp washing hanging on the clothes-horse in front of the fire, or draped on a line over the cooker, steaming up the cramped kitchen and filling the house with the stifling smell of drying cloth, paint a miserable picture.

I used to hate coming in from school on a Monday afternoon if it had been raining. Washing was always done on a Monday. You knew wet clothes would be draped everywhere. Even over the fireguard. It was so unwelcoming, wet washing. Worse than the smell of a wet dog. I never thought about all the hard graft for my mum, I just didn't fancy seeing it all hanging around. Or smelling it. Typical selfish kid!

Not every household's washing was done at home. There were the laundries, many of them having been started by Chinese immigrants who had settled around the docks in Limehouse.

The main washing was taken to a laundry in the next street, a bolster slip containing as many clothes as we could push in for half a crown. It reminds me of the Richard Murdoch and Arthur Askey radio show with the character Mrs Bagwash.

And, of course, there were the public wash-houses. The importance of these can be seen in the elaborate celebrations to mark the 'Order of Proceedings on the occasion of the laying of the Foundation Stone of the Baths and Wash-houses Old Ford Road, Bethnal Green', described in smartly engraved programmes produced by the Metropolitan Borough of Bethnal Green. The ceremony, which took place on 23 October 1926, included afternoon tea and a full orchestra 'playing selections'.

The completed York Hall Baths, as they became known, were opened three years later by the Duke and Duchess of York, the future king and queen.

The scheme was certainly a grand one, comprising an impressive three floors and a basement which would hold:

Swimming, Slipper, Turkish, Electric and Russian Baths, and a Public Wash-house and Laundry, equipped with modern labour-saving devices, and is estimated to cost £120,000.

On the ground floor alone there were to be:

First Class Swimming Bath, 100 feet by 40 feet (65 Dressing Boxes).
Second Class Swimming Bath, 75 feet by 30 feet 6 ins (42 Dressing Boxes).
Public Wash-house and Laundry (accommodating 170 Washers per day).
23 Women's Slipper Baths, Second Class, and 2 Vapour Baths.
Main Entrance and Crush Halls.
Cloak, Artistes' and Refreshment Rooms.
First Class Bath, when used as Public Hall: Platform, 100 Seats, Hall, 1,120.

Poplar Baths was obviously as big an attraction. In June 1953, it was reported in the local press that Mathias Joe, the 'Red Indian Chief' of the Capilano tribe of Vancouver, who was in Britain for the Coronation, paid them a 'surprise visit' and took advantage of the facilities, enjoying a slipper bath.

Such exotic distractions apart, for those who were responsible for the laundry, when the washing was eventually dry enough to iron, the work continued.

> When my mother did the ironing, she had to heat a heavy iron up on the gas stove. She would spit on the bottom and if it sizzled then it would be hot enough to use. The trouble was it didn't last very long and had to be continually reheated. There was no ironing board. Therefore two or three blankets and a sheet would be placed on the table to be used instead.

But regardless of the poor, or non-existent, facilities in the home, large families and multiple occupancy meant that, until the slum clearances and the building of the new estates in the 1950s and 1960s, overcrowding, with its ramifications for health and hygiene, would remain the major problem for the big, extended families that lived in east London. Yet despite the cramped conditions, the lack of privacy and the poverty, memories of living as part of those families are filled with genuine warmth and pleasure.

10

We all lived within a few streets. Nan and Grandad, from Mum's side, all her brothers and sisters and their kids, and all the brothers and sisters, cousins and that, on Dad's side. That was apart from all the neighbours who were 'Auntie this' and 'Uncle that'. That was usual. If you didn't call an adult Mr or Mrs, it was auntie or uncle. It was usual, but it got bloody confusing at times. 'Is that my *real* cousin then, Mum?'

Unless they were going away to sea or to join the armed forces, or, in an earlier period, into service, working people from east London did not usually leave home until they married. When they finally did leave, they didn't usually go very far, but would move to somewhere close by found for them by their parents' or a relative's landlord. This availability of affordable, if sometimes grotty, lodgings, meant that families would remain in the same area for many generations, only leaving the East End when they were in a position to 'better themselves'.

If there was any moving to be done by a young married couple, it was the man who most often did so, going to live near to, or even with, his wife's family. With their roots firmly based in the tradition of variety and music hall, the older generation of comedians who, now infamously, depended on mother-in-law jokes were reflecting on and observing the anxieties and predicament of the many young men who found themselves lodging with their new wives in a strange, matriarchal household with similar rules to, but different privileges from, their old family home.

Remaining close to their mothers, daughters could enjoy emotional and practical support.

I wouldn't have dreamed of moving away from Mum. I don't mean I wasn't capable of looking after myself – I'd been at work since I was fourteen years of age – but I still saw Mum every single day. I'd pop in to have a cup of tea, have a chat.

Nothing special. But she was always there, just a couple of streets away. And, of a Saturday, we'd go down the market, while my [husband] and his brothers went off to the football or for a few drinks, or something. It's not like you see now, with women shopping with their husbands. He'd have been a right nuisance while I was looking on the stalls. Like I say, I was capable, but Mum did a lot for me. I never had to worry, she was always there. Especially once I had kids of my own. That's when I realized how much she did for me. And how hard it is to be a mum. Especially a good mum, like she was.

Ours was a very typical close family, my mother being the eldest of fourteen children. One died as a baby and another died in the war, but all the remaining twelve lived in the East End with their own families as and when they all married.

If I had to do something, or if I'd managed to get myself a little job, Mum had [the children] for me. I wouldn't have fancied the idea of strangers having them. Not at all. I'd just pop them round to Mum and know they'd be looked after.

Extended families might have been a blessing for young working mothers, but the effort involved in raising a large family, especially during times of financial difficulties, could be exhausting.

Do you know, my mother was like an old lady when I was growing up – this was before the war, remember. There was a whole mob of us to see to, seven kids and my dad, and when I look back, I think of her, and, do you know, she must have been, what, only in her late thirties, but she was worn out. Thirty-odd – that's young nowadays. But she'd had seven children and there wasn't all the washing machines and that then. We must have worn her out. By the time a woman was in her forties then, well, she was elderly really, wasn't she?

With the experience of age [I was born in 1916] I think the parents of my generation were, in most cases, to be applauded for their efforts to raise a family under the circumstances in which they found themselves. It should be remembered that they themselves were born into an era of Victorian harshness when 'children should be seen and not heard'. Then to start married life at the beginning of the First World War, bring up children in the aftermath of a war that should never have been, to endure the Depression of the 1920s, with its unemployment and poverty, only to find that, in the late 1930s, when things were beginning to improve, they were plunged into another war, even more destructive than the first one . . . Is it any wonder that so many, like my good parents, never lived to enjoy retirement? Not killed by bombs, but worn out. They were the type of mothers and fathers of my childhood: good, honest, caring, hard-working folk, with little of the comforts of life we know today.

In spite of all the effort required to raise your family, there was a strong sense of pride in keeping them looking respectable.

My socks were white. Pure white. Mum used to pull them over her hand and scrub the heels clean with a nailbrush. She wouldn't have let me out of the house in grubby socks. And I had my hair put into plaits every morning, so it would stay tidy all day. I remember one of my older brothers, he must have been about thirteen or fourteen – I know he was already at work and he was a big old chap – but he hadn't washed his neck right. According to Mum, he hadn't. She was only little, but she dragged him over to the sink – it was one of the deep, old butler sinks – and stuck his head under the tap – brass and all nice and shiny, of course – and scrubbed his neck like he was a sock heel! She had him held there, and he didn't dare move or he knew what he'd get. 'That'll teach you to show me up with a dirty neck!' she said. Didn't matter he was old enough to be at work, she wasn't going to be shown up.

But caring for their families was not all that East End women were capable of.

The women then were amazons and had long hair which,

when they fought – oh yes, they could fight and swear like troopers in those days – was pulled out by the handful. Yet these women had eight or nine children . . . They were a hard-working lot, they had to be, looking after such large families.

Some of the women could fight as roughly as the men. They'd go at it like cats. Usually over someone taking exception to something the other one had said, or she'd been thought to have said. Rows over the kids were always a favourite!

My nan was a fat, jolly drinking lady and a notorious flirt. It was apparently a common sight to see her legging it along the street at turning-out time with my jealous grandad in hot pursuit with a broken bottle in his hand. As was the custom then [the early decades of the century], the men sat in a different bar from the women and grandad always said he could see her making sheep's eyes at other men. I would have thought fourteen children were enough for her. She was born in the Peabody buildings and her family were costermongers in the market close by. I think she must have been quite fun as a young woman. She had a home-made tattoo on her arm done by injecting indian ink into needle holes and always said she had done it to shock her father.

Physical strength, determination and a fighting spirit might be admirable qualities in some circumstances, but being strong and coping were not always virtues, especially when it meant you and your children's welfare were taken for granted by your husband, who conveniently complied with your pretence that all was well.

She hid any troubles from Dad. [As I got older] I used to say to her, 'You should have made Dad more aware of the troubles you had to put up with.' We know he knew that he wasn't bringing in enough money, but he still used to say to Mum, 'Can I have my dinner money for tomorrow so I can go and get a pint?' He got his money to go out to be with people, and that's where I think Mum went wrong. A man should share the good as well as the bad with his wife. There was more bad than good in her life. He had luxuries we never had. There was a butcher's that sold cooked meat. 'Go up and get two ounces of boiled pork for his sandwiches.' We never saw a bit of boiled pork. It's lovely to be affectionate [with your husband] but you can carry it too far. I'm not saying we were neglected, but she always put him first, [never] let him be worried about anything.

It has to be remembered that many people who spoke to me had parents or grandparents brought up in Victorian times, when rules were far stricter than would be considered acceptable today.

I'm nearly fifty years old. My mum smoked like a trooper, all her life, and so do I, but I never, ever dared smoke a cigarette in front of her. She'd have clipped me round the ear if I had. It was always do what I say, not what I do with Mum. You didn't answer back then. You just got on with it and did as you were told. Didn't do any harm, respecting your mum . . . My old nan was even fiercer than Mum ever knew how to be. I was frightened of her to tell you the truth!

You'd be picked up for 'bloody swearing' and told off for saying 'ain't'.

I was the eldest in the family. There were eight of us and, up to when I got married, I had to be in by a certain time, because then the lock went on. Many a time I slept in the passage or jumped over and slept in the shelter in the yard until next morning.

There was no vandalism as such, simply because when a boy got in trouble the father would give him a tanning with his belt. Children were seen and not heard.

Family rules did, however, vary, usually depending on your gender.

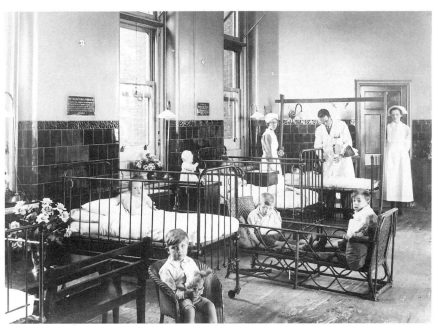

15. The children's ward in Poplar Hospital, 1906.

16. Poplar High Street, *c.* 1900. The labouring poor, the elderly and the infirm dreaded having to go into the workhouse.

17. Victoria Park, 1908. A place of both leisure and public protest, 'Vicky' has witnessed, over the years, the building and demolition of its glorious 1920s lido, gatherings of demonstrators ranging from Chartists to Blackshirts, and local people simply enjoying its many pleasures.

18. A family day out. *Front row from left*, 'Old Mrs Cooper' with baby Harry and son Percy; *next seated*, Maggie Cooper (Jamie Redknapp's great-grandmother) with daughter; *standing*, my grandmother Bridget Knight, pregnant with my dad, with daughter Sally, and the driver (Mrs Cooper's eldest son). *Back row from left*, Mrs Cooper's brother, Gerry Brown (Jamie Redknapp's great-grandfather), and William Griffiths, my grandfather.

19. *Above* Posing, 1934-style, at Poplar Baths.

20. *Right* The Russian vapour baths at 86 Brick Lane, *c.* 1910. Being opposite the Great Synagogue, they were very popular with the local orthodox Jewish community.

21. Bethnal Green, 1904. Following the Huguenot tradition of songbird and pigeon fancying, the Club Row and Sclater Street Sunday bird market was always packed. Wild birds, particularly goldfinches, which had been trapped in the Essex countryside, were sold illegally.

22. In the 1920s the Nastri family of Railway Street, Poplar, also sold ice-cream and ice, like the family shown here. They used a truck to tour the streets and in winter transferred their interests to the coal and coke business.

23. 'Chinatown': Pennyfields, Limehouse, 1927.

24. A different world: before the docks became Docklands. Dunbar's Wharf, Narrow Street, *c.* 1900.

25. A 'dock copper' checking that a dock worker isn't leaving with more than he arrived with.

26. The Royal Artillery unloading a ship during a dockworkers' strike in July 1949 at the Royal Albert Dock.

27. London Docks, 1961. Built at Wapping in 1805, they handled much of the valuable tobacco, wine and brandy imports.

28. Royal Docks, 1942. Despite the bombing and the danger, vital food imports still had to be unloaded.

Being a boy, even though I had four sisters older than me, I was allowed to get away with more. Stay out later and that. Mind you, they wasn't scared of me getting into trouble, was they?

Mum and Dad were much stricter with me than with my brothers. I don't think it was because I was the only girl. I think it had more to do with them worrying I'd *get into trouble*. The days I'm talking about, the 1950s, we didn't have the pill. Mind you, they wouldn't have been any different if we had have had it. Girls – *their* girl – had to be good, and boys had to be careful I suppose. I don't know who the girls were meant to be who they were being careful with though. *Trollops*, as my mum would have called them! Seems like the Dark Ages now, but that's how it was.

It wasn't just Mum and Dad who made sure me and my sister behaved ourselves. Our brothers, *including the two younger ones*, if you don't mind, watched us like hawks. They made sure we got up to nothing and that no one took liberties with us. My cousins were all the same. It was like being kept on a chain. Wonder we ever managed to meet any boys, let alone start courting.

Being male didn't always mean you would be treated more leniently, or that you could enjoy a carefree youth. Sometimes there was little choice but to buckle down and do whatever needed doing.

When my mum died, I was fifteen [and] the only one who had left school. My dad had charge of eight of us and, instead of putting us in a home, he kept us together. I had managed to get a lovely little job, and was well in with it, in a lorry firm that used to do waste paper as wrapping material. Dad only had work three days a week [but] I had to give it up to help look after the family. We lived upstairs and I used to get out on the windowsills to clean the windows. I had to scrub the floor – we had no oilcloth down – [and] I was in charge of the cooking and that. My dad also had to pay half a crown a week towards his father's keep, who lived three turnings away.

There were advantages in being part of a big family. Whether support, company or entertainment was being sought, having relatives around could be a bonus.

I loved it when I'd see my aunts or my grandad or someone else in the family sitting out in the street. I might get an errand to run and be able to keep the change, or a sweet out of their apron or waistcoat pocket.

Because there were so many of us, some of my uncles were not a lot older than me, a few years maybe, so when I was a boy they were like young men. If I got myself into one of my usual scrapes, I'd say, 'If you hit me, I'll get my uncles on to you!' [*Laughing*] It worked and all! Made me a right cocky little sod!

We sometimes would go and visit my [aunt and uncle] at their house in Plaistow. I thought they were really posh having a house with a garden, and when we were leaving [my] uncle would shake hands with me and slip me sixpence or a shilling, which seemed like a fortune to me.

It was good, when all the family came round. There'd be a house full, and you might get a few coppers as they were leaving. But that would always mean having to kiss every aunt and they'd smell all beery by the time they left, and you'd get a pat on the head from every uncle. You'd feel like a boiled egg being tapped by a spoon by the time they'd all finished with you.

You never wanted for company. That was a good part of being in a big family like ours. There'd always be someone you could turn to, someone who'd be there no matter how bad things got, or someone if you just wanted a bit of a natter. You wasn't ever alone. In good or bad times, they'd be there.

Relatives would definitely be there, or at least ready to celebrate at important moments such as weddings and the birth of a new baby or commiserate at funerals.

Taking part in the traditions and customs surrounding these rites of passage was an important part of being a member of an extended family in the close-knit communities of east London.

It was a bit like Christmas. All the women in the family flapping about and all the excitement. We weren't explained to, what was going on, kids were kept in the dark then, but we knew it was exciting. Then I had a little sister! There was even more coming and going, in and out, with all the family, than I'd ever seen before. I loved it.

Us kids would be sent along to one of the aunts to be minded by the cousins, while all the women got on with the business indoors and all the blokes disappeared down the pub, ready to wet the baby's head.

My nan was proud of the fact that she had delivered every child in [the street] except her own, and they had been delivered by her bosom pal and drinking partner, 'Auntie' Sally, at number 90. This, off course, was [around the time of the First World War] when a midwife charged about half a crown to attend.

I was so proud when I got my Silver Cross pram for my first. Mum and Nan had helped me pay it off weekly. But even when I'd paid for it, I never brought it home until I'd had the baby. You didn't then. It was like a sort of superstition. Just in case. But there I was with my new baby and my lovely coach-built pram. I used to keep it spotless. I hated to see a pram with all biscuit crumbs over the covers. It had a sort of lid in the bottom that you could lift out and, when the baby was old enough, he could sort of sit up with his little legs in the space underneath. Used to walk for miles with that pram, with my mum and my younger sister with me. Not showing off or nothing, I was just so proud.

It was always a joy when a new baby was born. If you didn't have much, your family would help out and you'd soon have a lovely layette for the little one. It wouldn't be all new, of course, though some of it would have been knitted for you, but there would be plenty of hand-me-downs, and you knew you wouldn't have to have your baby going without. Your family would see to that.

Sadly not all experiences of the birth of a new baby were as happy.

My brother's arrival, when I was four and a half years old, put my nose out of joint. Till then I had been the first, much-loved and welcome grandchild in both my parents' families. Now I was ousted by a baby! But I did not get to know him immediately. [When] my mother was pregnant, she was evacuated. I never asked why she did not take me with her. I went to a children's home in Essex run by the West Ham Central Mission, a large Baptist church in Plaistow. I remember [it] as full of space, big airy rooms, fields and playground. We were looked after by nurses in white uniforms and large flapping white veils. I remember eating good meals at regular times, having baths and wearing clean, comfortable clothes. Although the memories are good, I also have a memory of loneliness.

I lost my first baby. It was just after the war had finished, but I still had to be evacuated. I was twenty-seven. I couldn't get into a local hospital, and Mum said, 'You can't have it at home. I can't have you round me.' I suppose she'd had so many of her own, she didn't want to be bothered with babies. I had to go to this place in Cambridgeshire. Just to have the baby. And then I came home without him. He died after a week. But I managed to get him brought home and buried. So I know where he is. It seemed a hell of a long way on that

old steam train. And I never had many visitors. [My
husband] used to get over once a week. It was a terrible place.
It was a wing they had taken on from an old men's home.
The only place they could find to put us London mothers. It
was a terrible place, but you didn't know any different, and
you thought that's what you had to do, where you had to go.
There were a lot of faults in the birth, but I couldn't prove it.
I never had my people round me, my family, to sort things
out. All I wanted was my mum. I was so frightened. But she
couldn't get down to me. I don't hold it against her, but
when I came home all I wanted was a cuddle, [but] she said,
'Come on, you're not having all this fuss over losing a baby.
You can have another one.' That stuck in my mind for a long
time. When I look back, it was as real as yesterday. When you
hear how they sue for this and sue for that. But I didn't have
the know-how then. You thought [they] knew best. You put
up with a lot of things they wouldn't put up with now. I
admire people for speaking out and doing things. We never
did because we didn't think we could. You couldn't question
the staff, say, 'Why did my baby die?' The matron was
horrible. [The staff] were cruel to us London mothers . . . [I
didn't see him until] hours after the birth. He had a big graze
on his face. I said, 'What's happened to his face?' 'Oh, that's
nothing for you to worry about.' You didn't question it . . . I
had to stay in bed for a fortnight, and she used to come and
press and press my breasts to get rid of the milk. Never give
me anything to dry it up. I used to lie there, so weak. Sweat
used to pour off me. But they didn't do anything to [help
me]. They treated us London mothers as if we were the scum
of the earth, but we was the salt of the earth.

According to most of the people of around fifty and older to
whom I spoke, contraception and sex education were not subjects
which were widely discussed in their youth. In the pre-pill, pre-
abortion-reform days, the fear of pregnancy led to some terrifying
experiences, with a local woman 'helping you out' being the last,
desperate resort of a girl who would otherwise be shamed, or even
shunned, by her family.

If it hadn't been for my friend's aunt, I don't think I'd have lived long enough to have brought up the children I already had. I'm serious. It wasn't long after the war and it was all so hard. It's not something I'm proud of, but I'm not ashamed of it either. If she hadn't have helped me out . . . It's not something I had much choice about. I couldn't have gone through it again. Not only not being able to feed another child, but my health wouldn't have stood it either. I had to make sure I could look after the ones I already had. We'd been as careful as we could have been. It didn't work, though.

Young folk were not well versed in family matters. It wasn't talked about – unless, of course, a 'mistake' was made.

Close families and communities, so praised in other contexts, could be suffocating or threatening places for those who chose to go through with their 'mistakes'.

My cousin disappeared for a few months. It was only in later life that I found out she'd been sent away to a mother and baby home, and had had her child adopted. It seems so cruel to me when I think of it now. I've never discussed it with her, but we were such a big family and close neighbourhood, I wonder if my aunt, her mum, was concerned what people would think and say. Gossip can be very hurtful when you live so close to people. Not just hurtful, nasty. The family might have been kinder than some of the neighbours, but I'm not so sure. She has a husband and family now and it wouldn't be right to bring it up.

A girl at our school went missing for a while. When she came back, her mum had a new baby. None of us realized at the time, but the girl's new sister was actually her own daughter. It was all done to cover up. So sad.

I'm in my late forties now and I was very young when my periods started, about ten or eleven. I had on little

powder-blue pyjamas and when I woke up I thought I was
dying. My mum was sort of prudish. She could row and
swear with the best of them, but there was this thing that you
didn't talk about things *like that*. Most of the women in our
family were like it. Seems funny when you was all living on
top of one another, but there was a lot of whispering under
their breath in front of the kids. Things you didn't mention.
Women weren't even 'pregnant', they were 'expecting', in the
'family way' or were in a 'delicate condition'. And there was a
lot of disapproval of girls who were, as they used to say, 'no
better than they ought to be'.

You weren't told what it was all about, but you were expected
to know what they meant when they told you to be good. I'm
an old lady now, but I don't think you should keep people
ignorant. How can you know how to look after yourself if no
one tells you?

Getting married before you had children was expected, but, as
courting could last a while and so many were living in what would
now be seen as ignorance, making a 'mistake' really was a constant
fear.

When it [came] to the problems and fears of pregnancy, the
biggest fear was what would happen to me if I was the cause
of it.

I met my husband when I was sixteen, in Victoria Park. I was
with my girlfriend on our bicycles. I was engaged at eighteen
and married at twenty-one – a virgin. The fear of pregnancy
and 'what my mother would say' – the latter even more
feared than the former – prevented any premarital relations
. . . Girls who 'did wrong' and got pregnant were talked about
and frowned upon, her family was shamed.

But if you were courting seriously, it was usually with the intention
of being married once you had saved a little and had accumulated
a few things for your bottom drawer, so pregnancy didn't have to

be a disaster. Instead it could simply speed up what might otherwise
be a rather slow process.

> I met my wife in the park in 1929. They were playing ball and
> the ball came our way. We were chasing the ball and the next
> thing you know, we're chasing the girls. My life changed once
> I met my wife. I started thinking: I want to do this, I want to
> do that. I started thinking it's about time we thought about
> getting married, [but] it came to the fact that my wife was
> five months pregnant when we got married. We had been
> courting for seven years.

> Looking back, it was strange. You started going out with a
> local boy and he'd sort of *do*. You'd start courting and, so
> long as he was a reasonably respectable type of a chap, your
> mum and dad would be relieved. You were spoken for and
> they wouldn't have to worry. Cos, say you did get caught out,
> you could get married on the quick, couldn't you?

Many people spoke of a rather disciplined, formal approach to
the business of wooing which, though perhaps sounding as if it lacked
something in terms of romance, offered expectations of security and
longevity in the eventual marriages.

> There was a lot more discipline in the family in the 1920s and
> 1930s. People courted, got engaged and then got married;
> they did not just live together.

The charmingly formal language of the following description of
courting and sexual attraction in the 1920s clearly relates to the way
in which such matters were dealt with by this particular man's family.

> Whilst the appeal of the sexes has been a natural act since life
> began, time has changed the mode of approach to it. In the
> 1920s, we still had the Victorian, Edwardian attitude and
> concept of what was acceptable. I would not say there were
> no clandestine meetings of lads and lasses, but it was
> recognized that after a couple of meetings the parents of each

side would invite a visit in order to make an assessment . . . If satisfied, the [couple] were known to be walking out. Girls were lectured at great length on promiscuity – but in down-to-earth language – and the threat of banishment was a fear for all young ladies if found pregnant out of wedlock. I would think that there were a number of shotgun weddings, but to be a mother with no wedding ring was unpardon-able and divorce was only for the rich folk. The accepted procedure for the courting couple was for an engagement ring to be given and a set period of time to save, and for the girl to start a bottom drawer, collecting linen, cutlery and so on, with one of the mothers making themselves responsible for finding rented accommodation for them. It was always a local boy or girl that you married and it was accepted that they would remain living local . . . When considering the opportunity for youngsters to meet the opposite sex, there were no mixed schools or clubs back then and, apart from friends, brothers and sisters or parents' friends' children. The only place was the dance hall, but, nature being what it is, we managed. Because there were not that many venues for meetings then . . . the tendency to couple occurred a little later than today. Most of my generation were in their twenties. I suppose it could be that the age of consent, manhood, was twenty-one. You were not entitled to a man's wage until that age and the thought of leaving home may not have been so prevalent as in the minds of the young today. The one thing that stands out is very little effort was made either in school or in the home to prepare us children for sex education. Boys seemed to learn by innuendo and school playground gossip. Girls, from frightening lectures from mother.

Courting was not simply for the benefit of the happy couple and their 'relieved' parents; other members of the family could also profit from the loving relationship.

When our Alf started courting Margaret, it was like a miracle. From being a miserable sod who'd have begrudged me and me brothers the drippings off his nose, he started giving us ha'pennies for sweets and for the pictures. We loved it. Only when Margaret was there, of course. Did it to impress her, see. He wound up marrying her. Nice girl, and she made our life happier!

When my eldest sister started courting her husband, he used to treat her to sweets and things, and when she came home from the pictures she used to put them in the drawer. Rowntree's Motoring Chocolate. I used to love to go up there when she wasn't around and have a nibble of this chocolate. And I used to rub my teeth marks off so she wouldn't know. We never used to have any money, especially for sweets, so it was a real luxury to know we had chocolate in the drawer. Couldn't resist it.

Weddings were important social events, with even quite poor families doing their best to put on a 'good do'. I can recall my mother's horror when one of the pair of white, buckled shoes she had saved so hard for, for my brother to wear to a family wedding as part of his pageboy's outfit, was mysteriously flushed down the loo. The mystery was easily solved: the indignity of wearing those shoes was simply too much for my brother to cope with.

The wedding itself wasn't that elaborate. I couldn't afford a dress, so I borrowed one, but I had lovely flowers, and new shoes and a veil, and the party after! We had enough food to feed an army that night. And there were so many crates of beer out there, you could hardly get in the back kitchen. I don't know how everyone fitted in, but there was all our families and half the streets round there as well, all crammed in. Mum and Dad did us proud that day.

Weddings were a very big affair, with many guests, including lots of children. Weddings were always in a church. Catholic in our case. A hall was usually chosen for the reception, as this would have been the least expensive choice. As everybody toasted the bride and groom, guests would [give gifts of

money], as much as they could afford. The food would be
prepared by members of the family and would always include
jellied eels, mussels, rollmops, cockles and so on, which
would all be bought from the local fish stall, which would be
found outside most pubs.

Outside photographs – no flash bulbs then. My parents,
complete with wedding cake that had been heaved out
into the backyard, are standing there, beaming, for the
snapshots.

It was wartime, but we still did what we could to make it
special. And it *was* special. I didn't have a dress, I had a
two-piece costume, and one of the girls at work – we were
machinists – made me a new blouse, and my sister trimmed
my hat for me. The cake was made of cardboard, with a little
drawer at the side with a piece of real cake in it.

The wedding itself might have been something to remember, but
that didn't always guarantee romance.

I was twenty-seven when I got married in 1930. I had three
days' leave and we went to Sheerness on our honeymoon. In
all, the wedding cost twenty pounds. The bouquet cost seven
shillings and sixpence, and the rest paid for drink and some
furniture, which was not much, as we lived in one room only.
This was in May. When we returned home the bugs would
not let me sleep . . . We ruined the sheet using caustic soda
trying to kill them, but it was useless.

Or even that the marriage would last.

My grandfather had a pub in Hackney and he was carrying
on with the housekeeper. My mum said she was an ugly
woman . . . had all whiskers hanging out of her. Ever so ugly.
But she was very lustful and used to pour gin in the teapot
when she was supposed to look after my mother and aunt.
She used to say, 'I'll have a drop of tea now,' and used to be

> drinking this gin. My grandmother was very sedate . . . [she]
> knew what was going on with my grandfather and this
> housekeeper. It came to a bust-up and my grandmother left
> him.

There is an odd practice, mentioned when family relationships were being explained to me, of referring to married women by their maiden names. This might have been an aid to identifying people within large families, but, in my own family's case, it only added to the confusion. My mother, Dolly Griffiths, was often referred to by her single name, Dolly Sheekey, and my auntie, who became Dolly Sheekey when she married, was referred to as Dolly Stephens. The additional complication was that a brother and sister, my mum and her brother Charlie, had married two cousins, my dad, Tom, and my aunt, Dolly. In addition to these, there were several other relatives who also went by the name of Dolly, who would have to be identified in ever more elaborate ways, such as, 'You know her, the one who married your second cousin, on your nan's side.' But these interwoven family histories were not rare, as I was told by a man who is now almost ninety:

> In those days you couldn't afford a bike or anything, no
> transport, so you did your courting locally and married
> someone who lived close by. And because families lived near
> one another, not more than a matter of a few streets away,
> you'd get a mate going out with your sister and you might go
> out with his.

The growth of bicycle ownership, enabling marriage to someone more than a street or two away, must have had as significant an impact on the gene pool of the poorer, labouring classes in the East End as any amount of immigration into the area.

After the marriage, the next big do in many couples' lives would be a christening. It was something you did, as much a social event as a religious sacrament.

> You'd lay on a good spread for everyone at a christening. The
> baby would have had its head wetted down the pub, when it

had been born, and the mum would have been churched so she could go out again, then it was the christening. You wouldn't want to be shown up by not putting on a good spread and plenty of ale.

One family christening, my aunt insisted that my uncle had to return a little dog he had 'found', intending to sell it down Club Row the next morning. She wasn't so much concerned about him pinching it as the fact that it belonged to the vicar, and that didn't seem right.

Funerals, although obviously sad affairs, were times when preparations as extensive as those for marriages and christenings were made, with food, drink and appropriate attire all contributing to the self-respecting family's demonstration that they could give one of their members a proper and fitting send-off.

The reception for a funeral [would be] held at the local pub, with plenty to drink and similar food for weddings. People would start off very sad and sombre, but they would cheer up and often end up singing. This would seem strange behaviour to some, but this was the way we did things, and it would be regarded as a 'good send-off'. The deceased would lie in state in the front room of the house, where family members would come to pay their last respects. All the furniture in the house would be covered in white sheets to show respect. Everybody would wear black, which would include a black armband. These armbands were worn for several days. The coffin would be taken to the cemetery by horse-drawn carriage. This was always very slow and looked majestic.

You'd draw the curtains out of respect and cover the mirror – no vanity at such a sad time, you see. In the old days, when the hearse was drawn by horses, they would put pads over their hoofs and throw down straw to muffle the sound of them stepping on the cobbles. The horses were beautiful creatures. They've made a comeback lately. A lot of people round here are having the horses again. It's important to have a proper send-off. It was important even then, when no one had anything much to spare in their pocket, but you would make sure you had a policy to cover your funeral costs.

Everyone in the street pulled down their blinds on the day of a funeral as a mark of respect and sawdust was thrown in the road to muffle the sound of the black horse's hoofs that pulled the beautiful hearse with its elaborate glass sides. All the neighbours would stand in the doorways, dressed in their aprons, watching silently.

If the person who had died had been one of the old boys who used a certain pub, the funeral procession would stop outside so the landlord and customers could show their respect. They'd come outside and take their hats off. The hearse would wait there a while before moving on.

The East Enders were great ones for funerals: plumed horses and most artistic wreaths – the cushion, the empty chair, the broken heart. Everybody stood silently and took off their hats as they passed. [My friend and I] would go for a walk round Bow cemetery and read all the lovely things written on the tombstones. My little cousin was buried there. She was only five and had died of diphtheria. My uncle was heartbroken and on her grave he had put:

> She came, and it was light.
> Suddenly she went, and it was dark.

We used to cry.

At times of such sadness or of celebration it was accepted that gestures of sympathy or congratulations would be made by both the family and members of the local community.

A regular and accepted generosity was the street collection for a funeral wreath or a wedding gift. In our house, as in most

along the street, when someone died a few coppers was set
aside for the collection.

They were shared times. You'd want to show your respects,
so you'd make sure you gave to the collection. We was all one
in them days, you see. You might be crying, but you'd be
doing it together.

Displays of respect were seen to confer a decency on the arrangements and, regardless of your circumstances, you did the best you
possibly could at such times.

My nan never had much, but she paid her insurances regular.
Had to have enough put by for a good send-off, and didn't
want to think she'd be a burden when she was gone.

Being able to paying for your burial – a decent burial – was a
matter of pride. You'd have a penny [insurance] policy so
you wouldn't have a funeral that would show you up.

But with hard times and widespread poverty a decent burial was
not always a possibility.

Three of my playmates died of childhood diseases. The one
who lived next door was buried in a common grave. Such
was life, and death, in those days.

And, sadly, memories of such deprivation in the East End of even
recent living memory are not rare.

11

Grandad was gassed in the First World War and never recovered or worked regularly again. As a result the family was destitute throughout my dad's childhood. Dad was the eldest and, despite passing the 'scholarship' to go to grammar school, he had to leave education at thirteen to bring in money as the supporter of his siblings and parents. He told me that, at one time, he and his brothers took it in turn to go to school, because they had only a single pair of boots between them. A frequent meal was boiled rice, with a spoon of jam if they were well off that day.

When talking to people about poverty, it was sometimes difficult to believe that the stories I was recording were based on comparatively recent memories of life in the East End and not some Dickensian past.

While today we complain if the washing machine breaks down, or if the central heating isn't functioning quite as we'd like, or that maybe we can't afford that flash holiday we saw on the telly, or that we are 'starving' because we haven't had our mid-morning snack, older people recall tragedies and heartbreak which came from true hardship and hunger.

I never had a childhood. By the age of eleven I was caring for two Jewish children every night after school. Once they were in bed I had to clean their parents' shops. Every Friday, after their fish and chicken had been cooked, I was expected to dismantle the whole cooker to clean it. I never got home any night until eleven o'clock. I was paid half a crown a week; two shillings for my mum and sixpence for me. It was hard to tell Mum when there was no more cleaning work for me to do. They were bad old days. Hunger and hard work. We even ate starlings, and killed my own brother's racing pigeons to put in a pie. All the furniture was paid for on the weekly.

We'd lie on the floor to hide when the tallyman came round. There just wasn't enough to live on.

Stories such as this may sound, to modern, cynical ears, like well-worn variations of 'hard times in the bad old days', but when the human consequences are considered, they are far too affecting to be taken for mere cliché.

Really, you'd have children who were neglected. Dressed in rags and with sores round their mouths. No shoes on their feet, four and five to a bed, and freezing-cold bedrooms with old coats chucked over them. Chilblains and little chapped hands. They wasn't necessarily bad parents, they was probably doing what they could, but it wasn't always enough. Being hungry, really hungry, is a terrible thing. Having a hungry child must be worse.

My grandmother knew poverty. Her husband died young and she had five children, one born after his death, to raise. She took in washing and did scrubbing.

I wouldn't want anybody to have to put up with poverty like that. As children in the 1920s and early 1930s we never knew how hard it was [for our parents]. All we knew was we never ever got enough to eat. Parents must have had a terrible struggle to try and feed their kids.

There was never any spare money for presents and food at times like Christmas. My dad hung up his stocking hopefully and was excited to see it all lumpy and promising on Christmas Day. When he took it down, he found it was full of lumps of coal.

Between the wars, during the slump, Grandfather couldn't get work and was desperate, as they had nine children to care for. He went to Canada and worked on the new railroads being built there. It was so cold in the winter he nearly froze to death and had to be resuscitated.

*

Even among the very poor, there were those who were better off, those who were considered 'fortunate' to have even the meanest type of work.

> G. went blind as a young man – family rumour had it that Nana had tried a home-procured abortion. As was the way of the time, he was taught to play the accordion as a way of earning a living, and he and my mother would busk around the streets.

Children might be genuinely fortunate in that their parents had some form of regular work and could live that little bit better than their friends, even if 'that bit better' would not mean very much in today's terms.

> It was the summer holidays and I was raking the streets with a gang of kids from down our turning. We'd been playing over on the treacle barges at Long Wall [now part of the Three Mills Heritage site] when one of the boys found the end of a stale loaf that someone had chucked out for the street pigeons. He was from a right poor family and he dived on this bread like he was starving. He never kept it for himself, he ripped it up and passed it round. I didn't want to look like a snob, so I ate my share of this rotten old bread, but I was torn between what me mother would do to me if she found out I'd eaten it and keeping face with my gang of mates.

> My mother did dressmaking, so we were thought of as well off. A joke really, as she only earned a pittance and my father was often out of work. He bought Mum a second-hand treadle machine and, as she did mainly bridal work, he often used the hand-machine while Mum was on the treadle to get an order out! He would do the hems and so on. Us kids often went to sleep with the sound of those machines in our ears. If mum was doing a large order for a wedding, she sometimes *over-estimated* on the material so my sister and I could have a frock. Naughty.

*

Perhaps it was 'naughty', but it was also her mother's way of getting by, of seeing that her family did not go without. Others had their own methods of surviving and, demanding as those days were for so many, the memories are recalled not with shame but with dignity, because people somehow managed to get through it all.

> The Depression years were hard. Dad was out of work every other week [and there was] no unemployment money. We used to get coupons from the doctor to get a bowl of soup for us children. It was delivered to the local school and we used to take a basin down to collect our soup. Dad being the breadwinner had egg and bacon on a Sunday morning if there was the money, and us kids took turns to be given the bacon rind, which was a real treat. Once a week! We always seemed to have holes in our shoes, as there was no money to repair them or to buy new ones, so we'd stick a bit of cardboard in them to keep the weather out.

> Our mum used to take in washing and do a bit of cleaning. We got by in our own way. I was happy, though. But I was the baby of the family, remember. We was brought up the best [Mum and Dad] could manage. They did their best for us. All around us you could see people out of work but still proud and managing. Still getting by on a pittance. They were supposed to be the good old days. [*Laughter*]

> I'm one of nine children and times were very hard. My father was in ill-health, so Mother had a hard time bringing us up. We lived mostly through pawnshops. Any decent clothes we got off the tallymen. If they got their money that was another thing – 'Mum says she's not in,' we'd say and pull the strings through the door so they couldn't come in. But our clothes were mostly from rag shops and hand-me-downs. Everything was geared to getting money to feed you. I don't know how my mother got through it.

> The roads used to be surfaced with tar-covered blocks – tarry blocks, we called them – and you'd go down with a barrow or

an old pram and nick a few to burn on the fire. Full of
stones, they were, and they'd spit out at you. You had to be
careful if you sat too near, but they burned lovely. Gave out a
lot of heat.

Somehow our family managed to survive and, as I
remember, we were never short of food, because my mother,
whilst not very well educated, had an instinct for matters
financial. She used to buy pawn tickets from friends and
relatives anxious to obtain further cash on the article
deposited with the order. These she [would] convert into
cash by selling on the articles for a profit. She was also very
adept at bargaining over prices.

The memories of living in poverty were often recalled in a matter-
of-fact sort of a way. As most of the neighbourhood would have
shared your plight, neither they nor you would have seen anything
unusual in your circumstances – not at the time, anyway.

Having newspaper squares on a nail in the lav, with its
wooden seat shiny from use, was the same in next-door's
backyard as yours, and the same in the next-door's backyard
to them.

The school provided you with boots and they'd have a hole
punched in the side as a mark so you couldn't pawn them.

If I got some money as a kid, it was always spent on
something to eat. That was your main aim in life. I can't say
we was ever starving, but we could always do with a bit more.
Poor Mum, I don't know how she got through it. We went to
school mainly in white slippers [plimsolls] with red rubber
soles. I hated them. All the stitching used to come undone
and the sole used to flop. If we did have shoes – from the
tallyman – they were popped over at Uncle's [pawned] and
we used to have to put those slippers on. [To stop] Dad
finding out, Mum would say, 'Get behind the back of that
table. Don't let your father see you ain't got your shoes on.'

*

Organizing things to be taken to the pawnshop, as a way of stretching the meagre family finances, was usually the woman's responsibility, even if the task of 'popping' was delegated to the children and the actual cause of the shortfall in the budget could sometimes be found in the pub on the corner of the street.

> Quite often more money was spent on this [having a 'half-pint'] than could be afforded, resulting in a shortage of money on Monday morning. How are we going to get through the week? The answer was frowned upon by some [but was] the saviour to many. It was the pawnshop they turned to on Monday morning. These establishments with their distinctive sign, the three brass balls, would take any worthwhile article, lend money on it for a short period at a small rate of interest, and if not redeemed by the time stated, it became his property. In my opinion they were giving a useful service and at the same time helping to cut out the back-street moneylenders, of which there were many. Most streets had the wealthy little old lady with several large sons who would advance money but at an exorbitant interest rate.

Being poor did not have to mean that, as you stepped over the threshold of the pawnshop and set the bell above the door ringing to announce your arrival to 'Uncle', you had to leave your pride behind.

> Mum would always pay a little bit extra to have her pawnshop pledges wrapped in brown paper. This would keep the dust off, and kept your business private.

> [I used to go with my aunt] to the pawnshop on Monday mornings to pawn anything pawnable, including her wedding ring – which she used to replace with a brass one from Woolworths so [her husband] wouldn't know.

Others were not so bothered about trying to hide their poverty. Some even had photographs taken recording the circumstances of their deprivation.

Sometimes the pawnshop sold off stock it had collected and [there was] a picture of my dad as a boy in dreadful, ill-fitting pawnshop clothes.

People would say, 'Where's your wedding ring?' and you'd say, 'Oh, that's down the road this week. I needed a sack of coal.'

My job, when I was old enough, [was] to take a penny which was laid on the sideboard and the parcels to the pawnshop. We weren't old enough to put our own parcels up, we was under-age, but there was one particular lady, she was a bit queer to look at [but] she was there solely to put your parcels up, so they could go through. And she used to stop so much of the money from us for doing it. We couldn't have anything to eat until I came back with that money.

Business was obviously brisk in the pawnshops and a system of joining three pens together on a bar was used by the pawnbroker to produce the three tickets required for a transaction in a single go: one ticket to put on the item being pledged, one for 'Uncle's' records and another for the customer.

Even if you had nothing of your own to pawn, there were still ways of finding those few shillings until the end of the week.

We used to borrow one another's washing. You'd do a load of washing, dry it, iron it, make up a parcel and take it to the pawnshop. It might not be your clothes. It might have been the neighbour's, [who would say,] 'What washing you done for me, you can borrow to take to the pawnshop. Make sure you get it out for the weekend.'

When my oldest sister was courting she brought a bit of glamour into the house. Well, he seemed posh to us. He used to buy her jewellery. She had a lovely watch and a dress ring. Mum used to say, 'Can I borrow them for the week?' [And my sister would say,] 'Make sure I've got them back for the weekend so [he] don't know they're gone.' Once, I had to

go and get them out. I don't know where Mum got the
money from. On a Saturday it was, and getting near the
time when B. was going to come. Jewellery was up the posh
end and washing down the other. If you got half a crown on
a bag of clothes you was lucky, but you could get a bit more
on jewellery. Well, this watch, it was a lovely little thing, but
when I got outside the shop I dropped it on the concrete
pavement. I was so frightened, but luckily it was still
going.

The local moneylender was another, if more expensive and often
disliked, means of making ends meet.

There was an old girl who lived in the airy [basement] of the
house opposite. Dooky, her place was. Absolutely rotten as a
pear. But she was loaded. Moneylender, see. A lot of us
depended on that old girl in them days. She knew how to
charge us and all. She must have hoarded a fortune over the
years. Certainly never looked like she spent any of it. Not on
herself, anyway.

The housewives [coped] with grinding poverty, resorting to
borrowing two and six from the 'Lady' opposite, to pay that
three shillings [for rent] on Friday.

Popping something with Uncle or paying a less desirable visit to
the moneylender was preferable to going through the demeaning
experience of a visit from the Relieving Officer, but some families
didn't have a choice in the matter.

Before the DSS, if people were destitute they could go to the
Relief Office. There you would be supplied with tickets for
food, made out for a week's supply. These tickets were
handed to the shopkeeper, who supplied them with goods
according to the value of the tickets.

They didn't even give you the dignity of having a few bob in
your pocket. Bloody tickets they give you. Right show-up,

having to take them in the shop. Like being a beggar, going
cap in hand, so's your family could eat.

When things got really bad and you fell behind with debts
and you needed help, this man would assess what home
you'd got, what you could sell. They used to come round and
say, 'Well, you can sell this. You can sell that.' If you had
nothing you could sell, you got free coal, you got free
dinners. We used to have free breakfast. We used to come
from where we lived to another school that was set aside for
the free breakfast. It was quite a walk. And we got the free
dinner, which was good, because we wouldn't have survived.
It's not like if they can't get a job now – they stay on the dole,
but then the dole money was so poor. It wasn't through
choice. You got the RO. That was a pittance. And
demeaning. And my mum, being the person she was, it really
took her down, thinking she had to depend on it.

Despite the general view that poverty was a common state, not
everyone I spoke to agreed that times were all that hard, although the
following point was made by someone who lived in the comparatively
affluent area of East Ham, and he and the person speaking after him
both note that expectations have changed over time and that poverty
is always relative.

It all depends on what you call poverty. If we lived now the
way we lived in the 1930s we would think we were living in
poverty. But I don't think we thought then we were living in
poverty because we had one bath a week . . . or just bread
and jam for tea. In fact, it was probably better for us . . . In
the late 1930s you could always work. There were plenty of
jobs. You did not have to be hard up. My father was just over
eighty and he was working up to a week before he died. I
think poverty in this country is a matter of individual choice.

Compared with today's standards we were suffering, but most
of the country was in much the same boat. We managed, we
had to, and enjoyed it if a few extras came our way. Because

we were more or less all in the same boat, there was not a lot of scope for envy or jealousy of other people's possessions.

Your family did not have to experience poverty, however, for you to be aware of it in the community in which you lived and worked.

I was born in 1911 and have lived all my life in Plaistow and Canning Town, but, when I come to think about the East End, I feel I was almost a bystander. My father was a master baker from the First World War until after the second war. During that time he built up a business in Canning Town. But the poverty in those days impressed on me. They talk about the poor nowadays. To people then, they would have been well off.

You'll find this hard to believe after what I told you about my childhood, but I was considered well off by most of my mates. My family had regular meals. Nothing fancy, but regular. The poverty then *was* poverty.

The most vulnerable, as always, suffered the greatest during times of hardship. The following was the reaction to the financial and emotional poverty found by a nurse who, as a young woman, came from the country to work in London.

I remember most of all the bitter cold of that winter, 1947, the coldest and longest winter we have ever known; the lack of fuel; the food shortage – food was still rationed and the rations had become smaller since the war ended. I was seventeen that January, [the hospital] had been badly bombed during the Blitz and I had to thread my way between the stark, broken walls of the abandoned buildings to reach the wards where our children spent their entire lives . . . The walk was dark and creepy. I imagined the ghosts of all the people who had been killed in the bombing waiting to jump out as I hurried past in the dark. In those days before the Children Act, unwanted and abandoned children spent the most part of their young lives in their cots, or sitting on

potties – it always seemed to be 'potty time' – and they
suffered cruelly with prolapsed bowel. We young nurses were
not encouraged, nor did we have the time, to cuddle or show
love to our small charges. Their ages ranged from two weeks
to four years, and I presume after that they were moved on to
some other equally unloving regime. The ward sister was
kind in her way, and at Christmas bought them little woollies
and socks. These we proudly dressed them in, but sadly,
when they went to the laundry, they all came back stiff and
unwearable, because they had been boiled along with
everything else.

While I was there, there was an epidemic of dysentery.
Sister detailed me to take a baby to [another] hospital in an
ambulance which collected several of us. When we arrived
they told me it was dead. Everything was sad at that time. I
had a mouth full of ulcers, a head full of lice, and split and
bleeding fingers from the constant cold water we had to wash
them in. I had chilblains on my feet and legs. The lice I
caught from two children who were brought in suffering
from neglect. They screamed continually for their mother,
who was in prison. We had to bath all new admittances in
carbolic and cut off their hair.

Some were driven by their poverty to resort to crime and, while
deprivation is not an excuse for all who took this path, there are
memories of desperation as sad as those in the historical court
records, which show cases like that of the East End mother who was
deported for life for stealing a single reel of sewing silk in order to
feed her hungry children.

When [my dad] was about sixteen or seventeen, [his mother]
was so desperate for money she tried to commit suicide by
swallowing bleach, and [his sister] saw her being carried off
as she arrived home from school. To help out, my dad stole a
radio from a shop and legged it along the street. He wasn't
fast enough and was sent to Brixton Prison for three months'
hard labour. It was there that he heard a man being birched
and the memory never left him. I have his school testimonial

and it's really glowing. Apparently, his headmaster was
desperate to get him to grammar school but the money was
never going to be there.

Stealing something to eat, that wasn't thieving. Well, we
didn't call that thieving. Not when you looked at the poor
buggers who had nothing. What was a few tomatoes?
Suppose it was wrong now we look back. Suppose nowadays
they'd want to screw everything down. But it wasn't bad then.
Not too bad. People understood. I'd go as far to say, if you
wanted anything and you didn't have work, you had to nick
it. And there wasn't a lot of work about. I'm talking more
about for the older fellers, not us kids. [*Sighing*] That's how it
used to go on.

The local copper might even cock a deaf 'un if he knew that
someone wasn't doing any harm. I'm not talking about crime
now, I'm talking about feeding your kids.

Less poignant than turning a blind eye to the activities of the
distressed poor, less exciting than tracking down big-time criminal
gangs, the day-to-day routine of most police officers involved keeping
some sort of order within their own communities, whether carting
off a drunk too far gone to walk home to the police station on a
canvas litter, or making sure that local kids didn't take too many
liberties.

I regret to say that from the age of around eight, nicking
became a way of life. Sweets from a local shop, fruit from the
market. In those days the police were feared, if not respected.
It was always thought that they kept marbles in their white
woollen gloves, [making] a clip round the head for a
misdemeanour quite painful. And I should know!

There is a romanticized view of crime in the past: that people
lived in a totally drug-free world; that they were always safe in their
own homes – 'we had so little, who would bother with us?'; that
gang violence was exclusively limited to hard men sorting out 'their

own'; and that robberies were perpetrated only on those who could afford to be robbed.

People didn't take from their own. They took from people who had money and was well insured. Not from people that had nothing and couldn't cover their loss.

I cannot remember any burglaries – there was nothing for a burglar to take. No videos, no televisions.

You hear them talk about the gangsters, but ordinary sort of people like us could walk the streets without any trouble whatsoever. In fact, it was safer, if you want to know the truth.

But there were also recollections of it having been tougher then.

We might not have had that much to pinch, but they'd still have your brass candlesticks off the mantelpiece. There's always wrong 'uns, in every walk of life, who'll have whatever you've got from under your nose.

Bloody gas-meter bandits, that's what we called them. They'd break in when they knew you was down the pub or round your family's or somewhere, and they'd bust your meter open. Little bastards. You usually knew who it was, if you had any brains, and you'd go and have 'em.

You had to be careful in the markets, that was where they'd have your purse. I'm not admiring what they did, taking off their own, but they were clever all right. My aunt had her Loan Club money, one Christmas, and she was holding on to her bag, knew she had to be careful down the Lane, but they still had it off her. She was heartbroken. It ruined her Christmas. I hope their fingers dropped off.

Course there was crime, how else could you have bought a bit of this and that off someone down the pub?

*

It wasn't only pickpockets, thieves, burglars and fences who oper-ated in east London. There were organized gangs committing armed robberies in banks and post offices, and carrying out raids on goods being ferried to and from the bonded warehouses, and the Leman Street police station was equalled only by West End Central and Paddington in the amount of vice charges it dealt with after the war, when it became notorious for its red-light district.

After the war, when the Maltese pimps moved in around Cable Street, there were these twenty-four-hour cafés – so-called cafés. They were more of a front for the pimps, who would sit there drinking tea for hours on end so they could keep an eye on their girls. And girls was the right word, no more than children some of them.

A man was murdered off Cable Street. He was a very nice, obliging man who had a general shop that was open, literally, twenty-four hours a day. I used to chat to him, buy fruit and beigels off him. You couldn't get contraceptives easily in those days, but you could there. The toms – as the prostitutes were called – used to go to his shop for them. I don't think they ever found out who did it.

Up from Gardiner's Corner there was waste ground where all the toms used to hang out. Police used to go round there in twos, and they used to call it the 'rubber heel' because they'd wear very quiet shoes so the girls wouldn't hear them coming along.

It wasn't just prostitution round there, there was the gambling clubs, and where there's money there's violence, and there was plenty of both. You kept yourself to yourself if you had any sense.

There were other sorts of trouble that local people made sure they kept away from.

[When we moved in] we were warned by the couple who

lived underneath us to be careful of this one couple. 'You
want to watch him, he's got a record. Have you seen his
place?' His house was about three down from ours. 'Look on
his line.' I couldn't believe it: [hanging] on the line was all
the fur from where they'd got hold of cats and skinned them.

But sometimes you couldn't help becoming involved.

My brother got done over by some Teddy Boys and my mum
went crazy. He was about fourteen. Anyway, the police were
called, but my mum and dad had already gone looking for
them. They found them and Mum gave one a good fistful,
just as the police arrived. Mum really thought she would be
in trouble, but the police said, 'That's all right, missus, have
that one on us,' and marched the boys away.

You'd hear of fights or a row between a husband and wife
which would lead to violence, when the police would be
called by a neighbour.

Or you thought you couldn't.

I wasn't out looking for trouble, but it was a time when there
wasn't much else on offer for me. Too old to do a boy's job
on the cheapest wages, but too young to warrant a man's
wage, and when you see these fellers with their flash clothes
and pockets full of money down the pub, treating everyone to
drinks . . . It was too tempting. Why would I go and be a
messenger boy the rest of me life? Once I *did* have a chance
to do something else – someone offered me the chance to set
up in business with them – that's what I did. [*Laughing*] I
went back on the straight and narrow. There's a lesson there,
eh? And I didn't do too bad. Earned a living for the old
woman and the kids.

There is a joke that the Kray family must have owned the original
multistorey car park, because it seems that every other man over
fifty in the East End brags that he used to drive for the 'Firm'. But

not everyone considers that an association with the likes of them was something to brag about.

Everyone knew the name Kray. It was all over the place. Public. All that business about the Blind Beggar, where George Cornell was shot dead, becoming a tourist attraction. The film and all the books and that. But they were just one family. One family who spent a lot of time inside. There were plenty of others, more successful if you like, the ones what never got caught, never did much time, and never for nothing serious. Ones who are still around now, ones the public probably never heard of. Names I'd rather not mention.

Whoever the gangs were, it was by running illegal gambling clubs – the spielers – and protection rackets, committing armed robbery, living off prostitution and, later, pornography that they flourished.

The [X] family had a club next to our pub – it was a spieler, not a drinking club. All the boys [the known faces] used to go in there. I said to my husband that they'd got a right club there, but my husband was well liked and he never got aggressive with them when they came into our pub.

He'd say to me as they walked in, 'Trouble's here,' but if they turned a bit nasty he'd go over to them, put his hand on their shoulder and say, 'Come on, boy, you've had enough now. You don't want to get in a row with the missus, do you? When you come in tomorrow, don't forget, the first drink's on me.' He'd turn to me and say, 'Don't forget, when he comes in tomorrow, the first drink's on the house.'

They never paid for anything, but they always said, 'Your pub will never get broken up or gutted.'

I'd cook a ham for the pub; used to sweat myself up in the kitchen, breadcrumb it, egg it. Great big ham. I'd come down and it'd be gone.

I'd ask my husband where it had gone and he'd say, 'I cut it up for them two boys to take home to their wives.' We never made anything in that pub, but we never got broken into or smashed up. Never had to call the police once.

Others weren't as fortunate with the 'protection' of their property.

The pub next to the station, that was run by cocky people. They'd say, 'Piss off, we don't want your sort in here.'
'Don't you? Right.'
All the tables went into the cabinets, all the spirits and bottles smashed. Everything turned upside-down. Another pub, a little way along, she wouldn't stand them a drink or anything. They broke in in the middle of the night, and that was that.

They took liberties with us. If you're 'friends' with the likes of [them] you've got to hold the candle to the devil. On Sunday, we might have a couple of pork or lamb chops. We'd be open Sunday and they'd turn up from one of the spielers after being out all night gambling and losing their money, come in the pub and say, 'Come on, we want something to eat.'
'I haven't got any sandwiches today, fellers,' I'd say. 'It's Sunday.'
'Give us a cut off the joint then.'
'I never had a joint, we've got chops today.'
'Well, find us something.'
And my husband said, 'For God's sake, find something.'
And all of a sudden I'd have to come down with egg, bacon, tomatoes and fried bread. And they'd sit there and eat it.

It wasn't only local business people who were drawn, unwillingly, into the illicit world of the criminal.

It was as difficult, I think, being married to a police officer in that area as it would have been being married to a criminal. The way of life for them was almost the same. They had to mix with what has been called the underworld, do all their business in pubs. After years of that, the only difference is, one lot have the money from all their crooked dealing and the other lot wind up divorced because their families can't take it.

But there was a lighter moment in the life of this east London police officer.

I was amazed when I transferred to Thames Division [the river police] at Wapping. Instead of people throwing abuse or a punch at me, they were standing on the bridges waving down at us!

There were, of course, people who lived in the East End who were neither poor, deprived nor criminal, and who lived in comparatively idyllic conditions.

I finished up [living] down by the football ground. That's where we faced, all across the green. All the football pitches. We looked out on to trees. For the East End of London, that was living in luxury.

The majority, however, could only dream of such pleasures, living as they did far from grass and trees, and close to the polluting emissions of factories and chimneys, workshops and railways. With the additional burdens of poverty and poor housing, their health suffered accordingly.

12

Our parents would pay half a crown if a doctor visited. I know one thing, nobody called a doctor unless it was absolutely necessary.

Before the introduction of the National Health Service in 1948, sickness caused not only anxiety because of the ill-health of either yourself or one of your loved ones but also financial distress. When someone had barely enough to be able to pay the landlord and put a family dinner on the table, it was unlikely that they would have money to pay for the doctor or the midwife.

Even after the NHS was established, some older people recalled, the idea of going into hospital still caused real panic. My own grandmother, for instance, born in the 1880s, used to tell me how she would always associate the hospital with being absolutely, desperately ill, as bad as going into the workhouse, as you would be prepared to spend some of your precious food or rent money on medical attention, or accept help from the 'parish', only if you were so sick you were as good as 'on your way out' anyway. Like many, she would often prefer to employ do-it-yourself, home remedies.

If you had whooping cough they'd take you to where they were tarring the roads and make you breathe in over the tar barrels. Wonder we survived.

The time was when my parents had to pay the doctor a shilling for a visit, and most cures were old-fashioned remedies, some outrageous. My grandmother carried a petrified potato to prevent rheumatism, and the stocking filled with hot bran around the throat for mumps. Most seemed to be effective – either that or it was mind over matter . . .

There were all sorts of home remedies, I suppose because of

the cost of going to the doctor. Some I didn't mind, like chewing the liquorice sticks or drinking the liquorice water [from the sticks being steeped all week] of a Friday – mums seemed obsessed with you being regular – and a spoon of malt was more like a treat. But if you had a cold, that was it, a spoonful of Fenning's bloody Fever Mixture. God, it was horrible. It made your teeth go all furry. It came in a clear bottle with a sort of red wax-covered cork, and had a label with loads of little writing on it that claimed it could cure just about everything you could go down with.

There was this gear my nan kept on her shelf. You wouldn't dare say you had a gippy tummy or felt sick or you'd have a spoonful of this vile stuff shoved down your throat.

Some home therapy was remembered as being far more pleasant.

If we weren't well that was the only time we got to sleep with Mum in her double bed. We always had to go against the wall so we wouldn't fall out. Sleeping with Mum was better than all the medicine. You didn't get much of a look-in when you were one of so many. But when you weren't well you always got plenty of cuddles.

Doctors, accustomed to the poverty of the community in which they worked, understood their patients' situation and, at times, were prepared to forfeit their fee.

I was born during the First World War and I can remember Dr Jelly, who used to ride the streets of Hackney on his horse, which he tied to the railings. He charged you a shilling – if he thought you could afford it.

But where an adult could decide to forgo a doctor's visit for the sake of the few shillings it might cost them, a sick child was a different matter. With today's Health Service – no matter how we fret about it, it is still there – with the availability of antibiotics, vaccinations, decent housing conditions and nutritious food, it is easy to forget how even common childhood illnesses could be deadly.

> Mums would panic and call for the doctor for their little ones, but they'd suffer in silence when they were ill.

> I was only a child myself but I used to look after a little girl after I'd been to school. She had diphtheria and they never told me. I'd got home from school and they'd said, 'The little girl's upstairs, she's not well. Go and sit with her.'
>   I sat by her bed and I cuddled her and that. The next day when I went they told me she'd gone away to hospital. Two days after that I couldn't talk, I was choking. I had diphtheria as bad as you could have it. It affected all the back of my nose. They had to take all one side of my nose away.

> My mum was crippled with arthritis and I had to look after her as a child, but I don't remember any of us going to the doctor's very often as we had to pay [in the 1930s] for a consultation. I don't know how much it cost when I was admitted to Hackney Isolation Hospital during the diphtheria epidemic.

There were ways of making a visit from the doctor or a stay in hospital more affordable, but you needed some spare income to be able to make provision in the first place.

> We belonged to the HSA – Hospital Savings Association – also the Hospital Saturday Fund. These organizations contributed to any costs incurred. Both my sister and I developed pneumonia in the early 1930s, and Mum was happy with the contribution [they] provided.

It was little wonder that susceptible groups such as children and the elderly were often sickly. But the poor housing conditions, the burning of solid fuel, both domestically and in factories, and the proximity of so much other industrial pollution all contributed to the health problems of *anybody* living in the East End.

We used to get a lot of fog. It would just seem to appear. It was so thick that you couldn't see your hand in front of you. It was so black and dirty that, if you blew your nose, your handkerchief would be black. I am quite sure the weather was a lot colder years ago, because I constantly had chapped legs when I was a little girl. I would have to have Vaseline put on to soothe them.

A woman I knew worked in a chest clinic – there was a lot of TB around in them days. Consumption we used to call it. And she told me that when the fog was really bad you couldn't see to the end of the ward she was in charge of. Because of the fog! And it was a chest hospital! I know you sometimes couldn't see the screen properly at the pictures – I'm talking about the 1940s and early 1950s now – but not seeing the end of the ward?

There was a lot of TB about. The boy who lived downstairs [it was a typical, multi-occupancy house] contracted it and we all had to go to the hospital to be tested. Luckily nobody else in the house got it.

Oral testimony always throws up a range of views on any issue, and, according to this woman, the comparatively basic living conditions before the changes following the slum clearances actually had some real health advantages.

We didn't have carpeting, so didn't have dust mites and didn't have hay fever because they didn't have anything to live on. Everywhere got scrubbed and disinfected, you never had bits and pieces about. You was better off. Your scullery floor was concrete and that used to get scrubbed. None of these places that harbour everything. All these curtains and fitted this and fitted that. The vacuum cleaner doesn't get up half so much as a scrubbing brush.

Housing conditions apart, the great change in health care came, of course, in 1948. As with the reprivatization of the water supply, it is difficult to understand how, when we can remember the agonies that resulted from being unable to afford a visit to the dentist, we can stand back and watch the reprivatization of dental care.

> When the National Health came in, I couldn't wait to visit the dentist, *free*! I was born with chalky teeth, they were all broken and needed to come out well before the NHS, but there was no way my parents could have afforded to pay.
>
> They reckoned I lost all my calcium while I was carrying my first baby. Always had trouble with them. So, as soon as it came in free, I had all my teeth out, the lot. False teeth are a lot less trouble. Got rid of the lot of them.

Opinion again varied when I asked people about the benefits of the NHS and some of the views were rather robust, to say the least. One man claimed that it had created a nation of hypochondriacs who were never actually ill but were always 'a bit poorly', and another believed that it simply allowed anyone to spend their entire working life 'on the panel' (signed off sick). But widespread ill-health was a genuine problem in the East End and, before the introduction of universal health care, local authorities did what they could to improve matters by circulating public information on issues such as food hygiene, the care of babies and children, and the promotion of general well-being. One leaflet, produced in an effort to 'Help Your Council to Help You!' urged residents, as part of the National Campaign against Rheumatism, to go to the Poplar Baths on the East India Dock Road to:

partake of a Zotofoam Remedial Bath to rid the system of excess acids – the cause of rheumatic suffering – and expel the poisonous secretion through the open pores.

The treatment might or might not have been beneficial, but it was not free, although the council did stress, 'It pays in the end', just as did eating good, well-prepared food, which was also beyond the pockets of too many East Enders.

The following memories of the food people actually ate might not impress nutritionists, as what was put on the table was more a matter of what you could afford than what you thought would benefit you and your family's health and fitness, but that did not stop it being tasty.

> They'd stand there, down the Lane, with a big pole stacked high with beigels and a barrel full of pickled herrings on the side of the pavement. And they'd dip their big old red hands right down into the barrel and pull out the herrings and then stick them in a cone of paper with the beigels. All wrapped up for you. Not very hygienic, when you think about it, but they tasted lovely. Mind you, food used to then.

East London, like any area with a population of largely poor, working people, had a tradition of meals being produced from a few basic ingredients, but with great ingenuity. Trying to satisfy the empty bellies of a hungry, often large family when there wasn't very much in the cupboard, and even less in your purse, was a constant battle, and paddings of one sort or another – suet, split peas, bread, potatoes and so on – were used to stretch an otherwise skimpy meal into a filling plateful for everyone.

> My favourite food when I was a child was boiled stew with dumplings. The dumplings were made of suet and I used to save some for after dinner and have sugar on them – yuk! Bacon pudding with pease pudding was another favourite. Pickled herrings were a big treat with my grandparents. We often had bread and dripping and also sugar sandwiches.

> My nan was amazing. She could make a dinner out of nothing. A few bacon scraps and slices of onion rolled into suet pastry then wrapped up in a muslin cloth and boiled – lovely. She could stretch next to nothing to make a fantastic filling meal. None of this prepared stuff. What she could get for a good price down the market – that'd be what you'd have. And she made corned-beef hash; bread pudding; cut us great big doorsteps and toasted them, then smothered them in the jelly bottoms from the dripping pan. It was filling and

cheap, but it was smashing. She'd tell us how, when she was a little girl, kids were sent round the back of the London Hospital with basins to collect dripping from the big roasting dishes they left out to cool by the kitchens.

The one thing I never liked, that she always had, was the sterilized milk. It used to come in tall, thin-necked bottles and have a cap on it like a beer bottle. It was sort of a creamy colour and tasted sweet. I didn't like it at all. And she used to have a big cut-glass bowl on a stem, full of sugar, on the table. She'd have loads of sugar on stuff, even sprinkled on bread and marge. I suppose sugar had been in short supply during different times in her life and she was making the best of it now. It was like under her sink she had this cupboard, and she used to have tins of food, bags of sugar and that, as if it was all going back on the ration and she'd have to do without.

Visits to 'proper' restaurants might have been a rarity, but people did eat out quite regularly.

We went to pie and mash shops, but we never went out to a proper restaurant for a meal, except very, very occasionally to Lyons Corner House, where you could have the most glorious ice-cream sundae, a Knickerbocker Glory.

There was the coffee shop [in the 1930s] which had marble-topped tables in separate cubicles where my grandfather would take us for a meal sometimes. They served wonderful moist individual steak and kidney puddings, and, after the meal, he would take me round to the grocer's and buy me a penny 'Buzz' bar, which was a biscuit covered in chocolate, and with it I would get a toy which was a cardboard bee on a string tied to a short stick, and when you whirled it around it made a buzzing sound.

My family used to run a pie and mash shop. They used to make the liquor [parsley sauce to go with the pies and hot stewed eels] from the juice the eels made when you cooked them. You'd eat the pies with vinegar and loads of salt, always with a spoon and fork, never with a knife. It was a big deal when they started making tea in the pie shops, never mind the soft drinks and the fruit pies and custard, and the *vegetarian* pies they do in some of the pie shops now. That would have amazed people like my nan. The days of Nan storing the big enamel bowls of jellied eels under her bed have long gone. Can you imagine what the European people would have to say about that? It would make worrying about straight bananas and wrong-sized apples look like the joke it all is. I still love pie and mash, and if I've been up to London, I'll get a load and take it home to Kent. We all love it. It's a real treat. Daft when you think of the opportunities we have to go to some really lovely places nowadays, but pie and mash wins every time.

I've always loved pie and mash, but I don't eat meat now, I'm a vegetarian. But I take the meat out of the middle. My daughter washes out the inside of the pie for me. I couldn't bear the thought of not having pie and mash any more.

The pie shops were marvellous places, with their marble table-tops and huge etched mirrors with pictures of eels and seaweed and shells, and outside they had a stall with great metal trays of live eels all wriggling about. You'd sit on wooden benches, all bunched up together, with all your mum's shopping under the table between your feet.

Fish and chips were also a favourite, although, like saveloys and pease pudding, they were originally sold for home consumption rather than for 'eating in'.

Chris [Chrisp] Street market used to have this stall that sold the best saveloys in the world. They used to steam them in this big silver urn thing. And they were proper saveloys, real meaty sausages, not like you get now. And you'd have a scoop of thick pease pudden and a couple of roasting-hot faggots. You can't believe how tasty they was. Really peppery, sort of spicy. All hot and fresh. Lovely.

Fish and chip shops had no tables then, they were only for take-away.

The fish and chip shop near us was always packed. You would queue for ages for your penn'orth and ha'p'orth [penny's worth of fish and a halfpenny's worth of chips].

If you only had a farthing you could get a pile of crackling [the batter left in the fish-fryer] that you could cover with onion vinegar, left over from the pickled onions, and loads of salt. Really tasty, that was.

While our mums and dads were down the pub, all my brothers and sisters used to sit on the stairs or along the passage with all our mates from down the turning, with our coats over our legs to keep us warm, and we'd have bags of chips and crackling between us. Makes me feel hungry thinking about it!

If there was the money available, the boat would be pushed out on a Sunday.

Sunday was lovely, Sunday was roast dinner. Roast beef and Yorkshire pudding. They always had to put it on at a certain time and it used to take for ever. It never takes that long now. Why did it take so long? You had your dinner at least two or three hours after it was first put on. They did use to put those old vegetables on! And then the men would go down to the pub for their pint, and come home at about half-past two, and only then was the dinner put on the table.

My favourite Sunday dinner was salt pork or salt beef with pease pudding and carrots and boiled onions. It seemed to be a massive meal. I would try and join up the rings of fat floating on the top of the gravy with the tip of my fork.

Sunday was the one day we ate well. We always had to wait until Dad came back from the pub, because he had to carve. Us kids had to go out to the scullery [to eat] because there was only room round the table for the older ones.

Sundays, in your Sunday best [and] after church going to see Gran. She would have a big tray of lovely crispy roast potatoes in the oven for all us grandchildren. And we would have them all hot and floury. She made the most delicious creamy rice pudding and we would have some of that. She used to say, 'Don't tell your father.' It was our secret, and I'd go home and still eat all my dinner. My father's two young sisters used to take me out sometimes to Petticoat Lane [on Sunday mornings], and they would give me all sorts of forbidden things like cockles, pomegranates, and I'd spit the pips out, and they'd say, 'Don't tell your father.'

I loved Sunday tea, where the table, which almost filled the living room, was laid with small plates, each with a needle or pin on it and, in the centre, a pile of winkles and a large plate of bread and butter. When I was tiny, my aunts and uncles would remove the curly meat from the winkle shells and put them on my bread and butter.

With the presence of so many different cultures, cockneys were able to try 'foreign' food before doing so became a widespread habit. My father can still surprise waiters by asking for certain dishes in a Chinese dialect he picked up many years ago in Ching's Café in Limehouse.

East Enders also became skilled at adapting and adopting the various culinary traditions brought into the area by immigrants, and some types of food – from simple poultry to exotic fruits – once considered unaffordable luxuries, became generally available.

I was born just after the war and my dad was brought up
around Chinatown. I can remember eating Chinese food he
brought home from a café he knew there, and Indian curries
that a friend of his made. When I was really little this was.
Before it was popular like it is today.

Chicken used to be so expensive it was only for Christmas
[but] there used to be a little Jewish shop, down a side
turning, that sold chickens. If the chicken had a stone in the
neck, in the gizzard, the rabbi never passed it. It was good
chicken, but Jewish chicken had to be perfect; they'd put a
little mark on the leg to say it had been passed by the rabbi.
This chicken [that wasn't passed], there was nothing wrong
with it, and they used to sell it to me for half a crown. This
Jewish woman showed me how to do it with the *lokshen*.

But despite these memories of enjoyment and pleasure, many of
the strongest recollections are of food being in short supply and of
genuine hunger.

We had a bit of bread and jam, or brown sauce on bread for
a bit of relish. I used to watch my dad eat his herrings and he
used to look at me and break me a bit off. They were hungry
times, very hard times.

It was a big worry for the parents, how to feed their hungry
brood. It was, without doubt, a live-from-day-to-day
existence, because the amount of money available was never
stable and there was no convenient stock of food like we can
enjoy today. No fridge, freezer or pre-wrapped, not a great
variety of tinned food. I can only remember condensed milk
and corned beef in tins. So most food was bought and used
the same day.

Food was as filling as possible that Mum gave us. Mostly
bread and marge [in the day]. Occasionally we used to have
jam. We used to make it with rhubarb. Didn't wait for it to
set, you just put it on your bread as you cooked it. It was

always bread and marge for [breakfast] and to take to school wrapped in newspaper. And a bit to eat along the way – that was put on the top. There was five little newspaper packets, because five of us were all at school together. [At night] it might have been chips from the fish shop and a piece of bread. That was filling.

And when you were used to food being scarce, what you had, you valued.

My husband never bothered with drink, he was never a drinker. But he was a nosher. He loved all his food.

In them days we had all sorts of puddings and stews, and made them last for three or four days. You kept your own chickens and rabbits in the backyard, to kill to eat. We might not have had so much to eat, but what we had was wholesome.

We were not well off, so it was fish and chips or stew for dinner. I used to go to Oxford Hall for a school dinner sometimes, when we would get toad in the hole or stew. We also had breakfast, consisting of cocoa and bread and dripping. In those days – I was born in 1903 – if you were unemployed, you had to go to the workhouse and get bread and tea in kind. At the corner of [the] street there was a fish shop run by One-eyed Annie. The counter was too high for me to see over. To get the crackling and the chips was a nice occasion as I always seemed to be hungry. When we bought a loaf I used to get the 'make weight', a slice, crusty and hot, given to make the weight of the loaf up to two pounds, the legal limit. [You could buy] a cup of jam for a penny [and] white bread was twopence a loaf.

Even fruit peelings could be considered a delicacy.

We used to go scrumping as kids . . . Well, nicking, if you like to call it that. You know the stalls in Stratford market, well, when it was getting near the end of the night we used to get under the stalls for all the specky apples. They'd only have been thrown out. We'd bring them home, cut all the specks out and eat them. On Sunday, if Mum made an apple pie . . . I can see it now, us kids used to have to stay in bed till Dad and all the older ones got ready to go out – there wasn't room for us all to get down the stairs – she'd peel the cooking apples for the pie, then she'd put all the peel in an empty sugar bag. There'd be a few grains left in the bottom. She'd shake it and send it up to us children. We'd eat them as a real treat. Cooking-apple peels! We didn't care about the bellyache. Even now, when I'm peeling apples, I always have an empty sugar bag. I think to myself, 'Here we are, take them up to the kids.' We used to fight over them. 'Oi, you've got more than me!' And how about the condensed milk? When they used to open the tin with them jagged openers, the milk all used to collect along that jagged edge and you used to put your finger round it. Goat Brand it was.

Scarce or not, food was not always that appetizing, but it was usually still devoured.

[My brother] was in the Scouts and at one camp he learned to make damper, which was dough rolled out into a strip and then wrapped around a stick and cooked over the camp fire. Well, one evening he decided to make some at home and cook it over the fire in the kitchen. It may have been the difference between the camp fire and our coal fire, but it came out black on the outside and just about raw on the inside. But I ate it anyway.

Sometimes, though, it was simply too repulsive to contemplate.

There was a street running parallel to Hessel Street. They called it Chicken Hill. It's where they killed the chickens. The stink! Put you *right* off.

*

Food – tasty, unpleasant or indifferent but filling – had to be bought from somewhere, and whether it came from the market, a passing street trader or the corner shop, in the days before domestic fridges and freezers, buying it was another daily task.

13

All shops were handy, most were at the top of the street. We children were used to run errands, to get Dad's fags, or a penny ha'penny bloater, or a loaf from the baker, which had to be weighed – if it was under two pounds it was made up with an extra slice or a bit of cake.

There were many affectionate memories of the small traders who served their local communities, valued as much for the meeting place they furnished as for the goods they supplied. People spoke of the human contact which going shopping gave them – the chance for a chat, a laugh and a bit of gossip – and the passing of these businesses seems to be genuinely regretted, especially when the service they gave is contrasted with the impersonal experience that shopping has become today in the large supermarkets and chain stores.

When every street had a shop or a market within easy walking distance, and homes had a meat safe, a cupboard and maybe a larder, rather than having a refrigerator as a matter of course, doing the shopping was just another part of the daily routine, but it is remembered as a pleasurable one.

Corner shops were ever so friendly. They would have a chair by the counter for the older people to have a sit-down – and a good old chat, of course. Like a social centre as much as a place to get your provisions. A lovely white cloth over the cheese, there'd be. Fly-papers dangling down over the counter. And glass-topped biscuit tins. Children would put their heads round the shop door and shout out, 'Got any broken biscuits?' If the shopkeeper said yes, then they'd say, 'Well, why don't you mend 'em?' You could buy the broken biscuits cheaper than the others, but you'd be fussy and try and get the cream ones.

We did most of our shopping from the corner shop as there

were no supermarkets. Most things were wrapped up for you.
And you could get three pennyworth of stales. This was stale
cakes or biscuits. You could also buy yesterday's bread cheap.

These little East End businesses catered for just about every need,
offering a full range of goods and skilled services for their communities.

A shop with smells was the oil shop. It used to sell hardware,
and many kinds of oil. Paraffin [heaters] were used by a lot
of people. The oil shop was also the supplier of bundles of
wood for starting coal fires, and most household hardware
like kettles, saucepans, buckets, brooms and brushes.

The oil shop was wonderful. Lovely smell. And the corn
chandler's, that was another one. I'm nearly fifty now, but I
can remember this shop like I'd just been in there. We used
to sneak in there cos it was where we bought split peas and
corn for our peashooters. They were kept in big hessian sacks
on the wooden floor, leaning against the counter, with the
tops of the sacks rolled down and all the seed and grains full
right up to the top. My brother would make me go in,
because I was an innocent-looking little girl, and I'd get
served. 'It's for me dad's chickens,' I'd say if the shopkeeper
was a bit suspicious. There'd be a craze for peashooters, you
see, once a year or something, and suddenly all the kids had
them, and all the old girls would complain to the man in the
corn chandler's: 'Don't you go selling none of that to them
rotten kids, they're driving us barmy.'

On the corner of our road was the shoe mender's. He was a
nice man and I used to sit on the windowsill at the side of his
shop and watch him fill his mouth with nails and tacks and
mend the shoes. The shop always smelled lovely and he never
minded us watching. At the top of the road was the grocer's,
a real over-the-counter, old-fashioned lovely shop.

Alf's the barber's was along by us. He was a character. He did about two haircuts and would say he'd done enough for the day and let his assistant do the rest of the customers. One of Alf's regulars was another Alf, Alf the local undertaker. He would come and chat to us every morning after his daily shave and trim. If you thought undertakers were solemn people, Alf would prove you wrong. All my family went to him.

Miss S. had a little grocer's and sweet shop. If I had a ha'penny, I would go there and get a ha'p'orth of pickled cabbage. Miss S. would say, 'Does your mother know you're having this?' I would lie and say, 'Yes.' We both knew my mother wouldn't approve. It was like liquorice dabs, tiger nuts, sweet tobacco and sweet cigarettes. [My parents] were fussy about what you ate between meals.

From the shop that sold sweets and things, we bought Everlasting Sticks, long thin strips of toffee, and Chinese Coconuts, which looked like stones but were supposed to taste of milk when you kept them in your mouth and sucked them. I think they really were stones, because they never wore away.

Joyce's the baker's was just a few doors from our house in Stepney. By the smell, we knew when the bread was out of the ovens. Mum bought cottage loaves, crusty rolls and pies for just a few pennies. Sweets were bought at Balernie's. I can still see the women sitting there on lemonade crates talking to Mrs Balernie.

The women would take their Sunday meat and potatoes in a roasting tin to the baker's, and he'd stick it in his oven that was still hot from his baking and cook it for you.

As well as the friendliness and convenience of the small shops, they also offered an informal credit system for regular customers, who could balance their restricted budgets with the help of a 'slate', which allowed them to buy things 'on tick'.

*

We had a corner shop where my mother would pay weekly. Her account being written on the counter, if you know what I mean.

Across the road was this shop [run] by this dear lady. The people were so poor round there, they used to run up bills and she never got paid. 'Mum said could she have so-and-so.' I mean, it was a list this long. 'Well, she hasn't paid off last week's yet.' 'Well, when Dad gets some work . . .' That was how we lived. That woman, I don't know how she kept in business. Everybody owed her money. She was so obliging, everybody took advantage of her. 'Go to so-an-so's. She'll give you so much off the list.' You'd eat it as soon as you got it. You had nowhere to store it, [but] you never had it long enough to go bad or anything.

Mum would send me up every day with a slip of paper with the day on it and the things she wanted. [He] would give me the items and attach the slip to the others on a bit of string. At the end of the week Mum would go and settle her bill.

Not all shops in the East End were small, local businesses. Main thoroughfares had big parades of shops lining either side of the road, with stalls set out in front of them on market days.

In Old Bethnal Green Road were a lot of shops. Faulkner's the chemist, where Mum got her pink ointment, which stank, but she reckoned cured everything. Atkins's the newsagent, a cobbler's, a bagwash shop, a wet fish shop, Odden's the fruiterer and greengrocer, and the grocer's, where I used to watch them take a portion of butter from the large block and then, with the aid of two wooden paddles, pat it into a half-pound block and then wrap it in greaseproof paper.

On the [main road] there were all the shops you could want. The butcher's, greengrocer's, the barber, a corn chandler, the baker's, a fishmonger. Everything. They were friendly people who loved to chat and have a cheery word. One shop I hated

was M.'s, the cat's-meat shop. Horrid. Sights you wouldn't
see at a slaughterhouse. Animal lights strung up on the wall
with a notice '3d a bag'. The smell was terrible. But I had to
go there for a neighbour who had a cat and dog.

There were shops you don't hear of now: Home and
Colonial, Pearks and Cater Brothers. Benise's sold loose
vinegar from a wooden barrel, blue dolly bags for getting the
washing white, and bars of Sunlight soap. A stall outside sold
block salt – a penny would buy a good-sized piece.

And there were even grander businesses to be found in the East
End, with big department stores such as those in Whitechapel,
Stratford and Leytonstone offering a very different experience from
that of the corner shop.

The way they used to handle the money fascinated me. You
would pay your money over the counter and the assistant
would put it with the receipt in this little cylinder sort of a
thing, which she then hooked on to this overhead rail and –
whoosh! – it would take off across the shop like a rocket to
the cashier's booth, where it was dealt with, and the change
sorted out, before being sent – whoosh! – back across to the
assistant, who would hand over the change and receipt to
you. Stopped the assistants fiddling, I suppose.

In the 1930s I would go to Boardman's department store in
Stratford with my sister. They had what were called mannequin
parades as an inducement to buy what was on offer in the store.
It was where my mother, after leaving school – this is in the
Edwardian period – learned to trim hats.

Far less opulent than the big stores, or even the corner shops,
were the street traders and hawkers who once used to thrive in the
East End, and were still doing good business during the 1940s and
1950s, the time this next woman is describing. I believe the first trader
she talks about is actually my father, as he used his horse and cart
for collecting scrap iron from the bomb and demolition sites during

the week, and for selling shellfish at the weekends – shellfish being
a traditional East End Sunday tea – and his round had included the
street in which she lived.

There was the man selling shrimps and winkles. Then the
cat's-meat man. And the fresh-herring man – he used to call
out, 'Fresh Herring!' and we used to shout out, 'What d'you
feed your donkey on?' And we used to have Indians come
round off the boats. They used to come to the door with their
suitcase with all ties and scarves draped round their neck.
Knock at the door, open their suitcase and you'd sort out
what you wanted. The Indians were a bit of a rarity. It was a
novelty for us to see them.

We had a rag and bone man that used to come round with
his horse and cart. He would buy most old things from you.
If it was worth money he would give you a little, otherwise he
would give you a goldfish or, if you would prefer, a cup and
saucer. The goldfish went down well with the children. A
horse and cart would come round selling jellied eels and so
on. There was also a man that used to come around on a bike
with knife-sharpening equipment and people would pay him
to sharpen their knives. All this would interest the children,
[and] we would get a lot of canvassers knocking on the door
selling all sorts of things, from clothes to kitchenware. This
would be bought on the 'tally' – very often the only way of
acquiring new things.

For some reason, our rag and bone man was always keen on
getting jam jars. Maybe he took them back to the factory, but
whatever he did with them he'd give us kids a goldfish for
them. Smashing, that was.

There was a cart with a roundabout on the back pulled by a
horse. To get a ride you had to give some old clothes.

There was a constant stream of street vendors. A few had
special days, like the coal man, baker and fishmonger. I had

to sit at the door and wait for the baker and the coal man –
miss the coal delivery and you were in trouble.

A lady used to make toffee apples. I used to love them,
especially when you got the small ones with two on a stick.

I remember the muffin man with the tray on his head and
his hand-bell ringing. The beigel man. The salt man – you
bought chunks off a large [conical] lump. Hot chestnuts
baking away in that oven thing on the trolley on wheels. The
Neapolitan ice-cream man on his stall, cutting lumps off a
long slab and giving it to you in a bit of paper. Fresh roasted
peanuts in their shells. [And] our milkman, bringing the milk
twice a day on a hand-cart; the milk in a highly polished
churn. He used to ladle it out on a long ladle thing into your
pewter cans, which were supplied, and you gave them back
when you poured it out into your jug, so you saw you had
the right measure.

The cat's-meat man came round with a wooden barrow that
had a chopping block fixed across the handles and large
chunks of horse meat that he sliced and put on wooden
skewers. He came round calling, 'Meaty meat!' and I tried to
wheel his barrow, but it was much too big and heavy for me,
so all the meat got tipped over the pavement. The salt and
vinegar man came with a horse and cart carrying big blocks
of salt that he sawed lumps off with an ordinary saw, and
barrels of vinegar [from which he filled] your own bottle. He
also sold blocks of harsh yellow soap and washing-soda
crystals, which were wrapped in strong blue-paper bags.

The beigel man, with his beigels tied up with a piece of string,
[would hang] his customers' regular orders on their door
knobs. The coal man came round calling 'Range', which was
the name of the company. The Wall's ice-cream man on a
box-fronted tricycle [advertised] his presence with a type
of xylophone on the front which he banged with a little
drumstick. There was ordinary ice cream and what were

known as 'Sno-Fruits', which was flavoured water-ice in a triangular shape. Winkles, shrimps and whelks came round mostly on Sundays, and I used to try and get all my winkles out of the shell and make them into a sandwich, but mostly I couldn't wait that long to eat them. There was nothing like a winkle and watercress sandwich for Sunday tea.

A useful caller to the street was the insurance man. Apart from the doctor and the teacher, he was the only contact with the educated classes you would have, and he would read out letters for you or give you advice.

No matter what could be supplied to your door or how wide the range of goods in the corner shop, there was nothing to compare with the experience of 'going down the market'. Whether you favoured Chrisp Street, Roman Road, Whitechapel, the Mile End Waste, Hessel Street, Watney Street, the Lane or any of the other streets lined with stalls, going to the market was – and is – a favourite way of shopping for East Enders, a place to find bargains, certainly, but also as much an entertainment as a household chore.

The old Rathbone Market on Barking Road was a hive of activity. On Saturday night, Nan used to take me down there to do the shopping. She would park me by the hot sarsaparilla stall, while she went to the stall opposite and had her bowl of eels, then, to my horror, she'd shove all the jelly into me, which I hated! She said it was good for me. I used to love going to the button stall with all the scraps of material Mum had given us to match buttons for her dressmaking. There was a fortune-teller who told your future, and a ribbon stall, the delight of every girl going to the market.

We often went 'up the Road' – Bethnal Green Road – which was our main local shopping area, with its street-market stalls all along the pavements. Lots of things were on sale, and one could see the man making toffee and shaping it by hanging the semi-solid toffee on a pole and pulling it out and twisting it to make the shape. Sometimes the toffee would be two colours twisted together and when it had been pulled out to the right thickness it was then cut up into sweet-sized pieces ready for sale. There was the stall that sold horseradish and you could see the man grating the root into an enamel basin [and he had] barrels of soused herrings and *haimisha* [pickled] cucumbers on display. The stalls stayed out until late in the evening and when it was getting dark they would light up the pressurized gas lanterns. They couldn't link up with the electricity in those days, and the market took on a lovely, warm feeling with all the people bustling about.

We always used the butcher in the market. On a Saturday night we would get there at about seven, in time for them to auction the joints of meat. We always got our Sunday joint that way. A nice shoulder of lamb for two shillings.

The Roman Road Market, especially at Christmas time, was a wonderland of bright, lamp-lit stalls open until ten p.m., and all the traders calling out their wares. We didn't seem to mind the cold, and the smell of hot roasted chestnuts was mouth-watering.

We used to go down Watney Street Market, or Hessel Street. You could go down any of the side roads for beigels. In the markets you would strike up a conversation with somebody you didn't know. They'd say, 'Aw, yes, get that cut of meat, and do this or that with it.' You thought somebody was taking an interest in you. You didn't just hand your money over.

I loved going to Club Row on a Sunday morning with my dad. I think Mum used to get us out of the house so she could get on with the dinner. It was like a big production in those days, cooking a Sunday dinner. Anyway, I loved it. You could see all the animals and all the things for sale. I'd usually wind up with something – a little dolly or a jumping bean from a man with a big tray of them hanging round his neck, all wobbling up and down. There was this one time I remember when a man let me put this great big snake round my neck. I think you paid him to have a turn, but I don't think you got your picture done or anything – you just got a chance to drape it round your neck. I don't think Mum would have been very impressed if she'd known what Dad was letting me do – or that I'd sat outside the pub with a bottle of lemonade – with a paper straw, of course – and a bag of crisps, while he had a pint before we went home.

My sister, her late husband and I had pet stalls in Rathbone Street and Club Row – Sclater Street off Brick Lane. Club Row was a Sunday morning market only. We got there around seven a.m. and left around two p.m. Breakfast was a mug of tea and a roll, which we ate while serving bird seed, chicken and pigeon food, and birdcages. The tarpaulin sheets on the stalls were great green heavy things, not light plastic as they are now. The snow in the winter would need to be shovelled away to enable us to pitch the stalls. Customers came regularly and you got to know them well. They helped us girls – as we were then! – to lift anything heavy. Pets were also sold in the market then. Along with rabbits and chickens, all types of livestock. People lived in houses then and could keep animals.

Nothing like it, having a nose round the stalls of a Saturday afternoon with your mates, wage packet in your pocket and knowing you could buy something, a new blouse or a top, to go out in that night. You'd be broke by the middle of the week, but, with a bit of luck, your mum would sub you till the next weekend and you'd be after a new pair of shoes or a skirt again!

In the days before clothes had become something bought almost on whim and practically disposable, whether originating from a market stall, a clothes shop or even a posh gown store, they would, after years of wear, look more inherited than purchased. Older East Enders wore what could almost be described as a uniform.

You could see the elderly mums and grans wearing a long

black shawl and a cap and a white apron. Button boots were worn then. Many wore skirts right down to the ground and, of course, they caught the mud and dirt from dragging along the pavement. Most hats had a long hatpin to fix them . . . hatpins that were used in fights between women.

I don't think I can remember seeing my old nan without her cross-over apron on. And she'd have her thick stockings rolled down to below her knees with elastic garters and her hair in a net.

The men all looked the same: a cheese-cutter flat cap, moustache, shirt without a collar, muffler, waistcoat, jacket if it was cold and strong boots. Drab really.

In their childhood, men might be dressed more fancily.

I was shortened – my curls cut off, taken out of long petticoats and put into short trousers – well after I could walk. Can you imagine little boys in frills nowadays? They'd put the parents away!

Unlike young people in the post-war East End, with their teenage styles and clothes, after pre-war boys had been 'shortened' and had then passed through the age, or height, of wearing short trousers, and after girls had graduated from their baggy pinafore frocks, their clothing would not have been much different from that of their parents'.

I went into long trousers when I was eleven years of age.

I went to my first job, aged fourteen, in ankle socks. I must have still looked like a little schoolgirl, but that soon changed. Suddenly, you were a grown-up. No teenager stuff then. You went from school-type dresses to two-piece costumes.

Despite being short of money, mothers tried to keep their children respectable and to satisfy basic styling requirements.

*

[We] were always dressed in our best on Sundays. If my mother wanted us to look special she would put rags in our hair at night. This, I must say, was very uncomfortable to sleep in. [But] the next morning she would take the rags out and comb our hair into beautiful ringlets.

I think my mum wanted me to look like Shirley Temple, but I had hair as straight as a poker, so she used to use these home-perm kits on me. They stunk! All these little curler things and little packs of tissue paper. I've no idea what was in the mixture but it smelt lethal, and, let's face it, it didn't exactly look natural when she'd finished with me.

My mum would drag my hair back in tight plaits – little girls had long hair then. She said it would keep me from picking up nits off the other children at school. I don't see how, all I know is it bloody hurt and I had a constantly surprised expression on my face, like these women you see today who've had a face-lift.

We went to a children's outfitters in Burdett Road, Mandor's was the name – this is around 1955 – and I was fitted out with a new coat and matching hat for Christmas. The window had these posed, plaster models of boys and girls in smart-looking clothes. It all seemed so glamorous, really posh. Racks and racks of clothes. The woman took down things from the rails, took off the covering and held them out for my mum to consider. I loved this one cherry-red coat. It had a dark fake-fur collar and the hat had long ties with bobbles of the same fur on the end – to do up under your chin. I can still remember how scratchy that collar was on my neck and how the ties on the bonnet cut into me, but I didn't say anything, as I loved having something new, I loved that coat – it was a real special event. When my mum agreed I could have it, the woman in the shop put it to one side for my mum to pay it off, so it would be mine for Christmas. I'm not sure why we had something new at Christmas, but we also got vests and pants as well. Perhaps it was because the Loan Club paid out then and there was a bit of extra money for once.

Little boys did not always support their mothers' efforts to keep them looking decent – not when the streets were your playground and there were walls just begging to be climbed.

We used to get new clothes twice a year, Christmas and Whitsun, but if any of the good ones were too small for [my brothers], then I got them because I was always ripping my clothes or scuffing my boots. Dad would go potty if you didn't put your boots on properly without treading the backs down. One day I was in the entrance to the woodyard, calling up to the backyard of my friend, Eddy. The woodyard gates were held closed by a long iron bar which pivoted at one end on a ring set in the wall and when the gates were open it could be hung on a hook in the wall. I had to climb up on the wall to be seen from the backyard of Eddy's house. I was up there calling him when I saw Dad going past on the other side of the street. I quickly let loose of my grip on the top of the wall, but as I dropped down my jersey got caught on the hook. There I was, dangling on the wall, unable to quite reach the top of the wall to pull myself up, and too far from the ground for my feet to reach, desperately hoping that Dad wouldn't look round and see me. Somehow he didn't. I eventually managed to unhook myself, but my jersey was ripped and my toes were scuffed, so I was still in bother.

Having new clothes was a rare event in poorer households and 'making do and mending' were necessities.

Mothers were very good at keeping a garment wearable through their [different children's] ages, as clothes had to be handed down from one child to the next. Tommy's coat when he grew out of it was given to little Joe and patches on trousers were a sign of a caring mother.

Dad's clothes, when they were past patching, would be cut up to make trousers for us. And Mum would always turn the cuffs of his shirt. Clever.

Forced to wear things they didn't like, some children did not think their mothers' skills were so impressive, although they can look back as adults and realize that their parents were probably as unhappy with the situation as they were.

It was horrible. I had this serge dress for school that I'd had passed on from someone and it was just too big. Enormous it was. But Mum seemed really pleased with it, said I'd grow into it and it would last me ages and it bloody did. Couldn't get rid of the rotten thing. But she took this hem up on it – well, half the length of the dress, this hem was, and all thick because it was a sort of flared style. I made such a fuss. But when you think back, it must have been hard for her, knowing how much I hated it but not being able to afford something pretty for me, and trying to be positive and saying, 'It's lovely' but knowing it wasn't. Kids don't understand, do they?

But if you were lucky, as you grew older and found a job, you might be able to afford to buy something special to go out in, or even have something made especially for you.

I remember a lot of young women trotting off down the street with their high heels on [with] a fox fur draped round their shoulders. This fur would still have its head on! A lot of women worked in the rag trade at that time and my mother was one of them. Because of this, she used to make most of my and my sister's clothes.

And there was another way to have something new: saving with the Cheque Clubs, Clothes Clubs and Shoe Clubs, a tradition which stretches back to the Hat Clubs of Victorian times, when employees of factories with large female workforces, such as the Bryant and May match factory, would pay in weekly and then take turns in receiving the collective fund to buy a new hat.

*

My aunt used to run a club for Wickham's in the
Whitechapel Road. It was the main department store round
about that area. Each week, one of the club had a turn of a
cheque to spend in the store. So I always seemed to be
walking with someone in the family through Wickham's.

The club didn't buy things, it was more of a savings club.
We'd all want new things but didn't have enough money, so
we paid in an amount every week and once a month the next
name on the list would get what had been paid in from all us
girls to buy herself something. I always liked shoes, but you
could buy what you wanted and, with the numbers of girls in
the workshop, it was really worth it.

I've always liked to look nice. So, when I couldn't afford to
lay out for something all in one go, the club at work was an
ideal way of getting some new gear for going out in.

Having something nice to go out in was an ambition for East
Enders, who have always enjoyed 'getting done up' for an evening
out. After taking your turn in the tin bath of a Friday night, 'getting
yourself booted and suited' or 'all cased up' was just the thing before
going off to enjoy yourself.

14

The Monkey Parade, that was like the Spanish do of a night, you'd stroll up and down and show off your outfit, your hair-do, with your boy- or girlfriend, or in a gang. It was a place where you sussed out who fancied who. There was this trick that some of them played – they'd come up to you and slap you on the back, 'All right?' and you'd smile, 'Yeah, I'm fine.' You wouldn't know that they'd left a big, white, chalky hand-print on your back for everyone to laugh at. Right little sods, some of the boys. All harmless, but we thought it was fun. Our parents didn't know!

Pleasures such as the Monkey Parade – the evening saunter along the East India Dock Road, between Burdett Road and Blackwell Tunnel, when girls strolled arm in arm with their friends, hoping for a bit of innocent flirting, picking out who they fancied from the similarly occupied gangs of boys, and hoping the 'right' one would show his interest with a wink or a whistle – were definitely considered worth getting dressed up for, but, like most other ways of passing a pleasurable few hours, it was, out of necessity, an unsophisticated pastime and did not cost very much money, if anything at all, to take part in.

With most of our waking hours taken up with duties [both paid and domestic work] we would have had no time for all the home amusements that are available today. [Before] the wireless was available for the masses, we made do with the old wind-up gramophone with the big horn. The simple pleasure of life was to take time off for an hour in fine weather and sit at the front window or on a chair at the front door and pass the time with whoever was doing the same, [enjoying] the neighbourliness.

*

There was always a jigsaw on the go and everyone that called had a go at putting some pieces in. Nanny usually came round on Friday nights and always brought a bag of sweets – winter warmers – and, as she was going home, she would call out, 'Goodnight, Kidlets.' I said that when I grew up I would go out singing in the streets and buy her a pair of blue bloomers.

Although most amusements for working people were as modest as those described above, some were quite startling, and maybe the little girl who was going to buy her grandmother some underwear got the idea for earning money by singing from some of the exotic street entertainers who took their acts around the streets of east London.

I suppose it was not many years after the Great War finished – during the 1920s and 1930s – and there was this musical turn. There was plenty of unemployment about and this group of men, young men I think they were, it was hard to tell, they came round with a barrel organ. One used to play it and the other five or six of them used to dance. They'd link arms and dance in the street. They was men, yes, but they was all dressed as women. They had the lot. Long dresses, shoes, faces rouged, beads all round their necks. Gawd blimey, how they was dressed up! They had better clothes than the women watching them. And everyone would come out to watch and all the kids'd sit along the kerb looking at them. Dressed up they were and they'd be dancing and kicking their legs up. And we'd be shouting out, 'Show us your drawers, girls! Go on!' We called them the Gaiety Girls. They earned a few bob going round dressed like that. They'd go all round the East End, collecting the pennies and tuppences we'd throw to 'em. They didn't seem to mind. Least they was trying. And they were funny, they were. Used to be good and all. See, they'd come round and brighten up a dull place. I'm saying it was dull, but there was plenty of life to be had there. I realize now that I saw my first transvestites when I was a kid!

In those pre-politically correct times, others recalled the street dancers as going by the name of the *Nancy Boys*, or, more prosaically, as the *Jazzers*. Not everyone was agreed about the virtue of such talents, not liking the fact that they were 'posh' or from 'snooty' backgrounds, and one person actually expressed vehement opposition to their behaviour.

> After the 1914–18 war ended, jobs were virtually non-existent. Looking back, I recall with loathing the number of ex-servicemen who, in order to survive, dressed themselves up in outlandish women's clothing and, with the help of a barrel organ, sang and danced in the streets for the odd coins [that] others, in not dissimilar situations, were able to spare.

But during times of high unemployment, such as the inter-war years, many performers were eager to take their talents round the East End streets and even further afield, knowing that it was probably the only way they could manage to earn those vital few shillings that would keep the wolf from the door.

> There was plenty of street entertainment such as the barrel organ, which some of the children danced along to, though one man who came round would chase the kids with a stick if they started singing or dancing. Then there was the one-man band, who had a drum on his back, with the stick connected to his arms with string and cymbals on his knees, a mouth organ, a guitar and various other instruments around his body. Another group would take over a section of the road and perform an Egyptian sand dance or do a routine similar to snake-charming, but instead of a snake there would be a string of sausages coming up out of a tin can. All the audience would sit on the kerbstones at the side of the road and traffic would just about cease while the performance was on. Accordion players often went round playing outside the pubs in the evening, and I remember one artiste who played what he called a nose harp.

*

One or two artistic types would set up a stand in the street –
usually in the market – with a board and a big wodge of
putty or clay. You'd pay them a penny and they'd do your
face, make your likeness out of it. It would amuse us. It
might not seem that special now, but we loved it.

My dad was a boxer. Not a professional [but] he used to go
to different parts of the country for these exhibitions. They
didn't get money because they weren't allowed to pay
amateurs then. But he used to bring home different gifts and
things that were worth money and that made things a lot
easier for Mum.

Even though the majority of the people were not well off, and
there were not today's commercial pressures inducing them to spend
money, Christmas was still a special season when every effort was
made to have a particularly good time. There were the same feelings
of anticipation as the big day approached and of excitement when
the morning itself eventually dawned.

We used to know it was Christmas in the East End when we
used to start making paper chains in school out of bits of
paper. Glueing them together – what a job that was. I don't
remember seeing a Christmas tree then [in the 1920s] but
you'd also know Christmas was coming because of the smell
of the oranges and the fruit being brought up the river in the
boats, and when the dockers unloaded them.

Christmas morning, [*laughing*] we'd wake up to a big old
army grey sock hanging on the bottom of the bed, with an
apple, orange and a couple of nuts. Maybe a few sweets. And
that was Christmas. But the one thing I remember, always,
even now, at seventy-six years of age, there wasn't one
Christmas, not one, that I went without a toy. I don't know
how Dad done it, but he did. I had a tank one year. I
remember that tank – bloody thing was made in Germany
and all! Still, I had Christmas. I got a train set, clockwork.
Couldn't have been electric then anyway, it was all gas in our

house with pennies in the meter. My parents never let us go
without. Dad used to just have his pint. And Mum . . . I don't
know what Mum had, she never had a lot. But *we* never went
without. We would sit round the fire and Dad would have his
jug, warm the poker up and stick it in the beer. 'Have a drop
of that, boy,' he'd say. [*Laughing*] Oh, God, we used to sit
round that fire and we'd sing some old song me mother
knew!

Do you remember the paper that oranges used to come
wrapped in? We'd have orange tortoises made out of them at
Christmas time. Dad would screw the four corners of the
paper into little legs so it made the tortoise's shell, then put it
over the orange and roll it, scuttling on its way, across the
lino.

The spending might have been modest compared with our present
frenzied seasonal consumption, but just providing a few simple toys
and putting a decent spread on the table still entailed a big outlay.
To help spread the cost of the celebrations, Christmas savings schemes
and Loan Clubs were set up in church halls, pubs and corner shops.
A few pennies a week, more if you could afford it, would make all
the difference.

We had a neighbour who used to come round on a Sunday
morning selling sixpenny savings stamps so at the end of the
year you had a few bob for Christmas.

The Loan Club was an ideal way of saving as you could take a
sub out during the year, pay it back and you'd get interest. It
worked out well, as it wasn't someone earning out of you,
you were making money for yourself. The couple who ran it
made a bit, but that was only fair.

But sometimes Loan Club administrators weren't always so fair
and were not satisfied with making just 'a bit'.

Just before the Christmas pay-out, my friend's dad ran off

with the Loan Club money. The whole lot. And all those families that had been saving with him all year so they'd have a bit extra for Christmas . . . It was awful. Her family were so ashamed. But people got by somehow.

And they did, some of them on very little. The idea that pleasures were simpler 'back then' is well illustrated by this childhood memory.

We didn't live far from Spitalfields Market and I'd go with Dad with a sack. He'd have just a few bob and we'd mooch about the stalls, get a bit of cheap fruit, a few nuts, apples, tangerines and that, or a few oranges. Used to make a bag up, you know. For three or four bob you could get a decent bit of fruit then. Then we used to come away from the market and cross over the road to this big pub. I used to sit outside on the step with an arrowroot biscuit and a glass of lemonade. [*Laughing*] Dad used to be in there knocking it back, his couple of pints. Why not? Five o'clock every morning except Sunday he'd get up. He earned it. Why shouldn't he have a drink?

Drinking has always been an East End leisure activity, although not all drinking was done in the pub.

As a kid, your mum or dad would send you down the Bottle and Jug – that was like the off-licence bar – to get a jug of beer for them to have indoors. We used to call it the four ale bar as well. Seems strange now, letting a kid go in a pub and buy beer. We used to run errands for cigarettes as well. [*Laughing*] 'Dad said can he have twenty Players, please?' Nothing was said, it wasn't thought strange then. My friend who went to school over Canning Town way used to go out at dinner time to get her teacher a jug of mild from the pub over the road! The mothers'd all be up the school complaining if they tried that today.

If you wanted to go out for a drink, with a pub on almost every street corner you were always in walking distance of somewhere you could go in for a pint of mild and bitter or a glass of port and lemon, as well as some entertaining company.

> I spent many hours waiting outside for my parents. This was not as bad as it sounds. We actually used to enjoy it. The doors were always opening and you could see and hear all the fun going on inside. There was live music, [with] some relative or other who would get up and sing. Every few minutes we would call a family member to get us some crisps or a drink of lemonade. Outside the pub there was a stall selling jellied eels and cockles.

> Pubs, or beer shops as we termed them, [were] divided into several bars, each one with a name. There was the private bar, the public bar, saloon or lounge, and a snug used mostly by the women. There was also a Jug and Bottle, for take-away beer. The different bars would tend to classify its drinkers: workers and labourers in the public; shopkeepers and council workers in the private; bosses and councillors in the lounge or saloon.

There was always the chance of a hand of cards or some other game of chance you could take part in, then, at chucking-out time, there was the opportunity to go on to a do – a knees-up – with your neighbours.

> You could always have a game of cards, darts, shove ha'penny, or a game of crib – that was always popular with the old boys. Didn't matter if you had no money, you'd play for matchsticks, but you'd take it just as seriously.

> Many homes had a piano, and most women and many men could knock out a tune on the old joanna. These parties were never prearranged, they mostly erupted from a Saturday night meeting of friends and relations in a pub. [At closing time] they were in the mood to carry on, so, off to the nearest home for a sing-song.

*

You didn't even have to go to the pub first, or at least the women didn't. They might stay at home, getting things ready, while the chaps nipped out for a 'swift half'.

> I remember being in the front room of my nan's house. The radiogram was on and Kay Starr was singing 'Wheel of Fortune'. All the adults were dancing, and us kids were sitting out in the passage on the stairs, peeping in at them. We were supposed to be up in bed with all the coats, but I don't think they'd have minded. The men had been up the corner to the pub for a few pints and had brought back crates of ale, while the women were in the kitchen making sandwiches, all laughing. It was lovely to see them dancing. Not in pairs, but in a big circle, with all their arms around one another's shoulders, heads back, singing at the tops of their voices.

> It wasn't sort of private then. We all got involved. You wouldn't think your neighbour was a nuisance cos they were having a party – you'd be in there with them. You'd be part of it. It was your party as much as it was theirs.

But drinking alcohol wasn't to everyone's taste.

> [My dad] was a strict teetotaller. Having seen the damage caused by alcohol in his own family, he took the pledge early on. So, although he was my mother's parents' first son-in-law, he wasn't the most popular one. Everyone else brought a bottle of spirits or some beer for Grandad when they visited, but my dad, of course, did not. I think Mum's family found it a little difficult to relate to this gentle, serious young man who was uncomfortable at an East End knees-up and who didn't enjoy a drink.

Parties were not the only indoor entertainment, there was plenty of other fun to be had in the home, some of it with the latest innovation – the wireless set.

> We got a wireless. My uncle was a nutter on anything like

that; he had what they called a Cat's Whisker. You would
touch something and you'd hear it: 'Two, hello. Two, hello.'
Gawd knows what they was on about, but I was a kid and it
was all a wonder to me. Like going up in a bloody rocket
now, I suppose. Then we bought a wireless. Where the hell
Dad got the money to buy a wireless from I don't know, still,
that was his business. I'll never forget, it was called a Cosser.
And it run off a battery, an accumulator. He had it on a shelf
in the corner of the room and he messed and fiddled and
buggered about with it for hours and couldn't get a bloody
thing on it! In the finish he sent over for my uncle – he was
the mechanic in the family, the old 'Two, hello' man with the
Cat's Whisker. If he don't know, who do? Anyway, over he
come. And they was still messing about, both going at it now.
And we're all sitting here waiting. And waiting. And waiting.
All that bloody night. All of a sudden – bang! – 'Here it is!
Got it! Got it!' What was it? They was playing 'God Save Our
Gracious King'! It was bloody twelve o'clock, it was going off!
Me uncle shot out of the room. He knew what was going to
happen. He done his nut, the old man. Messing about all
night and the bloody thing's gone off! [*Laughing*] They was
the days eh? Bloody accumulators!

We were fortunate that Dad had managed to afford a radio
set. It was a Cosser which had to have an accumulator and
two batteries to make it work. One battery was a Winner 120
volt, the other was a Grid Bias, and the accumulator had to
be taken to Glickman's when it ran down, to be exchanged
for a fully charged one. One evening [my brother] and I
wanted to listen to *Monday Night at Eight* but as we were
living in the kitchen at the time and the radio was in the
front room, Mum said we would have to sit and listen in the
dark, because she couldn't afford to light the gas in another
room. The first item on the programme was 'Sid Walker', a
character who was a rag and bone man who was always
solving crimes. They first played his signature tune: 'Day after
day, I'm on my way, singing, rags, bottles and bones.' Then
there was a crash of glass and a scream, which sounded as

though it was just outside the window, and we both rushed for the door back to the kitchen, scared out of our wits, deciding that it was better to be in the warm and the light and with Mum.

At a time when you usually 'made your own fun', even a potential disaster could provide a few hours' free, and highly memorable, entertainment.

Me and a few friends, mates, you know, we got on top of this big building, where you could see right over the top of the railway. And we stood there and we watched the Crystal Palace burning. In the 1930s, it was. We could see from where we were in the East End of London across the river to Crystal Palace, right across on the other side. Blimey, what a fire that was.

The night of the Crystal Palace fire, my father and I went to watch with lots of other people. I was in tears, remembering a wonderful day there earlier in the year, when I was among hundreds of schoolchildren who were there for 'A Festival of Song'. We were all dressed in white, and it was marvellous, singing our hearts out, ending with 'Jerusalem', which has remained my favourite even to this day.

Annual outings and beanos – for which you would pay in every week at your local pub or social club and which involved taking a charabanc to the coast or the countryside, with crates of ale on board to provide refreshment for all the stops you would make on the way – might have been less spectacular than watching burning buildings but were just as diverting, and not only for those who were privileged enough to be going on the trip.

Holidays, for the people of the East End, were something to look forward to with great enjoyment [even though] the majority could only enjoy the odd day's outing to the nearest coast, like Southend. They were charabanc outings run by the local pub, usually either all women or all men. These were a great time for the kids of the neighbourhood to gather round and shout, 'Chuck out your mouldies!' when a shower of halfpennies and farthings would be thrown from the charabanc. The children had a chance to visit the countryside with the Country Holiday Fund. Mother would pay what she could afford, but I think there was some kind of means test involved. People living in the country would offer to take one or two London children for a week.

Another annual event which was recalled with enthusiasm was a visit to the funfair, which would pitch up and stay for a week of gaudy diversion and entertainment. With its exotic travelling fairground people, running their hoop-la stalls and rifle ranges, boxing booths and the Wall of Death, brightly painted steam gallopers and reckless dodgem drivers, the fair was a wonderland of twinkling lights and danger.

It seems horrible when you think about it now, but at the fair we used to go to of a Bank Holiday there'd be these booths. They would have, well, freak shows. Bearded ladies. Two-headed animals. Mermaids. All that sort of thing. All made up, I suppose, but when you think about paying money to see people just because they're really ugly or they look nasty . . . Makes you ashamed of yourself. But we would queue up to see them. Same with the bare-knuckle boxing booths. Not very nice at all, really. But we loved it all. It was sort of magical at night, with all the lights and the smell of all the food and the oil on the machinery.

These were places of free fun. Even if you had no money, as was often the case, there was no entrance fee, so you could get enjoyment watching the people taking part in the amusements, and wander around the roundabouts and carousels, all being driven by a great big steam engine that played pipe music at the same time.

There were more solemn annual events in which people took an equally enthusiastic part. These were celebrations for St Patrick's

Day and the huge Catholic parades held on your local church's saint's day which wound round the streets of the east London parishes, drawing crowds of many thousands of spectators.

> The processions went all round the streets, carrying the statue from the church, and with all the kids from the Catholic school dressed in white, with coloured sashes, and carrying flowers and wreaths with banners across them, and holding on to ribbons tied to the statue. All the women from the Catholic families would set a shrine up outside their street doors. They'd cover a table in a nice lace cloth and then put a crucifix, any religious pictures they had of Mary or the saints or the Sacred Heart and that sort of thing, their rosaries, and a nice bunch of flowers, and the priest would bless it and their home as the procession passed through their street. It was a bit of a competition between the women. Who made the best shrine, had the whitest lace cloth, that sort of business. But it was a marvellous thing to see, all those little children. The mothers must have saved hard to buy their outfits. Thousands of people, and I mean thousands, lined the streets to watch them. It was a really big do, you know.

St Patrick's Day was celebrated, *very* enthusiastically according to my dad, by my Irish paternal grandmother. She was a clever woman, but unable to read or write, and did not know her date of birth, so she had, a bit eccentrically, picked on the movable feast of 'Pancake Day' to commemorate it. Apparently, her annual birthday merry-making was just as exuberant as that which marked her homeland's saint's day.

> As Roman Catholics, [St Patrick's] was a big day in our calendar. Not all the family went to mass but they all joined in the fun. This was very much a big drinking occasion. Sometimes the drinking would go on all night and on till the next night.

> Always a good excuse for a do, St Patrick's. We'd have a right old knees-up. Lovely parties in them days, all in together,

didn't matter if you was Catholic or Irish or not. Most of us had a bit of Irish in us round there anyway.

The street party was another celebration in which all the neighbours would take part, doing their bit to make the day – and the evening – a success for everyone concerned.

We had street parties for very special occasions, such as the Silver Jubilee of King George V or the Coronation of King George VI. The people in the street would join in to supply the food, and the children all got a Coronation cup, saucer and plate, and a tin box with the royal family on it filled with chocolate. Tables were borrowed and laid out down the middle of the street with Union Jacks as tablecloths and bunting all across the street. Everyone had a great time.

Even the most organized of days didn't always run to plan.

I was eleven years old at the time of King George's Jubilee, which was the highlight of 1935. Our parents were putting up bunting and flags, and setting up tables for the street party, and the food was all ready. On the Saturday, King George and Queen Mary were driving in an open coach so that all the crowds could see them and cheer them on their way. Our school had been chosen to be in the Mall, where we were in the stands. We had been there waiting for some hours with our sandwiches, taking in all that was going on in the Mall. About an hour before the cavalcade was due to arrive, we were told to line up for a drink of water which was being supplied from some containers. By this time we were very hot and eager for a drink, but just as I was going to take my turn I fainted! When I came round one of the teachers was delegated to take me home, which she did without a word about having to miss the parade. Of course, when we arrived home I wasn't allowed to go to the street party, but was put straight to bed. Wonderful day!

A frequent outing was to the cinema. Popular with all ages – as recalled in the stories of children's Saturday morning shows – adults would attend during afternoons and evenings, with the keenest film-goers sitting through two and three showings a week.

We would go to the flicks with a few pennies' worth of sweets, sit on old wooden benches and be transported to wonderland.

There were so many cinemas, La Bohème – the Labo – the Coliseum, the Palladium, the Tivoli. Live shows would be put on before the films. Jolly good ones, too.

The Odeon had wall-to-wall carpeting and they had big settees upstairs. A beautiful place. Carpeted, settees and all beautiful pictures on the walls. You'd get a box of chocolates, sit down and wait for the show to start.

The highlight of our existence was on Friday night going to the Seabright cinema in Hackney Road. Oranges and peanuts were sold outside. I used to get a headache every time from sitting at the front near the screen and having to look up all the time. [But] it was the high spot of the week for us.

I used to work as a waitress in the posh restaurant at the cinema. I was all in black and white. It was a lovely atmosphere. You walked in and there was an usherette at the door with a torch, and you had the [double] back seats when you was courting and the front ones when you weren't. The screen was one whole wall, the stage and curtains. You used to have turns and an organist. If you was posh enough and could afford it, you went upstairs. It was an atmosphere you could lose yourself in. When I worked in the restaurant it was all carpeted, all fitted out by whoever owned the cinema. We had to wear black and a little white frilly apron and that. I loved it. [The food] was all dished up posh – but if you went behind the scenes and saw what went on you wouldn't say it was posh. You hoped you were going to get a tip, because the wages were terrible.

*

Cinema-going could prove to be a far more rowdy affair than it is now.

> All you could hear was the sound of people cracking peanuts, noshing on sweets and fish and chips, talking to the screen – 'He's got a gun!' That sort of thing – and reading out the writing [the captions] to one another. That was without the row from the piano.

> The crowd would get so noisy when the projector went wrong – which used to happen just about every film. And some of the more devilish ones would throw things at the screen.

But it was a more formal business in another way.

> When you'd seen the films, you'd always show respect. You'd stand up at the end for the national anthem.

Despite the rapid spread of cinema-going and radio-listening, the music hall and the variety theatre still enjoyed wide popularity both before and during the war.

> I used to go to the Hackney Empire a lot on a Monday, because our [family owned] coffee shops and used to display the showbills and would get free tickets for Monday nights. You got them for Monday nights because they reckoned they hadn't rehearsed anything and they were doing it for the first time. Six days a week it was on, they didn't do it on Sundays. I saw Max Miller many times, saw a lot of the famous music-hall artistes, G. H. Elliott, Monsewer Eddie Grey, Jewel and Warris. I saw the Crazy Gang many times. Big bands, even dog acts, it was true variety. They used to have these high-wire acts, paper-tearing, someone playing a one-string fiddle, things that these days people would take the mickey out of. The thing that interested me most, being wartime, each time the alert went up, nobody would budge. I always remember that the conductor, Paul Clifford, would raise his

baton and, instead of them all coming in together, they used to come in one after the other. It was a wartime orchestra!

Even the lining up to go in was amusing, with street buskers who would entertain the queue from the gutter for whatever odd coppers you might give.

My dad, a good, loving man, was a London City Missionary of the evangelical persuasion, so we didn't go to music halls or cinemas, as they were 'worldly places'. However, we did go to Christmas pantomimes at the People's Palace, because he saw that as family entertainment, though I wasn't very old before I understood the *double entendre* of the jokes. Some of my earliest memories are of sitting in the dark, entranced by the atmosphere, totally involved in the story, shouting louder than any of the other kids. 'He's behind you!' I thought it was magical. I was so impressed by the glamour of the fairy godmother, startled by the flash of light and plume of smoke with which the baddie appeared and disappeared with a flourish of his cape or twirl of his devil's tail. I loved it.

And, as this memory shows, even post-war the enthusiasm hadn't waned.

I must have been about five, so it was in the mid-1950s, and I can remember the excitement of being taken to see a variety show. The Hackney Empire, I think it must have been. I was only little and the place seemed really posh. I can't remember all of it, but I know there was Tony the Wonder Horse, a beautiful palomino that did sums and counted out the answers with hoof beats; a woman who just tore up news-papers and made these fantastic, intricate patterns, and ladders and palm trees, all from newspaper; and a bloke with a musical saw. I wasn't so impressed with that, and nor were most other people. A lot of them were laughing, but I'm not sure it was meant to be funny. And then these men came round, little tiny men with big papier-mâché heads. They scared the wits out of me. Big grinning faces. But the fact I was so young and remember so much of it, it must have made a big impression on me. They should have that sort of thing now.

Another very popular pastime in east London was speedway racing.

We lived in Custom House, right down by the docks, and we were at the speedway one night, when the Graf Zeppelin came over West Ham Stadium. This was about 1928. It came so low, you could see the people looking out of the windows. A hundred thousand people used to come down that stadium, and on special nights they used to put up £100 for a trophy. If we couldn't afford to pay to go in, we used to go round the corner and jump over the fence.

A little less spirited than speedway, but just as appreciated, was the practice of hiring bicycles.

This would be the 1920s I'm talking about now. We used to go to this old boy who had a load of old bikes that you could have out for a penny or so. Right old bone-shakers they were. And the saddles were so hard. But we used to think they were lovely. Go for miles on the bloody old things. Down to Essex, to Hadleigh Castle and that.

We used to go to Grimshaw's in the Beckton Road and hire a bike out for a couple of hours and then say to a boy, 'Do you want to take that back for me?' Sometimes we would go as far as Southend.

An even more tranquil leisuretime activity was fishing, although the concept of how to actually catch a fish escaped some would-be anglers.

They used to be lined right alone the Lea and the canal, sit there all day fishing. It was relaxing, and you didn't need expensive gear, just the basics, and it was a bit of fresh air, a chance to be out and relax. Didn't matter that you weren't on some posh river-bank, that you didn't have a motor to take you out into the country, it was a working man's pleasure, and plenty of us used to enjoy it.

We were quite young – good excuse! – but my friend's dad told us that if we went down to the canal – the Regent's Canal ran along the bottom of our turning – and sprinkled salt on a fish's tail, then we could catch it. We sat nearly all afternoon on that canal bank chucking a whole box of Saxa salt we'd 'borrowed' from Mum's scullery. And, no, before you ask, we didn't catch anything.

Gambling as a pastime could be taken quite seriously, especially when money, rather than matchsticks, cigarettes or cherry stones, was at stake.

Puk-a-pu was this gambling game they played round Pennyfields – Chinatown, Limehouse, you know – it was full of gambling round there. And we'd go there if we was feeling flush and a bit lucky, but you wouldn't take any liberties, wouldn't try and cheat or not pay your debts.

Pitch and toss was a popular way of trying to win a few shillings. You'd see men out of work, admittedly with nothing better to do, but just standing there in the street playing until they'd lost everything, thinking they'd win. Nearly as bad as the mugs who believed you could win Chase the Lady, and the pea under the cup game. You never win them things. Only the stooge who's working with the bloke with the cards wins, the one who draws in the mugs. They think, 'If he's won, then I've got a chance.' Mugs.

There was big money involved in flapping. That was, let's say, *private* dog racing. Used to go on over the Marshes. Remember, this was when gambling away from the official tracks was illegal. Lot of money in it, there was. A lot of money.

*

29. Sheltering from the bombs for the night became a part of wartime family life.

30. The docks, vital to the life of the country, were continually targeted by enemy bombers.

31. Royal Docks, 1944. Admiring a consignment of canned meat from the United States during the hard days of rationing and shortages.

32. 'Bombed out': Lydia Street, 1940. Moving whatever could be salvaged from the wreckage.

33. VE Day celebrations, 8 May 1945. After nearly six long years, the East End was ready to celebrate.

34. Women enjoying a chat in Whitechapel, 1938. Note the 'uniform' of cross-over aprons and hairnets.

35. Teatime, Whitechapel, 1938. Having a professional photographer in the home meant a nice cloth and the best china would be brought out.

36. *Right* Scrubbing the step ready for the Coronation party, 1953. Beware anyone foolish enough to actually put a foot on a freshly scrubbed step.

37. *Below* Like most other turnings in the East End, Morpeth Street held a weekly collection to pay for the food and Coronation souvenir china for their street party, June 1953.

38. *Left* Attracting the punters, Petticoat Lane, 1936.

39. *Below Left* Attracting the punters, Petticoat Lane, 1998.

40. *Above Right* Likely lads, 1951, by an advertisement for the ever-popular Troxy.

41. *Right* A celebration 'knees-up' at Bill Cannon's 'pigeon do', 1960s. My mother, Dolly, is on the right, and next to her is my aunt Doll.

42. Using a length of rope, a lamppost and their imagination, two girls, without benefit of expensive toys, delight in their shared game, *c.* 1950.

It was a Christmas morning pigeon race run from the pub. All of us who had entered took our baskets of birds to the station the afternoon before, so they could be sent that night out to a station in Essex, where they were going to fly from the next morning when the stationmaster released them. But one bloke thought he was clever and crept round to the station Christmas Eve night, before they were sent out to Essex, and nicked one of his birds back. The next morning, Christmas Day, he worked out the flying time and run round the pub with the pigeon to say he'd won and to claim the winner's prize money. What he *hadn't* worked out was that it was winter, it was snowing out in the Essex countryside and the stationmaster hadn't been able to liberate the birds yet! He hadn't thought to phone through first to check. All the birds were still sitting on the station platform. Silly sod. And *that* was *your* uncle!

As with children's gambling games, not all racing bets were placed in money – especially when cash was in short supply.

Because unemployment was rife in the 1920s and work, when available, was by no means permanent, it left a lot of men idle at times, resulting in them finding something to do. A number of men might group together to form a pigeon-racing syndicate. A relative of mine was captain of one of these and had sufficient space to build a sizeable loft. Many times, my cousins and I would take a basket of birds on the train to Epping Forest and release them to fly back home, while the men would have cigarette bets on who would be first and second home.

Parks provided a more local opportunity for adults to enjoy a flavour of the countryside experienced by the pigeons and their young couriers out at Epping Forest.

The attractions of Vicky Park were many. The really hot hothouse that contained many tropical plants that very few in the East End would see themselves, unless they were sent abroad to fight a war. A super attraction, especially in the winter, for the hundreds anxious to inspect those strange plants. Just round the corner was the parrot house, with Polly, an exotic visitor from the Far East to the East End of London. Then we could visit the deer and peacocks, and cross over one of the bridges which spanned the lake. Only one thing spoiled this wonderful park and that was the soccer pitches. [They] were laid with gravel and it was quite common to see dozens of lads with their legs in a terrible state [after] they took a tumble. A more peaceful sight was the young men in the summer playing cricket, and the older generation enjoying their bowls. There was netball galore for the girls and tennis too had its devotees, and many folk loved the Saturday evening and Sunday [events at] the bandstand. Also supervised were the children's swings and a well-kept running track. Also the two swimming pools, which were later replaced by the super modern, well-supervised lido. It seemed there was no end to the joys of the park: the wonderful Chinese pagoda, the fabulous work of art that was the fountain. [Then] there was also a little gem tucked away in the north of the park, the truly super 'old English' garden, tended by highly skilled gardeners, an area of true tranquillity. The park was really the great asset of the area, the green lung of the grey East End.

We would get a number 56 bus to the Isle of Dogs. It was exciting. If you were *lucky*, all the lock gates would be shut. It made the journey longer, but very interesting watching all the boats and so on. Then we would walk through the tunnel [the foot tunnel under the Thames] under the river to Greenwich and go to the park.

It didn't matter that we weren't little kids any more, as we went through the foot tunnel, we'd always shout to each other and run along all excited. We were going over to Greenwich! It was a beautiful place, but a bloody climb up that hill. And I was fit in them days!

*

Even work, when it involved a sojourn in the hop gardens for the annual harvest, could count as leisure for East Enders keen to get away from the foggy, overcrowded London streets to the fresh, autumn countryside of Kent.

> Hopping was a paid treat, a way of earning a few bob – to pay off the tallyman, to make a few extra pounds for Christmas, or just to make already overstretched ends meet. But it was also a holiday, a break from the fog and the dirt, the overcrowding and even from the old man!

> My [family] used to go hop-picking in Wateringbury in Kent. A lot of people used to do this as it was a way of having a holiday while earning money. Every family was given a hut to use and you were paid by the basketload of hops that were picked. My mother and sister and I used to go, and thoroughly enjoyed it. We would all pile in the back of one of my uncle's lorries and off we would go. We had straw beds to sleep on which were supplied by the farmers. But my grandparents used to take their own feather mattress with them! The women worked all week and the men would join them at the weekends.

> Hop-picking, that was our holiday. A paid, working holiday, and we all loved it. Looked forward to it from one year to the next. I'd still go if I could. Wouldn't even mind using them horrible lavs, though I'm used to a bit better nowadays!

But, as the memories in the next chapter show, not all work was as pleasurable as the annual trip 'down hopping'.

15

You had to work a twelve-hour day, six days a week, one o'clock on Saturday, for a small wage, perhaps a pound per week, less in some cases. You have no conception of life as it was lived in those days – I was born in 1903 – but we endured and enjoyed ourselves in our own fashion. No tea breaks, no days off unless you were sick, no holidays except the statutory holidays. You were lucky if you could keep a job then . . . you worked, and you earned your wages.

Formal working life began early for the labouring classes, when even a young person's miserly wage was a welcome, sometimes vital, addition to a tight family budget. Regardless of whether a child was bright and had maybe won a scholarship that might have opened up opportunities beyond the dead-end jobs for which they would otherwise be destined, there was little choice but for them to leave school and go out to work.

Once a youngster had found a job in a local factory or workshop, there was little security. When they reached the age to warrant being paid a few shillings more per week, it was not uncommon to be sacked and replaced by another, cheap, grateful and undemanding school-leaver, who in turn would stay for a year or two until it was their turn to be supplanted.

My childhood, I think, ended when I was thirteen. Knowing that it would not be long before you were leaving school and working alongside people like your mum and dad, life took on a new meaning. For months before leaving school you had to be thinking of what job you could get, and childish games began to get less interesting. I was waiting for my first long trousers and stopped playing in the street so much. By the time I reached my teens, I had already, like most of my friends, found several part-time jobs, [such as] helping the local baker on Saturdays. As our needs for money grew with age, parents soon found where there was a need for likely lads.

In 1930 I left school as a fourteen-year-old and started work. There were a number of jobs available, most of them dead-end – short-term cheap labour for a couple of years, after which they would expect an increase in wages to cover the few pence they now had to pay for the 1924 Insurance Act. So it was cheaper to employ another school-leaver in your place. These jobs with no future included errand boy; tea boy and general cleaner; van boy, to stay at the back of the van to stop joy riders and help with the delivery; telegraph boys, to deliver telegrams on a bicycle – they never did seem to make the job of postman; [and] even those employed by building firms were usually put off before they were twenty-one, when they had to be paid a man's wage.

I left school at fourteen. I got a job in a sweet factory in Stratford. I was so small they weren't going to employ me – they didn't think I was old enough. So I borrowed a pair of my older sister's shoes with high heels and one of her cut-down frocks to make myself look older. I was only wrapping broken rock. I used to walk to work, along the sewers [usually known as the sewer bank, and now as the Greenway] from West Ham. Go up the steps, along the sewers, and you got to Stratford from that end. I used to hate walking along those sewers when it got dark.

In what, according to the people I spoke to, was a comparatively rare instance, this young woman could have continued with her education and postponed beginning her working life, but she chose not to.

Annie looked after her husband's niece. I [was a child and] remember her as a daring teenager who wore make-up and was always out late. 'Boy mad,' Annie said. Sometimes she was cheeky or sullen, and clearly didn't want to be dumped with Annie. She wanted to leave school [but] the school leaving age was being put up from fourteen to fifteen years. Pupils of fourteen, that year only, could choose whether to leave after their fourteenth birthday or stay on for another year. I remember pitched battles between the niece – who wanted to leave – and Annie, who thought she should 'stay on and better herself'. The niece won. She got a job behind the counter in Woolworths, which I thought was ever so glamorous.

With little spare money in most households for such luxuries as 'staying on', children finding paid work, even before they left school, was generally welcomed by both youngsters and adults.

There was one lady who always needed someone to run errands. We'd go mad to go for her, as we knew she was generous, and always gave you at least a few coppers or a slice of cake. Maybe both.

On Saturdays we would hang around the part of [our] street known as Jews' Alley, because it was where the Jewish people lived and had their tailoring shops in the big houses. There were Lithuanians and Latvians who had come to escape the oppression in their own countries, and their religion did not allow them to do anything on a Saturday, which was their Sabbath. So they would ask us in to maybe put a piece of coal on the fire and then tell us to take the money which was left on a table, because they were not even allowed to handle money.

As children, we were what was known as Sabbath Goys, non-Jewish kids who were happy to earn a little something by going into our Jewish neighbour's home and turning on their gaslight and making up their fire for them on their Sabbath.

My aunt [lived in] a small downstairs flat opposite the back entrance to West Ham football ground at Upton Park. The windowsills of the houses were about three feet away from their front walls [and], whenever there was a match at the

ground, fans would come on pushbikes and leave them in the
space between the windowsills and the front walls. Children
were able to earn threepence for looking after them
throughout the match. I begged to be allowed to do this, but
my aunt would not let me. It was *common*, she said, and not
much better than begging. She was a real lady, in my eyes.
Before her marriage, she had been a 'Nippy' in Lyons Corner
House. She'd worn neat black with a lace apron and a cap
worn tidily across her brow.

As had been the experience of earlier generations, those people
who spoke to me remembered jobs as being difficult to find, and,
when they did find work, it was frequently unreliable.

I know some have got it hard now, but, believe me, we had it
harder back then, especially before the war, I'm talking about.
You might get a few days, but nothing you could depend on,
and you still had your family to feed and the rent to pay. The
kids and the landlord didn't go on short time, did they?

Employment was a constant worry. Very few were sure of any
permanency. A craftsman with a trade could feel a bit safe, as
could those we called the white-collar workers – those in
council offices and postal workers. What money was given [to
you] when [you were] out of work was very little, and one
had to sign on three times a week, at different times, to make
sure you were not employed.

It was hard in the 1930s. We didn't know that – the children.
Well, most of us didn't; I suppose a few poor buggers did.
Dad used to go out at five o'clock every morning; stand with
a group of others waiting to be called on to get a day's work.
If your face didn't fit, you didn't get it. And that's how it
went. But he brought us all up, all five of us. And Mum used
to take in washing and do cleaning. So we could get by.

There were periods, however, when things looked up for the lucky
ones who either had appropriate skills or were simply in the right

place at the right time. In 1910, for instance, West Ham was booming and, so strong was its position as a hub of chemical works, food and tobacco processing, metal and engineering plants, that the council distributed a leaflet referring to itself as the 'factory centre of the South'. Workers flocked there and, two decades later, the area was still prosperous, with technological innovation now really beginning to benefit consumers and workers alike.

> During the 1930s industries increased as the new amenities like electricity arrived [and] with telephone and wireless expansion. The motorized van and internal combustion engine were replacing the horse and cart. Public transport was expanding, more modern buses and the trolleybus were replacing the old trams, doing away with the tramlines down the centre of the road, [and] the underground was being extended to the outer suburbs. All adding to the need for more workers, [although] at the same time some jobs were becoming obsolete. With the introduction of electric streetlighting, away went the old lamplighter's job. With the progress of the delivery van, the horse and cart was seen less often, and with them went the driver – the carman or drayman – who managed the horses, with their gleaming brasswork. [Also under threat were] the tram driver and the canal bargees, with their string of barges carrying timber and sand. With the improved sewers and drains, the street water-cart was no longer to be enjoyed by children walking along behind with no shoes and socks. Expansion in employment, I think, outnumbered the jobs lost. I remember mine and other families feeling a better lifestyle in the later 1930s. Even though wages were kept stable, prices were steady.

The furniture-making and allied trades had been traditional employers of large numbers of East Enders from as early as the eighteenth century, and, to a far lesser extent, they still are today.

> At the back of the yard was a big, glass-roofed shed which was used as a workshop for furniture-making, and there was

a small hatch in a wall from the scullery into the shed. There was a double glue pot standing in a big open fireplace [and] work benches. On the other side of [our] street were the factory buildings. Some of them were three or four storeys high. On the corner was where they did French polishing. Then came the entrance to the woodworking shops. There was a factory that made cane furniture and another that made cardboard boxes, they used to tie them in packs and drop them out of the window for someone to catch. In the basement of the factory on the corner, they polished and bevelled mirrors, and you could watch through the basement window as they operated the grindstones with the water dripping over the glass.

Other trades and industries, now vanished from the streets of the East End, are nothing more than memories.

There used to be huge live turtles arriving at Lusty's to be turned into soup at the factory there. The smell was awful.

I was a lamplighter. I moved to the basement of a shop to be near my work, as time was important where the lamps were concerned. This was a seven-day-a-week job, and you had to light, clean and tend to 120 lamps. You had a long steel pole with a brass guard on top to protect a flame from going out. A trigger was at the bottom of the pole, about four inches up, which was fixed to a rod that actuated the gun to light the flame. I think the oil was a mixture of calza [sic] and paraffin. We had matches issued to relight the torch should it go out. We had boxes of mantles of different sizes, and a leather and scrim to clean the glass in the lamps. In summer, you went out at about five a.m. to turn out the lamps, then you picked your own time to clean them and renew broken mantles. Again, at ten p.m., you went round to light up. In winter, the times were earlier to light up and later to turn out. The foreman went round each man's round to check up on his work. It took about an hour to light up once you got used to it. You also had a ladder and a safety rope which was used to prevent you falling. Some men did window-cleaning between lighting-up times. When it was foggy by day, we had to light up the main road only on the council's orders, as the council set the time when to light up and turn off. In summer the painters painted the lamps and it was a job to clean the glass, owing to the paint on them. As my section was to be electrified, I had to leave, being the last one to join the muster of lamplighters.

Work wasn't important only as a means of earning a living, it also kept you out of mischief – the devil notoriously making work for idle hands.

Grandad was in the docks, but he packed up work when he was about fifty and his wife died, said his kids could keep him. [So] he used to go out and get pissed, and would get brought home in a barrow. Mum would be out with her mates and they'd see someone wheeling a wheelbarrow down the road with her dad in it. They used to say hello to her, but she'd look the other way as if to say, 'Nothing to do with me.' She'd say, 'I don't know him, bloody bloke.' He was always going out on the booze.

If there was no work about, you'd get bored. Me and my mates, all young, fit fellers, we'd hang around, kicking our heels and playing cards, or stretching our last few coppers for a half a pint. I never got tempted to do nothing dodgy. I was fortunate. My old man had a regular job and used to give me a few shillings. But others weren't so lucky and wound up getting into bother.

Despite the idea that 'women didn't work then', many, of course, did do paid work, many *had* to, often doing long hours of boring, back-breaking piece work, or being employed casually for cash in hand, in much the same way as their mothers and grandmothers before them.

I used to do all odd little jobs because my husband was in the tailoring trade and didn't earn much money. I'd do a bit of cleaning. Any little job.

She used to go along the street, knocking on people's doors – the ones who had paid her – to wake them up for work. I don't know who woke her up.

Women who didn't go out to work [but had] outdoor work could bring a few more shillings into the home. These [jobs] were numerous and varied: feather-sorting and grooming, for the ladies' hat trade; matchbox-making; hand-sewn gloves; and, because of the local tailoring businesses, there were many outdoor jobs to be had for the homes that managed to acquire a Singer sewing machine. [And] apart from helping with outdoor work, it was a must for the mending of clothes.

[My brother] and I often used to play boats in the upturned lid of Mum's sewing machine [as] the machine was nearly always in use because Mum did lots of outdoor work when she could get it, sewing shirts or blouses to help get some money. Any bits of material that were left over, she would make things for us or something to sell.

Others did 'proper', regular jobs, even if they were not always treated that well by their employers, or were naïve regarding the ways of the world in which they found themselves.

If you worked in the print, you had to be in the union. We were well looked after by the publishing companies: doctors, hospitals, everything the best. Anyway, women were OK until they married, then the union chucked you out. When I rejoined the union, in another job on a trade paper after the war, some cocky union bloke found out I had been a union member and wondered why I hadn't kept up my subs. I took great pleasure in telling him, 'Because you chucked me out.' They wouldn't let married women work then, but during and after the war they were glad of us.

*

[My husband] would have been in his thirties then, but he wasn't fit to go to work because of the terrible experiences and injuries he received as a fireman during the war, so, I thought to myself, I'll have to get myself a job. They were advertising for postwomen, because all the postmen were away in the army, so I got a job in the Whitechapel post office, delivering the letters. Being a new woman, they put you down on the hardest routes: 'You'll deliver round X Street' where all the prostitutes lived, all the slums.

Well, I was a bit simple . . . well, I was about prostitutes. I've got a registered letter to deliver and you got to get their signature. So I went up these flats, right up the top, and I rat-tatted on the door, and a voice shouted, 'Come in!' I just stood there. 'Push the door and come in.' And in I went. It was one of these flats where you open the door and you're in the room. And when I went in, there was this woman sitting up in bed. All painted: rouge on her face, hair all dyed, black eyelashes and all black under one eye. Lovely silk dress and a nice cover on the bed. But, on top of that cover, she had two great big sheets of newspaper. And she was plucking a chicken.

I said to her, 'Registered letter. You got to sign for it.'

So she said, 'I thought you was my customer.'

So I said, 'What do you mean, customer?'

'My man friend,' she said. 'I'm waiting for him. I might as well pluck my chicken for my dinner while I'm sitting here.'

I didn't know what she meant, and when I got back to the post office I was telling one of the women there, about this woman who was all done up in bed, and she said, 'She was a prostitute!'

When finding work was particularly difficult, potential employees could be impressively resourceful, if not always entirely honest, in their search for a job.

After the war, when my husband tried to get a job and couldn't, I went up the Labour Exchange. They wanted women in the Ministry of Pensions and National Insurance, changing the insurance cards.

The woman there said, 'I don't know if you'll get it because you've got to have a very good education.'

I said, 'I've got a good education. I was very good at school.'

She said, 'Did you go to secondary school?'

Well, I never, but I said, 'Yes.' I actually went to Ben Jonson School, but when she asked me where I went, I was going to say Raynes Foundation School, but, I thought to myself, they'll start inquiring. I knew the school in Coborn Road was bombed a bit, so I said I went there.

'Well,' she said, 'you can go and try for it.'

I was scared stiff when I went there. There was all different rooms and all these men walking about with all different books and paper. I thought to myself, 'Oh blimey, I'll never do this job.'

I had to go and see the manager. He was a stern-looking man but he was all right. He asked me if I was a good reader – 'Yes' – and what school I went to – 'Coborn Road'. I got the job *and* I was good at it!

Once they were fortunate enough to land a job, hard-up employees would have to be just as resourceful about how they got to work in the mornings.

You'd troop through the ticket barrier at the station, all mixed up with the other passengers, and you'd say, 'He's got the ticket, him behind.'

I saved money by walking to work. All the way to Stratford. A good few miles. I wasn't so keen when it was dark and cold. But it saved the money, which was important if you haven't got much in the first place.

A lot of our mates did this trick. Wonder we all got away with it, but not many did it to get to work, it took too long. Still, when it was only a day to payday and you had no money left, me and Dolly would try it on. We worked together up Whitechapel, so we'd get on a bus going in that direction and do our best to avoid the conductor, dodge upstairs or downstairs – where he wasn't. Then, when he eventually come up to us, we'd go, all innocent and flapping our eyelashes, 'Two to Stratford, please.'

'That's the other direction, sweetheart,' he'd say.

We'd be all shocked and surprised, and we'd get off at the next stop. Course, what we'd do is wait for the next one to come along, and do the same all over again. I'll have to admit, it wasn't the quickest way to get to work.

As well as doing their paid work, women and men came home to all the domestic chores that had to be done in order to keep their households clean, fed and in reasonable shape.

Women were always busy. Even when chatting on the doorstep they would be shelling peas or peeling sprouts.

It was non-stop, keeping the place nice. You had different jobs for each day of the week. You couldn't save up your washing and stick it in the machine when you felt like it, it was all a big deal. You'd have to prepare for every job. Know what you was doing. Like cleaning the mats. No vacuum cleaners. Drag them out the yard and give them a good whacking. The dust used to choke you.

Women were tough then. They seemed to get everything done. If you think about it, today you've got a washing machine, a Hoover. Back then you used to have to get down on your knees and scrub your floor and scrub your step. Washing was done out the back of a Monday. And when you think about bathing the kids . . . You had to be pretty strong. When my mum was at work I only used to wash that bit of lino that showed round the mat. Never washed under it, just round the sides. Mind you, if you'd have polished that bit under it, you'd all have gone arse over head!

*

[As well as going to work] Dad had jobs mending the kids' boots and shoes; sweeping the chimney was a Saturday morning job. It was also his job to beat the mats and carpets. With no Hoover, mats had to be hung on the line and beaten with a broom handle. One of his worst jobs was ridding the place of vermin.

Dad wasn't always in [paid] work because of the slump, [and so] he did a lot of decorating, wallpapering and painting. I can still see him sitting on a chair in the kitchen with a roll of wallpaper over his knees, with a big pair of scissors cutting off the unprinted edges of the paper. It took ages to do the amount of rolls it took to paper a good-sized room.

The docks and their allied trades were still thriving right up until the beginning of the transformation of the great port and its docks into the Docklands of today (see Appendix, pages 309–18). So busy were the docks that, in the mid-1930s, my father, in a fit of pique after arguing with his mother that he wanted fish and chips for his tea rather than the stew she had made for the family meal, was able, literally, to run away to sea. He met up with a cousin, went down to the docks and found himself a job on a ship that same night. And I, born in 1951, can remember being on the Isle of Dogs, looking along a side turning that led to the water and seeing a massive ship looming up as though it were parked at the end of the street.

In 1948 I went into the docks for twenty-two years. My dad and my grandfather were in the docks before me. My uncle as well. Call-on was at quarter to eight every morning, or afternoons at quarter to one. Stevedores were called on outside the docks. A stevedore was a man who worked on the ship, and the docker worked for the stevedore. Eventually, I worked on the ships as well as on the quay. My dad was in the docks, so he went through his branch for me. There was a bit of a fiddle about that, I think. A year and a half and we hadn't heard anything. I talked to my brother, he belonged to the same branch, number 5 branch of the Stevedore and Dockers' Union, which used to meet near the docks. It was a blue union, called that to separate it from the white union, the Transport and General Workers' Union. He found out that people that had put their names in after me had got their names down, but I was still waiting. It came all of a sudden, after he made inquiries. It seems to me that a lot of people had been getting backhanders, that had been the hold-up. You know, even if you got prosecuted for theft or something, you could still go back afterwards and work in the docks. All sorts of people worked there. Once you were in a gang you were guaranteed work. There were twelve of us in a gang. The top hand, who does the signals to the crane driver; the crane driver; perhaps two of us would be on the quay doing the loading; and the rest of them would be down the hole.

My family came from the docks. It was well-paid work but you had a job to get in unless you already had a family member in there. These things sort of passed down through family members. My uncle wasn't liked by any of the rest of the family, so he never got in. No one would ever put his name forward or give him a ticket for work in the docks. He had to go on a day-to-day [casual] basis. When he got there, they'd all line up, but if they didn't get the day's work, they didn't get in.

There was no one to beat the London dockers for tonnage. We were working eight o'clock till seven o'clock at night with an hour's break. Eleven hours a day, five and a half days a week. Sometimes Sunday as well. We were earning what was perhaps two weeks' money in a week. It was hard work. I used to put a handkerchief covering my face, Vaseline up my nose and in my ears to stop the asbestos we were working on, going down my chest. Even doing that, I used to have to go to East Ham to have my chest X-rayed for years.

My brothers and me father used to go to the docks and stand in line, waiting to be chosen [for a day's or half a day's work]. My dad was better off because he was a stevedore, and my eldest brother was able to pass off as eighteen when he was fifteen to work on the ships as a stoker. When the other boys were old enough, if they couldn't find work, they'd join the ships and go abroad.

There were plenty of stories about how well the dock employees did for themselves, many from people with no family association with the work but who knew all the gossip and the rumours, and probably wouldn't have minded the opportunity to have been involved as one of the recipients of such bounty.

When whisky was being unloaded, it was arranged for bottles to be broken on purpose and the dockers would rush forward with enamel buckets and catch the liquid. Later they strained it carefully and a good time was had by all.

During the war, when tins of scarce items were being unloaded at the docks, some were *dropped* and badly dented. No prizes for guessing who took them home.

In an echo of the old song 'How you gonna keep 'em down on the farm after they've seen Paree?', this man remembers his first trip working as a seaman.

One January morning, I'll never forget it, I had the pleasure of joining one of the ships I used to watch as a boy. I joined it at Woolwich. I was rowed out by a boatman. The ship hired him, I never had to give him nothing, and he dumped me on the ship and that was it. And before we knew where we was, we was going. Sailing down that London river. To where? I didn't know at the time. But I knew I was leaving the East End behind me. I looked back and I could see familiar landmarks going by as we was going down the Thames. I remember thinking, the East End all lies back there. This will not be East End where I am now. I'm going out towards the sea, leaving the East End behind. All my mates, Mum, Dad, brothers, sisters. I was leaving them all. Where the hell I was going, I didn't know. I soon found out, and, nine months later, we was coming back. I knew the East

End would still be there, but I knew I had changed. I'd seen things that I never thought possible. I'd seen parts of the world I'd only dreamed of, or had seen in the geography books in school. I'd had so many experiences and I was still only fifteen. I knew the East End wouldn't have changed, but I had. How would I ever be able to settle down again after seeing all them wonders, places and people? It was remarkable, marvellous, how a snotty-nosed kid like me . . . from the East End of London. What was I doing on bloody Copacabana Beach? Or Rio Harbour? Or bloody Buenos Aires? Montreal? New York? It was unbelievable.

But the East End itself did change, and not only because of the dismantling of the docks. The two world wars were to cause irreversible changes in both the place and its people.

16

The war changed everything.

The closure of the docks would eventually cause a radical transformation of the whole social and physical fabric of the East End, but before that the defining moment of change was the devastation brought about by the Second World War.

As in the Great War, the docks, railways and high-density population made east London an obvious target for German bombers, and very quickly anti-aircraft measures, including barrage balloons, searchlights, guns, air-raid shelters and the blackout, and evacuation were introduced. The East End was under threat.

> That Sunday morning in 1939 when the Second World War was declared, I was ten years old. The news on the radio, and then the sounding of the air raid siren was so frightening. That sound still turns my stomach.

> When war was declared, we'd all gone out to an all-night party up in Stepney Green, and everyone ran out into the street because the siren had gone off. They were all shouting, 'I haven't got me gas mask!' We all thought we were going to get gassed that same morning.

Yet with all the precautions and the initial fears of air raids and even of imminent invasion, life in the period which would become known as the Phoney War soon settled back into a routine, returning almost to normal.

> [It] started very quietly; rationing began but still no expected air raids of any strength, so it began to lead us into a false sense of security. Men continued to be called up – I received my papers to start at the beginning of February – but it was the Phoney War. Life seemed to go on as usual, although

rationing began to bite, and industry was fighting to retain key workers, which, in a lot of cases, was allowed if they were reserved occupations. It was a shame for these men, who felt self-conscious with so many other men around in uniform.

The attitude of my generation was different from that of my parents'. While they had experienced the first war, we, in our ignorance, were treating it as a new experience, and, with our indoctrinated, childish pride in the nation and our Empire, and not knowing what war was all about, we had a kind of sang-froid attitude towards it when called to the colours. Like the young of all times, [we were] full of our own importance. The wives shed a few tears, but were soon just as embroiled as their menfolk. So, the 1930s ended with uncertainty as to the future, but with changes minimal compared with what was to come.

Many homesick cockney children and their mothers were happy to return from the strangeness of evacuation in the 'sticks' to the familiarity of their own London streets and homes.

I hadn't wanted Jimmy, my youngest, to be evacuated in the first place, so, when it seemed safe, I fetched him home. It might not have been the right thing to do, to keep him with me once that bombing started, but I didn't want him to be away with strangers. But the bombing did get bad.

She was not exaggerating. The bombing, as anyone who lived through it knows, was more than bad. On 7 September 1940, on a clear summer's day, the Blitz began to wreak its vicious havoc on the men, women and children of London's East End.

If the war changed everything, then it was the Blitz that changed the war.

The Blitz was the most traumatic thing of my life in the East End. My school was in East Ham [and] because where I lived [was] in such close proximity to the docks and Beckton Gas Works, it was number-one danger zone for the aerial bombing which was expected. They closed the school within weeks of the war starting. I was nearly thirteen years old when we evacuated, but no Blitz had started at that stage [and] things were so bad where we went that Mum brought us back. Because there was no school and we were so close to leaving at fourteen years, the town hall said we would have to go into the ARP. We were employed on filling sandbags and looking after the stirrup pumps. This was around the chemical factory, Beckton and the docks, or wherever they decided to send us. The Blitz had still not started. That summer, up to the September, when they bombed the docks, we were filling sand buckets and having a good time, a lot of lads together. The bombing of the docks and Beckton was horrendous. I was there when it started. I ran home at about four p.m., absolutely terrified. We had an outside toilet and I sat in it and cried. I would not come out. That was the beginning of the real war for us. As a family, Mum and Dad decided we would stay together.

While we were in London [on 'holiday' from evacuation] the Blitz was starting in earnest. With raids every night, we had to more or less sleep in our clothes to be ready to dash to a shelter. We ran along the street to a neighbour's house, where they had built an Anderson shelter in their yard. One night, the siren went and we dashed along to the shelter, but as we were running through the house we heard some 'screaming bombs' coming down and stopped in the back doorway until they had landed and gone off. They were a frightening weapon, designed to cause panic. They had things attached to the fins which made this screaming noise as they rushed through the air and they sounded as though they were about to land just in front of you.

The docks, a primary focus for the Luftwaffe, were attacked relentlessly: 400 German aircraft bombarded the area, in full view in the bright sunlight, with a further 250 bombers returning after dark. They came in wave after wave, leaving homes, docks, warehouses and factories burning. These sustained attacks lasted into October –

fifty-seven days of bombing – with surface shelters offering little protection.

> When you saw the damage that high explosives could cause, you just knew those flimsy surface shelters would have been as good as useless.

> We either went to Bethnal Green tube or the surface shelter they had built just outside our house. I preferred the tube, because you could buy a baked potato under the railway bridge at the Salmon and Ball, or you could sometimes buy crisps in the shop in the tube. Not only that, it was much warmer than the surface shelter. [But] the surface shelter saved my parents' lives one day. They heard the siren and were just going out of the front door when a German plane swooped down and started machine-gunning the street. They managed to run behind the wall of the shelter and the bullets went all along the pavement in front of the house.

People flocked to underground stations, cellars beneath local factories and, if they had them, shelters in their backyards. But there were stories of the domestic shelters being little more than death traps for those who entered them.

> My older brother took our house when we moved, with his wife and two children. They were lucky. They had the Anderson shelter in the garden and it got a direct hit. All they found was my sister-in-law's knitting, but they were out shopping in Stratford. They were very, very lucky.

> On my eighth birthday, my mother's sisters and brothers came to tea. There were jellies and a cake . . . In the middle of all the laughter and fun, the siren sounded and we all trooped down to the shelter in the garden. [My] auntie laughingly said, 'You know what it is – Hitler's heard it's your birthday and he's sending you a birthday present, a bomb with your name on it.' I took her seriously. I really believed that Hitler was being particularly malicious because he knew it was my

birthday. It almost did have my name on it. A huge shell exploded about 200 yards from our house. It made an enormous crater. If it had hit our house and garden, being in the Anderson shelter would have been no help.

It might seem odd, but for those who were children at the time many memories of the war were of the excitement at the tumult that was going on around them. The disruption of normal schooling, sleeping in air-raid shelters, kindnesses shown by strangers who quickly became friends, and even the novelty of queuing for rations were all remembered with childlike wonder.

Adults were very good at helping children feel OK and not terrified at what was happening all around them. I have good memories of air-raid drill in class, where we all squatted under our desks, and of sing-songs and games, I-Spy and reciting the multiplication tables in the school shelter. It even had a piano in it! Everything was made light of, so that sitting in the damp shelter at home, with a candle in a flowerpot, comments were made about the feebleness of Jerry's aim as shells whistled down and exploded nearby. We got used to the blackout, to glass with criss-crosses of tape on them, but I was sorry when the bus windows were fitted with obscure safety glass. I liked to sit in the front and 'drive' the bus. How could I 'drive' when I couldn't see out?

One of the buildings that got blasted and couldn't be used again was a pub called the Crocodile. In the pub was a stuffed crocodile, which the kids managed to get out. It was around the streets for a good few weeks. Then we had the bright idea of leaning it against someone's door when it was dark and then knocking and running a safe distance away to listen to the shrieks as the person opened the door and the crocodile fell in on them.

Our spare room was filled with gas masks, which [my father] fitted and issued to all the families in our street and those close by. People came to try them on, bring them back and so on. I had one in a case that I took to school; my brother had a toddler's one in coloured rubber with Mickey Mouse ears. My baby sister's was a closed box like a carrycot with a lid, a grey, wrinkled hose pipe with a pump that was meant to be worked by an adult. I remember wondering if a reliable adult would be around should we ever need it.

When war came in 1939, shelters appeared in the streets and gardens. We went to shelter in the railway arches near Cable Street and also in the Free Trade Wharf, sleeping on orange boxes. I was never afraid – you don't know fear at the age of seven. Coming from the shelters in the early mornings, the streets were always different from the previous night: houses were just a pile of bricks, craters, dust and glass, and there was always a smoke haze.

One of my most vivid memories is of German bombs accurately hitting an old ammunition dump near our house. Every piece of glass and china in the house broke. We spent the rest of the war drinking from jam jars. My mum mourned the loss of her wedding present cut-glass bowls. I was lifted from my glass-filled bed by a fireman, without a scratch. The blast had made wardrobes and sideboards, cupboards and tables all fall over. But we were alive and OK. I remember the fireman carrying me outside. Even though it was dark and cold, the bedroom was brilliantly lit from the oil-dump fire. The fireman held me and we stood and looked at it, great plumes of smoke and fire lighting up the sky. It was one of the most beautiful sights I have ever seen. I cried when they took me away from it. Dad was praying, thanking God we were all alive and safe, [but] Mum was furious – angry for ages – because of all we had lost in the blast.

I was a twelve-year-old boy being bombed. I saw aircraft plunging out of the sky, on fire and in bits.

I remember the incendiaries coming off the roof when I put my head out of the shelter. My father wasn't there with us because he was running around Whitechapel, driving an ambulance. I saw many a dog fight in the Blitz. You could hear their guns firing overhead.

Every self-respecting kid had a collection of motley metal pieces – shrapnel from exploded bombs or falling aircraft. Once, when I was visiting my grandmother, I was playing out on a bomb site with my youngest uncle when we found an unexploded bomb. We took it home to Nanny and showed it to the adults, who screamed at us. It was put in a galvanized bucket of cold water – as if that would have prevented an explosion – and carried by my uncles to the police station, where they confiscated it, much to the relief of the adults.

Among the excitement and adventures, of course, there were the tragedy and horror that even a child could not avoid seeing around them.

There had been a direct hit in the night at the end of our road, and there was rubble and chaos everywhere. Ambulances stood quietly and the firemen were frantically scrabbling at the rubble, trying to rescue whoever was entombed in it. I dared not be late for school, so I only stopped to watch for a few seconds. My eyes lighted on the pavement. They had found a severed arm and it lay there, mutilated.

Some wartime events in the East End stand out as being particularly terrible. One such occurred on 10 September 1940, when a school in Agate Street, Canning Town, that had been taken over as a centre for bombed-out families awaiting rehousing, received a direct hit. The tragedy was made worse by the fact that if the transport which had been promised to take them to temporary housing had arrived at the time arranged, the school would have been empty. Instead, all the occupants were killed. The official figure of seventy-three dead was questioned by local people, who believed that far more lost their lives.

Local people have also continued to question the official version of events that became known as the Bethnal Green tube disaster. Theories, some more shocking than others, have been put forward about the cause of what was the worst civilian incident of the Second World War, when, on the evening of 3 March 1943, the air-raid warning sounded just after eight o'clock and an estimated 1,000 people hurried towards the supposed safety of the underground. For some reason, panic ensued and the disaster happened. People close to the entrance stumbled and fell forward, crashing on to those already at the bottom of the stairs, and 173 people were killed, with another sixty-two seriously injured.

> It was the sound of these new anti-aircraft guns in Victoria Park that started the rumour that enemy bombs were dropping and people took fright. They surged forward to get down the steps to safety.

> Do you know, there were lots of stories around at the time about what really happened at Bethnal Green. The worst I heard – my dad told me this – was that some bastard was trying to dip people [pick their pockets] while they were preoccupied trying to get down to safety with their kids and that. Someone realized and the cry went up, and the struggle that started – as they tried to get hold of the bloke – caused someone to fall, and then, well, you know what happened next. Terrible, whatever the cause.

> Dad was in the heavy rescue service and had to work on some pretty horrible incidents, including the one at Bethnal Green tube, where lots of people were crushed when someone tripped as they were going down some poorly lit steps and the guns went off close by . . . People were piling on top of each other in the rush to get to the shelter.

Like those in the rescue services who had to deal with the conse-quence of the tube disaster, supposedly ordinary young men and women showed themselves to be heroes and heroines. The simple fact was that there was work to be done, no matter how difficult, upsetting or demanding. It is sometimes hard to believe that so much responsibility was put on the shoulders of such young individuals.

The first woman is speaking about when she was a nurse of just nineteen years old, and the others were not much older.

> We had to do one night duty in five at the hospital and had to prepare lists of casualties for the police to distribute. I was not so afraid when I was working.

> I saw the destruction . . . whilst the bombing was taking place. I will always remember how people I had known all my life were coping with that destruction, and could still clear up and carry on with the cocksureness of the cockney. I was proud to be one of them.

> Although we often came close to losing everything, we never expected it to be us who would take a hit. Everyone must have been constantly living under stress, but we . . . were protected by warmth and closeness and neighbourliness.

> It was 1941. Our place had just had a blasting; all the windows were in. And we'd just been to the pictures and his brother came in, saying, 'Here you are, here's your papers. You've got to go in the army.' So he said, 'Shall we get married?' And I said, 'Yeah.' Very romantic it was, we'd just been to see *Love on the Dole*! We got a special licence and had four days to prepare. As you know, we were rationed and couldn't get a drink or anything. If you went to the pub you were allowed one tot per person, [but] we took bottles and managed to get them filled up. Goodness knows what went in it. A drop of everything. They all got blotto! Anyway, we got married and off he went to the army.

It could not have been easy for those young men and women who had to leave home and join the forces, but, in different ways, the war was as difficult for those left behind on the home front.

It was hardest to comfort those women whose men were

'missing, presumed dead'. Half-news is always worse than certainty.

Some of my brothers would come home on leave and we'd have an air raid, and they'd say, 'You're putting up with far more than we are in the forces.' Nobody dreamed it was going to last for six years. We had a lot of near misses. On one occasion, when they'd come home on leave, we were sitting down having something to eat. All of a sudden a buzz bomb came over. Me and my sister made a dive outside for the Anderson shelter. It dropped and the blast blew us both right into the shelter. When we came out, the men were all covered in soot. [My husband] had been blown right up against the street door. All the sausage and mash was covered in soot.

Having to find somewhere to stay if you had been bombed out was just one of the problems.

We'd heard there'd been a really bad raid in Poplar and I just wanted to get home to see if my family were all right, but they said at work [near the City] that I had to wait in the shelter till it was over. As soon as the all clear went, I was off. I don't know how I got there, I don't remember, but I know when I did I saw our place had had a direct hit. I nearly died on the spot, but a neighbour came over and said, 'Don't worry. They're all right. They were out. They salvaged some of your stuff and they've gone looking for somewhere to stay. I said I'd tell you.' I was so relieved. It wasn't an unusual sight where we lived, close to the docks, seeing someone with their stuff on a barrow looking for somewhere empty after their place had copped it.

In June 1944 the East End was confronted with a new horror: the V1, the first of which fell by a railway bridge in Grove Road, Bow, a matter of yards from my childhood home, killing six people and injuring and making homeless many more. They had a particular place in people's wartime memories.

*

When the characteristic whine of the doodlebug, the pilotless, flying bombs, stopped, you would count to ten and then know it was about to hurtle to the ground and explode, causing terrible damage.

We were in the shelter and heard a buzz bomb – doodlebugs, we called them – coming across the sky. Suddenly the engine cut out and we could tell it was going to fall close to us. There was a massive explosion and we found out afterwards it had fallen only two streets away.

We suffered damage as a result of the bombing, but escaped being driven right out until the buzz bombs [and then] we lived on the dance floor of the town hall for some time.

I was at [a relative's house] when the sirens went off. She had cooked a tasty stew for our dinner. We heard the sirens, then ran out the back to go into the Anderson shelter. I was aware of a doodlebug – one of the pilotless German planes targeted on the docks – right above us in the sky. I gazed up, transfixed, and, as I looked up, my plate of hot stew and dumplings tipped down my front and on to the path. Annie, already at the shelter entrance, screamed at me and I ran, counting to ten as I heard the engine stop. I got inside the shelter with seconds to spare. The doodlebug dived into houses a few hundred yards along the road and exploded. Many people were killed and the houses flattened. There is now a park where those houses were. When the all clear sounded and we came out, we did not yet realize how close a call it had been. I was really upset at the loss of my stew. Like everyone else, I was really relieved that, once again, we had not been hit, but the loss of the stew really distressed me. Then, all the rest of the day and throughout the night, I watched the emergency teams digging for survivors. It felt like an invasion of privacy to see inside bedrooms, where the walls were ripped off. The mirrors still hung on walls, wallpaper flapped, fire-place and chimneys open to the sky, and, everywhere, scattered personal belongings.

*

Listening to some stories, it might have seemed that the war was
no more than a nuisance through which normal life had to be lived.
But I had been told so often by people that they had no stories to
tell, that they were just *ordinary*, and then, after a few minutes of
listening to what they had to say, it would become obvious that if
there is such a thing as an ordinary person, I had yet to meet one.
Whether it was the casual way in which they described an undeniably
frightening time in their lives, or the humour and generosity with
which they had somehow managed to retain their dignity, all the
people who shared their memories were extraordinary in one way
or another.

> Where we had moved to, there were just surface shelters, they
> didn't have room to put Anderson ones round there. In our
> little house we had gaslight and some of the houses further
> down only had oil lamps. We only had two up and two down
> and the scullery, and my brother and his wife and children
> came to us when their house was bombed. So we had a
> crowd. But I was seventeen then. We took that sort of thing
> in our stride, but we were scared. You couldn't say you
> weren't, but you deal with it at that age. We used to go down
> to the church, go underground. The barrage balloons were
> above on the ground and we were underneath. It was like
> going into a tunnel, all concrete. You slept along with
> anybody then. There were three tiers of bunks and you got in
> where you could. You didn't know who you were sleeping
> with. We only stuck that for a while and then we thought,
> 'Oh, well, we'll go back to bed. Chance it.' We used to go up
> the pub. You could hear the [anti-aircraft] guns from in
> there.
>
> Sometimes schools were hit. Twice during the war I was sent
> to a different junior school because of bomb damage. Classes
> were doubled up, with teachers having to teach more than
> sixty children. We sat on the floor, on benches, in the hall, in
> shelters, we sat three to a desk. I don't remember us being
> naughty. We realized times were difficult and accepted we
> had to get on with it.

*

Bombs were simply a fact of life and no one could do anything about them and we just did not worry about them. But there were far greater terrors. One day, I saw a rat suddenly whisk by me on the path and shoot down the shelter. I told my dad and he began a frenzy of banging with a stick and shaking the blankets in the shelter. He swept and poked, thumped and hollered, but no rat was revealed. Later, when we were in the shelter and I was thought to be asleep, the rat episode was discussed. My aunt told very graphically how, if a rat feels cornered, he would try to escape by jumping over your shoulder but was much more likely to go for your throat with his sharp teeth. She told stories of babies in prams having their faces gnawed off and of whole armies of rats marching down the street when their sewer home had been destroyed by the shells.

I was getting ready to go out, we were courting then, and he was coming round to collect me. I was standing doing my make-up, with my mirror propped against a sandbag, and the Battle of Britain was going on overhead. I said, 'He's a blooming long time getting round here.' Well, of course, they'd got bombed down the docks and there were no buses.

One night we were in the shelter and there was a fairly heavy raid going on. The guns were firing and bombs were dropping. It was damp out on the road and Dad was wandering around outside, and we could hear the shrapnel falling and sizzling on the wet road when we heard Dad's footsteps across the street. He stopped and then we heard him say loudly, 'Sod it.' He had been to pick up a piece of shrapnel and it was still hot and burnt him.

When there was a raid we would get up when the siren sounded and go down in the damp and the cold to the Anderson shelter at the bottom of the garden. If the weather was really bitter, we would get into the Morrison shelter instead. This was a thick steel table. We would be put to bed under there and the mesh sides would be put up [around us].

We would often wake to find our parents were there
squashed in with us too. Dad was knowledgeable about
bombs, as I'm sure all adults at the time were. He could
identify each whistle and crump as a shell, an incendiary, a
hundred-pounder or whatever else it was. We [children]
learned to do the same, but less expertly – we knew when
they were close. The house shook and the china and windows
rattled. It was often too noisy to sleep, so we played I-Spy
and other games. I wasn't very afraid. We often needed to go
to the shelter in the daytime. At school we learned to crouch
beneath our desks when the siren sounded. We ate our
school dinners so often in the shelter that I thought ground
rice was, in fact, 'underground rice' and that you only had it
when you were underground.

When the bombing was at its worst, a lot of the women and
children who had come back to London during the Phoney War
were evacuated again. While it was the safe option, it could still
prove disturbing enough for a child to want to plan his own return
home and for adults to be willing to risk the bombs.

I started to save my pocket money to pay my fare. I hadn't
realized how homesick I was. I eventually saved sufficient to
be able to write home and say I could pay my own fare, so it
was arranged and Dad came down to collect me.

My mother hated being evacuated. She hated village life.
There were no shops, no buses, no electricity and you had to
walk everywhere. She missed her sisters and was glad to get
back to London, even though the bombing was bad and we
spent a lot of time in the air-raid shelters.

I was in the ARP and had to look after my elderly mother,
who stayed in the East End. I didn't want my children
evacuated, but I was persuaded. I think I was as unhappy as
the kids. I used to try and visit them, but I only had Sunday.
One boy was evacuated to Wales, my daughter was near
Uxbridge, and the one of nursery age was at Bury

St Edmunds. I'd go to Wales and my husband would go to another one. We used to go by train and it got too much. I couldn't get them all together. The youngest was in Lord and Lady X's house with all other little children. It was more like a children's home. I used to take sweets and loads of things, but they were only allowed one and then they'd be put away. Very strict they were. I said to the welfare lady that I'd like my two youngest together, so they said the girl could go to Bury St Edmunds to keep an eye on the boy as she was four years older. That was the worst day's work I ever done. I went there, this day, and I'd bought her a big doll like a baby. When I got into the grounds with the other mothers all the children were crying. What an alteration I saw in my daughter. Her hands were raw – where she'd been before they'd rubbed her hands for her when she had chilblains. They were all crying. And they'd cut off all her hair. And they were all hungry. I gave her this lovely big doll and I'd got sweets for her and everything. And she kept saying, 'Give us the sweets, Mum, don't give them to the lady and the man.' But they wouldn't have it. They said they had to be distributed.

Evacuation was a short-lived experience for different reasons for this little girl.

The war began when I was two and a half years old. When the opportunity came for evacuation, my dad's sister, Annie, accompanied my mum and I to Devon. I was in the field one day when I heard a shout. It was my beloved dad coming over the stile. His shout echoed up the whole valley. He had walked miles from the station. It was a surprise to see him and what happened after is a blur. He had brought dreadful news. Annie's husband, Arthur, had been killed in the docks, and he had come to tell her and to take her back for the funeral. So we all returned to London. Our evacuation had only lasted a few months. I don't remember the journey back, but I do remember two policemen with tall helmets coming to tell us what had happened. It seems Arthur had had a load

of timber dropped on him. The crane driver, who was too
old to be called up, had suffered a stroke or a heart attack
and had let the timber go. I remember Annie crying bitterly.
So did my dad when the policemen left. Seeing my dad cry
was terrifying.

Even so, she remembered her time in the countryside with great
fondness.

We went almost immediately to Lincolnshire on an
evacuation scheme. We were only there a few months, but it
is a shiny, idyllic time in my memory. It's a curious thing, I
can recall the tough times in my life fairly easily, but when
I reach a happy oasis like the time we spent in Lincolnshire, I
am instantly overwhelmed by tears. At first we stayed with
the village postwoman, who went on her bike delivering
letters and much dreaded telegrams from the War Office
[around] the village. I remember her kindness . . . Her
cottage was small and dark, without electricity or running
water. I helped fill galvanized buckets from the well. But I
wasn't good at carrying them and always got wet socks. I
suffered with chilblains, but most people did then.

The experiences of this boy, his brother and the unfortunate J.
were rather different.

The evacuees weren't liked and I suppose it was to a degree
understandable, when we were just dumped on people, and
when one considers the effect it must have had on their quiet
village life, but if anything went wrong it was usually 'those
Londoners' that were to blame. I've no doubt we did cause
chaos at times with the things we got up to, but in the main
we were too young to appreciate this. Some of the evacuees
were poorly treated by the people who were looking after
them. There wasn't much we could do about it, because our
parents were too far away. One of our billets was the vicarage.
We had to live in the servants' area and had our meals in the
kitchen, except J., who had to eat in the dining room on a

separate table in the corner because he was a 'naughty' boy.
[His] family never sent him any clothes, so we were made to
give him some of ours, and when Mum found out she went
potty, because it was enough of a struggle clothing us two. I
don't know if J. had a mother, because she never came to see
him, and his father only turned up once. Because we were
kept separate [at the vicarage] we had some of our rations
given to us individually each week. If we ran out there was no
more. As J. had to have his meals in the dining room,
because he was a bad boy, he wasn't served by the maids in
the same way as the family, but had his meals put on a plate
in the kitchen and had to carry it in himself. Well, one day
his plate got broken, either by him or one of the maids, and
they wouldn't give him another, so he carried in half a plate
with the gravy dripping off it. If we broke anything we had to
make an appointment and 'confess' our sin, and we were told
to pay for a replacement or do some jobs to pay for it.
Because J. couldn't read very well, he had to go into the
nanny's room to have reading lessons, and while he was in
there he saw she had a cupboard full of tins of fruit and
things and packets of biscuits. We never saw those things on
our plates.

Another little cockney boy found himself isolated in a village in
deepest Devon.

When I started at the school, all the other boys kept looking
through my hair. I was upset, because I thought they thought
I had nits, but the teacher explained they had never met a Jew
before and were looking for my horns.

Others remember their experience of being evacuated in a matter-
of-fact, almost businesslike sort of way.

In September 1939 [my brother] and I were evacuated with
the school. Mum made us haversacks, which had our spare
clothes and some other things in, and, with these on our
backs, we marched from the school to Bethnal Green

Junction and caught a train. I was only nine years old and [my brother] was eleven. It's only now that I realize the responsibility he had of having to keep an eye out for me. I thought we were going away on a holiday, little realizing how long we would be away from home.

There were only two shops in the village. We went [in one] to buy Gibbs Solid Dentifrice, which we ate instead of sweets, which were rationed. There wasn't a barber's shop in the village so we had to go to 'Smoker' to get a haircut. [He] did the hair-cutting on a kitchen chair in an alley between the houses, and one of his sayings was, 'How's your father's leg then?' God knows what he meant.

Being the older boys, we got the job of making all the evacuee labels: cardboard cut up to size on a guillotine – I cut my finger and still have the scar – punches for the eyelets and then folded over, doubled cord for the tie. Indian ink to write the names.

Village life was strange and quiet for children who had been brought up in the bustle of the East End, but we managed to find lots of new things to do. The only sign of the war they knew of down there was if the Germans were trying to bomb the sugar beet factory at Bury St Edmunds, which was five miles away. We would hear the sirens in the distance and go to the Morrison shelter under the living-room table, but I only remember this happening a couple of times. The only other incident happened when [my brother] and I were on holiday in London and a couple of stray fire bombs fell in some bushes but did no real damage, though, of course, the villagers thought it was horrendous.

After six long years, it was at last time for all the evacuees to go home, not just for a holiday but for good.

It was strange at first, being back in London. I'd become a bit of a yokel, I suppose. But you couldn't beat being home with your mum.

*

Adults too were returning to their East End homes.

> One of my earliest memories – I was not quite three – is of
> my uncle coming home from the war one Saturday morning.
> My aunt was waiting in our house, and I can remember the
> excitement but not knowing why we were all excited. Aunt
> Marie gave a loud scream and a strange man in khaki was
> running down the street with a kitbag over his shoulder. I
> rushed ahead, having no idea who he was, [or] why I should
> be so pleased, and he scooped me up in his arms. I can still
> vividly remember the roughness of the material of his jacket
> against my legs.

At last, it was really over, and the celebrations and congratulations
could begin.

> Luckily, every one of our family came through the war. All
> six brothers were in the forces. I was doing 'special work' . . .
> making direction finders for the ships and submarines. The
> work was secret and we had to be locked in the room,
> unlocked when we came out. We were not to divulge what
> we were doing. We had our family record in the *Stratford
> Express*, the family's war record. All our names: the six
> brothers, the three brothers-in-law, and all us girls on war
> work. We were proud of that.

> People must have been preparing for street parties and
> celebrations everywhere. In a few hours, all the men in our
> street put together a wooden platform with a stage. Everyone
> dragged out timber they had been saving for a huge bonfire.
> We kids had been roaming the bomb sites for weeks,
> collecting anything that might burn. Every street had a fire.
> All the neighbours were up on ladders, hanging out bunting
> and Union Jacks. One neighbour's piano was pushed out on
> to the platform. As the day wore on, the preparations for the
> street party were frenzied. Every household provided
> something. There were sandwiches, cakes, jellies and trifles,
> and we children ate until we ached. A fancy-dress

competition was announced for the young ones. The bells rang out and, best of all, the streetlights came on. We no longer needed to cover our torches with crêpe paper to see our way home in the dark.

We had heard that Walthamstow town hall was to be floodlit and my dad took me for a walk to see it. It's a plain, municipal building, bureaucratic and boring, but on this night the fountains and the ornamental ponds were all floodlit. After the blackness of the blackout, I thought it was fairyland. Fireworks exploded in the sky above it, searchlights danced around it, and the water in the fountains rose and fell in sparkling drops of light. I was totally entranced and wanted to stay there.

Everyone sat out in the street on chairs or on the windowsills. We saw a bonfire and celebrations at every street corner. Many of them were burning effigies of Hitler. One in particular was most realistic. It had a moustache with black hair plastered down and a full German uniform. He hung on a gibbet over the fire, waiting for dark to fall and the fire to be lit. I shivered, despite all the joy and relief all around me. It had been light when we left home, but as we returned all the fires were up. The sky that was usually so black was now full of dancing sparks, glowing orange from all the thousands of bonfires throughout London. It was magical.

The bonfires burned all night. People brought out the fireworks they had been saving. Us children had never seen fireworks before and we were very excited. Even now I can't begin to describe the beauty of those fireworks. For all my living memory, until that time, nights had been really black, darkness was really dark, and now it was exploding with light and colour all around me. The war had ended.

A future without air raids, sirens, shelters and shortages beckoned.

I was allowed to stay up as long as I liked and I could eat as much as I wanted. I managed to stay awake until one a.m., protesting, 'No, I'm not tired. No, I don't want to go home yet.' It would not have been any good going to bed anyway. The whole world was awake and singing. The relief was almost tangible. Being woken at night for several air raids was much more exhausting than if we were awake all night long. The prospect now of having unbroken sleep at night was wonderful!

Even after the parties were over, there was more fun to be had for cockney kids liberated from the restrictions and rigours of a London at war.

In the morning, the bonfire was a great smouldering pile of hot ash with a glowing red heart. The streets were deserted, absolutely no traffic on the road, quieter than a Sunday. With a group of friends, I trekked from street to street to see if the other bonfires were still alive. It was a piece of new information for us that fires could burn all night; our coal fires at home always needed lighting in the mornings. For a few euphoric days it felt as if we could do as we pleased. Adults were too tired, relaxed or too hungover to pay much attention to us kids. So we went around collecting spent firework cases and looking for shrapnel, because we knew we would not be getting any more.

If it is inevitable that the number of people who can share their memories of the Second World War is decreasing all the time, how much truer this must be of an even earlier conflict.

While living at Finnis Street [Bethnal Green] the Great War broke out in August 1914. I was still at school at the time. I remember Victoria Park being taken over by the army and the troops digging trenches, signalling with semaphore flags, and Lord Derby's army of volunteers marching to Bethnal Green station with their red armbands with a gold crown in the centre, but no uniforms, headed by a band. We had plenty of warning of an air raid, as the lights on the station would go out, then a policeman would ride round on a cycle blowing a whistle to take cover, then the maroons would go

off and we waited. The Zeppelins would fly high, but one
night a searchlight caught one and it was shot down by
Lieutenant Ball of the Royal Flying Corps. The Zeppelin came
down in flames near Cuffley and we stood on our landing
and cheered. The air raids were not as bad as the Blitz of
1940, but bad enough. One Wednesday, in school, there was a
daylight raid by German planes and a school was hit. Then,
on a Saturday, I was cleaning some knives and forks when I
saw six German planes flying over. Again damage was done.
These were the only daylight raids I remember. We had
potato rationing, so we had swedes instead, which were like
turnips. I liked them. In Bethnal Green Road there were some
German-owned shops, Stoltes by name, and a pork butcher's.
[When, in 1915,] the *Lusitania*, a liner, was sunk by U-boats,
German submarines, it caused such bitter feelings amongst
the public that a crowd of boys smashed the windows of
those shops and, before the police could interfere, ran off
with legs of pork, sausages and joints of all kinds. There were
loaves of bread, cakes and flans scattered on the pavements.
Some families had a nice dinner that day.

After 1945, the people of the debris-strewn, bomb-ravaged East
End would experience massive changes in their lives. Following the
period of post-war austerity, there would be increasing affluence and
opportunities for working men and women; promises of decent
housing; a National Health Service worthy of the name; universal
education and a welfare net to catch those who had previously been
in peril of falling through to the bottom of the social heap; and real,
if slowly achieved, improvements in living conditions that came with
great hopes of full employment and prosperity for everyone.

But not all change was a cause for celebration.

17

I consider myself a thoroughbred cockney. There's not many of us left now.

By 1950 there was an overall decline in the population of London, with increasing numbers of people moving out of the war-ravaged East End to make their homes on the new, outlying estates which were being built following the London County Council's promise in the 1930s that the slums would be cleared in ten years.

Regardless of whether you were going to a new home with all mod cons, an indoor lav and a street door that you could call your own, leaving the East End was not always something done by choice. If it had not been for the war, many would not have considered moving away, but with the bomb damage leaving less housing than ever available for rent, and overcrowding becoming intolerable, new lives in places like Dagenham were embarked upon.

This post-war depopulation left the way open for another wave of newcomers ready to take the place of those moving away to the suburbs.

Bengali-speaking workers, at first mostly male, began to arrive with the intention of earning, saving and then returning to their families. But with the tightening of immigration rules at the beginning of the 1960s making the future uncertain, families were sent for and brought to London. It was with the arrival of wives and children that an identifiable community began to evolve.

As the previous residents took the post-war opportunities – and their skills – and started their new lives elsewhere, the movement of manufacture out of the East End, which had begun after the First World War, was accelerated. These changes, followed by a national industrial decline, saw Britain wasting its post-war opportunities and moving away from a manufacturing-based economy to one which focused on service industries.

Traditional East End trades and crafts all but disappeared, or were being shunned by locals and taken over by newcomers. There was a feeling of abandonment among older people, who talked about the loss of their old neighbourhoods. It was not simply a dislike of change but a case of no longer understanding the meaning of what was going on in what had once been their world.

I spoke to a group in a library in Newham who were not alone in expressing regret that Neighbourhood Watch has to exist.

> *I'm* in it, but I think it's sad. It's bad enough we need it to stop the little buggers breaking into our places in the first place, but what's sadder is we're not looking out for each other without having it as a sort of club. You used to look out for one another because it's just what you did – the right thing to do. What's happened to people?

> It makes me sad and all, these Neighbourhood Watch schemes. Not only the fact that there's so much crime that you practically live in a bank vault, with the number of bolts and chains on your door, but the fact that you need to actually ask people to keep an eye out for you. That should be done automatically, not because you've got a sticker in your front window.

But, as the history of the East End shows so clearly, communities do change: they grow, evolve and, in some cases, dissipate. In the autumn of 1991, the Soup Kitchen for the Jewish Poor in Brune Street, Spitalfields, was closed, after operating on the site since 1902 and having served the needs of locals for over 130 years. From the Second World War, hot meals had been replaced by weekly food parcels and then, as the Jewish community grew smaller still, the final blow came, with the premises being closed and the food replaced by monetary payments. The money no doubt filled a need, but, as an elderly local, Leslie Simmons, said, when interviewed in the *Jewish Chronicle*, 'You can't talk to a pension.'

The Soup Kitchen is now a private apartment block. Of course, memory is selective, and we are maybe forgetting the shame of having to queue for charitable hand-outs, but it is the meaning, the understanding, of that lost past which highlights people's anxieties about what is happening to them today.

The following quote is from a woman I interviewed who had moved from east London to Kent to settle in the area she had grown to love while hop-picking in her youth. She missed the community that she can now observe only second-hand through soap operas.

> You know, you coming here and talking to me like this, it's the first time in I can't think how long that, once it started getting dark, I didn't lock up, draw the curtains and sit and watch the telly for the rest of the evening. I like telly, [*laughing*] *EastEnders* and that, but you can't beat sitting having a chat like this, can you? We used to go round one another's houses and play cards and have a laugh. Nothing special. Might cut a few rounds of sandwiches and that. Nothing special, like I say, but we'd just enjoy the company and having a laugh. We got together round here for the street parties, for the Jubilee and Diana's wedding, but that sort of thing's once in a blue moon. Not like just going round and having a laugh of an evening.

She wasn't alone in her feelings of isolation and regret.

> I feel we were better off in them days. There was more community spirit, more give and take. Today, you only got to say something out of the way to your neighbour and he'll punch you in the earhole. Them days, there was nothing like that, was there? I worry about my grandchildren. I've got twenty-six grandchildren and twenty-seven great-grandchildren. In days gone by, the mum and dad used to take their kids round their grandad's three turnings away. My relations are all over the place. In future, we'll be going to visit them on the moon.

> I think the people who moved just a little way out, to live in blocks of flats, would have been much happier if they'd stayed in the heart of the East End. The people that moved right out, to nicer homes and pleasant scenery, would probably prefer their surroundings now. In many ways, I think they left because it seemed ridiculous not to try and

better themselves. But are they happier? If they went back now, they certainly wouldn't go back to what they left thirty or forty years ago. The old community spirit, from what I can make out, is not the same. I know that, as much as I had a wonderful childhood growing up in the East End, there is no way I would ever go back there to live – even if it hadn't changed so much. The fact is, it is not the same as it was.

What I miss about the old days is the genuine care of one neighbour for another and how they would all help in times of trouble. You can live in a place now and not even know your neighbours' names. Everyone sits indoors watching the telly. I don't want people in and out all the time, but a friendly word wouldn't go amiss. It's moving away, you see. You leave all your old roots behind. It takes time to put down roots. It was good when you could get a place near your mum and dad, and see all the old friends and family, but people move away. They want different things. And then there's the waiting lists. It's so hard to get a place now.

When people look back, I suppose it's to their time as a teenager, or a young married couple just setting up home. For them it was good, it was their youth. [But] I also think people appreciated things far more then. For one thing, you made more of your own entertainment. It was many years before I had television. And people didn't shut their front doors, did they?

The fear of crime – the need to 'lock up' once it gets dark and to 'shut your front door' – is a real concern. Statistics suggest that it is young males who are most at risk from violence, but it is older people who are frightened by the representations of reality presented by the press and on television – in drama and *Crimewatch*-type programmes – a world where there are masked muggers and house-breakers lurking in every shadow.

This is not to deny that terrible crimes do occur. I spoke with one woman whose elderly mother had died as the result of a street crime which netted the perpetrator a few lousy pennies. But it is the frequency of such events which can become exaggerated and make people prisoners in their own homes, believing that the East End has become a lawless place, a place of fear and lack of control.

They're all taking drugs and saying it's the only way they can enjoy their life. They don't even try to enjoy it any way other than with drugs, drink or whatever. If you're taking drugs [you're not] thinking about your family, what you're doing to other people. [To get money] today, it doesn't matter [to them]. You can nick from an old lady out on the street.

It seems to be a thing that is round every corner now; always somebody that is a child abuser. The community policed itself [then], and if anything happened, they would get hold of them and bash them. If you touched [them] today, they'd have you up. You can't touch that person because they can sue you. The same as when we was at school, you could be hit with a ruler, pulled up by the back of your hair or your ear. But you do that today and they'll sue you for it. I think to be able to do that to a teacher is wrong. You've got to have some discipline. If you don't do that, when you let them on the streets, they'll be hooligans, not decent people.

We won't go out of a night-time, not even together. A lot of things you don't do now, because you are frightened to go out. On the odd occasions you have to go out, I was terrified. To wait outside for a bus, you feel as though you are taking your life in your hands. All these yobs and mobs – just walking past, they frighten you. You didn't hear of drugs then, did you? Drugs and alcohol, they're too free to get hold of. Alcohol is just as bad. Even children at school can get hold of it. They're *encouraging* youngsters to get hold of it. We got a drop of lemonade powder put in a bottle of water.

People did not express concern only about the ways in which their own lives were affected by changes in the community.

*

I was born here. My family had a shop. [But now] everything is totally unrecognizable. People are frightened to open their street doors. Being the warden of a settlement, I go round a lot visiting pensioners. I do hospital visiting and home visits if needed. Only the elderly people. I go round and visit and you hear 'bolt, bolt, bolt'. They are petrified round here, the pensioners.

A lot of the trouble is all the news. They have to fill the papers and the news with something. There's local papers, local news on the television, local radio. As soon as anything happens it's a major story. I know it's their job, but it puts it all out of perspective. You hear people like my dad saying, 'It never used to be like that round here.' Yes, it did. You just never heard about it so much. When there was just the one lot of BBC radio news, why would they bother with what was happening in Stepney unless it was something 'juicy', like the Blackshirts? A riot, that interested them. Papers need sensation, not 'Mrs Smith's lost her budgie.' So they make something out of what might otherwise have been heard of in passing from a neighbour, not seen in the headlines. Now it's *all* happening on your doorstep, *all* the time. It's like all the 'Devil Dog' stories. There are a few dogs round here, and the panic! It's terrible that children got hurt, but I'll bet there were no more than at any other time. Except maybe some nutters saw the stories and thought, 'I'd like one of them' and then didn't know how to handle them or train them, or got one of the really dangerous ones that they'd never have even heard of if it wasn't for all the panic in the papers. But no one thinks about them now, not now they're off the front pages. They're just dogs again. Owned by the people who always had them. Still a bloody nuisance when they poo, but just dogs.

But there are things of which undoubtedly people have every reason to be scared.

Drugs is an acute problem here. Not only for white children, but for our Asian children too. The parents have no understanding. Drugs? It is one of those injections. They have no idea about glue-sniffing and things.

It used to be other parts of London, but the reality is, is that guns are moving to east London. Guns were used for robberies and things like that, but nowadays they buy them to kill each other. I was actually offered a gun the other day. The guy pulled out like a whole panel of the things. *He had a little pink lady gun for the ladies*. The prices were amazingly low. I think the drug dealers realize that the sentence is going to be pretty much the same [armed or not], so let's go the whole hog.

Crime was blamed on greed, selfish materialism being what has spoiled everything: conditions might be better, but the mood, the spirit, has changed.

People are more interested in what they can get and what they can have, rather than about the people around them. They're always striving to get something more, rather than [worrying about] their family.

So many things were different in those days. There was no snobbery like today, no greed, because people never had much anyway, certainly nothing to pinch. People had time for each other, respect for people and property. Children were more content and loved to spend time with their families. We had no telly until I was thirteen. We'd play games or read or listen to stories about the war. Today, people are obsessed with money and status symbols. They see something and have to have it, regardless of the cost. Kids have no respect, and, yes, I do believe they were the good times. OK, they were hard, and our parents worked and fought like tigers to put a meal on the table, but at the end of the day they were happy. I have nothing against progress, but I despair at how some families go on. It seems the more some people get, the more they want. [People are no longer]

quietly content, happy knowing they've done the best for
their kids, the way our parents did for us. That was the
typical East End way.

It was such a nice feeling that everybody was the same. It is a
real sadness that this has changed. You've not got the feeling
that everybody is the same any more, that nobody's better
than anybody else. They're all out to do one another now.

Ours was a big family and they stuck together. There was a
family feeling that is not there now. Seems to me that's the
trouble, you know. These children leave home and live on the
streets. How can a parent allow that to happen? My mum
went without food more often than not to feed us.

There was also a feeling that the way people are housed has caused
yet more change for the worse.

I don't think there is an East End any more. Not as we knew
it when I was a kid. I do not like the idea of my
grandchildren playing out. They never play out in the street.
There is no community spirit any more. You used to be able
to have your doors open all the time. No more. Everybody's
got their door locked. Most people don't know their
neighbours for the simple reason that you don't have
long-term neighbours any more. Older people don't stay in
the same house for years, or have their family move into the
street with them. They all moved out. Or the council
changed. When they built estates or knocked others down,
they changed the people that lived in them. They moved
them out and moved other people in. You don't have that
same community. The ones that have moved in either don't
want to know you or you don't particularly want to know
them. They have moved in a lot of problem people; they
think if they move them in with people that are not a
problem, everything will be all right. But, instead of that, it
makes everybody's life a problem.

And when asked if she was glad about anything that had gone, this same respondent had an emphatic answer.

> No. I think slum streets weren't slum streets as they called them. They were communities.

> The lack of affordable – *decent* – housing is what has killed the community off. The kids move away. They have to. They are not going to get housed round here unless they wait. And wait. And wait. Unless they do something about housing, I can't see the old East End community surviving. People want dignity and a decent place to live.

The problems that housing policies were seen as causing – children being forced to move away from their elderly parents, the destruction of extended families and the break-up of communities – meant that someone had to be blamed. But instead of demanding that politicians begin acting in the interests of locals, people go by the evidence of their eyes and blame those who are often as badly off, or worse off, than themselves.

> My daughter can't get a place, yet you see all these foreigners when you're queueing up for your pension.

> If one of the neighbour's daughters needed a flat and somebody had a house with a couple of rooms upstairs, bomp, you moved in there. So you had the mother, the daughter, the granddaughter. But you can't do that now. The kids can't get a place for love nor money. They have to move out. They move away and then the nan and grandad either have got to move with them, or stay where they are and just get left. I think that is what has absolutely killed it. You can't just pop in and know that Mum and Dad are all right.

> The pubs were a focus for the community, somewhere where everybody could go for a chat. But most of them have gone from round our way. They knocked them down when they started the rebuilding. Then they knocked down the local

school and put up this horrible-looking thing. Down a rotten
alley, where it used to be a big wide alley with shops each
side, so when you walked down there you didn't feel worried,
because there was life with the shops. But now there's two big
high walls and one lamp-post stuck in the middle and all wire
fencing above it. It looks [*sarcastically*] really wonderful. Like
a concentration camp. No sort of place for people. Just walls
and alley. The council did what they thought was making it
good. They built all these flats, one on top of another, and
greens round them where no one can play ball, because that's
what it says. You don't know who people are and now you
are shut behind a security door. I find it bloody ridiculous.
Why build them in the first place? Making you a prisoner in
your own home.

When I see the changes in the street where I was brought up,
where there were good, brick, three-storey houses that are
now demolished, and what is there now? Flats! It seems
absolutely soulless.

After the war, with its destruction of so much living
accommodation, there was a need for quick and durable
living quarters, which resulted in the prefab – preconstructed
dwellings made in sections, which were erected on-site,
containing all modern plumbing and toilet facilities, and with
a guarantee of at least ten years. These were a masterstroke.
My sister-in-law lived in one for twenty-five years, loved it.
They even had a little garden.

Then came the disaster. High-rise flats. There were
tragedies in some instances [such as the Ronan Point
disaster], with a loss of life. That was bad enough, but what
was never considered was the mental effect these monstrous
mountains would have on people. They were being asked to
live most of their life away from the markets in an
environment that was a psychological mind-bender for
people who had lived at ground level. Not only the problems
caused by lifts not working and having to climb several
hundred stairs, but many other characteristics in humans

changed because of this new way of life. There was the lack of playing space which affected the young; neighbours becoming a torment because of noisy children; daughters and their families now in another building, or, if lucky, ten floors higher and losing family closeness.

In the 1950s and 1960s they'd started to knock down all the little roads. All the little back turnings and terraces. The people weren't rehoused where they lived, but further out. So the people that moved in when the estates were built knew nobody round there and nobody knew them. But when my daughter was looking for a place, I said to them couldn't she get a place round here? They said, 'We don't do that any more.' Years ago, when you put your name down, you'd get something in the same area. But they said, 'We don't do that now.' You haven't got priority now. You move wherever they get a place. That breaks the community. If you want to move, you don't go near the family, you have to go somewhere else. All the families get broken up.

Moving away did prove successful for some families.

Why wouldn't we prefer a nice, clean home, with an indoor toilet, a bathroom and a bedroom each for the kids? I missed things about the East End, course I did, it was where I was brought up, but I didn't miss trying to keep them bloody old rooms clean. No matter what you did to them, they were slums. My husband would put a coat of paint on the kitchen walls and they'd be mouldy again in a few weeks. You couldn't keep paper on the walls of the front room, it was so damp.

We were moved to live on the Becontree Estate. The house, or cottage, as the then LCC called them, was new and seemed like a palace to us after one room, and, best of all, no bugs!

But it was not the answer for everyone. As people usually moved with only their immediate nuclear family, there was an absence of a wider familial and social network, and, with the need to travel considerable distances to work, life on the new estates presented problems that did not start to disappear until roots took hold and the next generation had been born and had grown up there.

So many people thought they were moving to little palaces when they moved out. They were going to have a fitted kitchen, with lovely hot water and central heating, which they'd never had before. In their terraced houses they'd had an outside toilet and a scullery. Them people died when they moved. They'd got nothing. What can you do in your palace? You can cook a dinner, you can go to the inside toilet, you can be warm. But you ain't got nothing. You can't sit at your door, sit there shelling peas, talking to people.

When I was [a girl of] about eight [in the 1950s] the council rehoused us in one of the brand-new slum-overspill estates that they had started building in the then countryside. It was very typical of the period that the reason given wasn't that our current house was bedbug-ridden, rat-infested and home to various species of flea, but that my brother and I shared a bed. It meant that I was torn away from my beloved nan and transplanted into the countryside. We went to a new estate in Aveley, Essex, which at that time consisted of about four roads surrounded by fields. It was a complete trauma. I was enrolled in a small country school with only two classrooms and must have looked and seemed a complete freak to the other children, who had probably never left their village. I was a smelly, dirty cockney child with no social graces, but an awful lot of street ways. Imagine their reaction. I can remember wearing a pair of fur boots all through summer term because we couldn't afford sandals. When I mentioned to my mum that I was getting stick for wearing fur boots in July she [said] that the other kids were jealous. Probably my only advantage at school was that I was obviously clever. We all know how other children admire you when you're clever, don't we . . . Because of the rush to rehouse Londoners after the war, houses were being built in satellite towns like ours, but there was no work, so both Mum and Dad continued to work in London. The only transport was a coach which left at about six a.m. and arrived back at about seven p.m., so I hardly saw either of them during the day. *Faute de mieux*, at the age of eight, I had to take responsibility for my brother and myself. I got us both up for school, did toast for breakfast and prepared toast for our tea in the evenings. In retrospect, we seemed to live on toast, usually burnt. I also washed and ironed our clothes: very badly and very infrequently. It was here that I began to realize that other children didn't normally have potatoes in their socks or holes in their shoes. They also bathed occasionally. It was here I started to play truant, because there was no one at home to stop me or even know, and I could forge my mum's writing easily. If mugging had been invented, I would probably have ended up in jug.

Moving to Dagenham was the worst day's work I ever did. It was a lovely little place, the house, but I didn't know a soul. It was lonely. No friendliness. I tried, but it wasn't like living up home. You felt you needed a long-service medal, that you had to be one of them who moved in at the very beginning to fit in. And the ones who had jobs in Ford's – the better jobs – had cars, which was very unusual for an ordinary person, and they'd be out there night and day, polishing. Right snobs. But they were only the same as us, they just thought they were better. Full of old bounce, you know the type. I was glad to get back. Got myself an exchange.

Those who stayed behind in the East End had some strong views about those who had left.

Corned Beef City we called it, because a lot of them who moved down there [to Dagenham] thought they were *it*, but we all knew they lived on corned beef, because that's all they could afford. Kippers and curtains, see. They'd have nice lace curtains up [at] their windows – that's important, because it's what people see – but then they have to have kippers every night to pay for them. All show.

There was the story that the families who moved on to the estates from the East End kept their coal in the bath, because they weren't used to having a bathroom. You could believe anything of some of those families.

   The isolation, the absence of community, was not blamed solely on housing. How people were now expected to shop was also a cause of concern.

Think about it. You can shop in supermarkets without saying a word to another living human being. Put your shopping in your basket, carry it round, not know a soul, go to the till and the girl runs it over the light. That's it. Not so much as a 'Good morning', never mind a 'How are you feeling now? Is your chest better?'

You went up the corner shop and bought a bit of cheese, the bloke behind the counter used to have a chair. You could go in there and sit down. He'd serve other people and it would go backwards and forwards. 'Here, did you hear about so-and-so over the road?' You'd go in there and get your gossip. But there's not even any talking in the supermarkets.

I worked in shops and restaurants and you made contact with people. I enjoyed it. You had all kinds, good and bad, stroppy ones and not so stroppy. But you was integrated with people and not a machine all the time. One day I went down [the supermarket] and it was all closed up. I asked what was going on and they said the computer had gone wrong. That put the whole shop out of action. When I worked in [a grocer's shop] it was the old type, where you chopped the butter and cut the cheese with a wire. You served people. And there was a seat for you to sit on while you were being served. And you could have two ounces of butter, when they didn't always want a whole block, or couldn't afford it. You could have two

ounces of this, a quarter of that. It was lovely, serving people.
You talked to them. You wrote [the prices] down and added
it all up in your head as you went to the till. Nothing was
done for you, you used your brain. I think that's why I can
talk and think as well as I do now. You had interesting
conversations with people. Now you walk all the way round
the supermarket in a daze looking at all the stuff, [worrying
about] sell-by dates.

I miss the East End markets. There's none round our way.
You have these boot sales of a Sunday, but it's not like going
for your potatoes and greens and a bit of fruit off the stalls.
You'd go most days of the week. All nice and fresh. And
you'd have a laugh and a chat.

There was also a perception that any future changes will not be
for the better either, that conditions are worsening, that it is somehow
'too late'.

We won't ever get them times back that we had in the East
End. And it's frightening but I reckon we'll be thinking that
these are the good times when we look back on them in a few
years' time, when we're all stuck indoors the whole time by
ourselves and never ever go out and see people. It'll all be
everything done by machine, like you see on the telly. You
see.

When I first came to work here [as a professional in the East
End], I would not have believed in the erosion of the welfare
state. I would not have believed in the erosion of provision of
education. In the erosion of the NHS. In the erosion of
housing. The main problem for people in this area, in
practical terms, is not having enough money. It has an
economy with a very low wage structure. I really don't know
how they survive. Even if there were jobs for them, people
can't break out of their cycle of poverty.

In some cases, those people are 'foreigners', recent immigrants to the East End. This comment was made by someone who is himself from an immigrant family.

> You get an Indian or a black person moving in, never white. The balance has gone. One community's getting built up and the other one is going down.

And not all of the foreigners are from abroad. 'Yuppie' was a term used by people I spoke to to describe incomers of any age who were gentrifying homes in east London.

> There are a lot of what you'd call more middle-class types moving in here and pushing up the prices. The yuppies come in and buy up the old places that used to house a couple of families, now they're just a couple living there, not even kids. And look at their motors. Look at the way they drive. Look at him [going past the window]! Speed he's going down this little turning. How am I meant to walk along here?

> The docks. That area has changed into a posh people's place. I liked it when it was a working area – the docks how they used to be. People working, big ships coming in. The blokes had work. Now there's the yuppiefied businesses. Marinas and boat-fitting. All geared around people who have got a few bob, rather than normal people who work for their living. You don't need airs and graces. I don't think your voice should make a difference. It might make a difference to you getting a job in some places, but it doesn't stop you being intelligent.

The antagonism to newcomers was described to me as being the 'last-off-the-boat syndrome', when earlier arrivals in an area resent the next wave of immigrants, but not everyone felt that way.

> My London was a competition between Jews and Mosley, the National Front and ordinary East Enders. Now it has been taken over, partially, by immigrants. But I get the impression that they are part of us, have *become* part of us, so it is OK.

After all, we did take their countries away from them. If only we had thrown all the guns away, what a wonderful world this could be.

I live in a really mixed area. There's people with a few bob, others with nothing, and all sorts of different colours and backgrounds. It's great. It's like being on holiday with all the different things in the shops. I never even saw an avocado till I was in my twenties, and now I see all sorts of things! And there are little shops round our way where you can get anything you want and where you get to talk to people. And buy just a bit of this or one of those, instead of a great big packet of stuff.

But, it has to be said, the majority of older people I spoke to felt that the East End was a place where they were no longer relevant, where they no longer had a say.

It does make me sad that that way of life [associated with the river and the docks] has gone. Since I stopped working there, I have only been down the docks a couple of times, and I'm amazed at the changes that have taken place down there. We went down there when they had the celebration at the new airport. I think the Millennium Dome is going to have a big impact round here. They say people are going to have to park up here, to visit over there. I'd have thought that that amount of money could have been used elsewhere. They're spending more each week. I've always said – if they can make that Channel tunnel, why couldn't they spend money on straightening the river? Something useful to local people. It would have made easier access and saved the docks. Do that, instead of the Dome. They won't even allow the council to build their own houses. It's all housing associations.

They decide who's going to live where. You start sorting out a life for yourself, after all the changes you've had to go through. You think, that's it, this is where I'm going to spend me last years, and then they come along and muck it all up again. Bring in people with loads of kids, problem families and that. It's not right. It really worries me. I don't want to have to start again.

Perhaps it is a function of a world where individuals over a certain age feel increasingly redundant – in every sense of the word – rather than a problem that is limited just to those from the East End. The speed of change *is* alarming – in one century we have moved from Victorian values to the Internet – so is it any wonder that older people, from all cultures, sometimes feel confused or left behind?

This computer business. I don't understand none of it. Young children know all about these things, but is it a good thing? Even before computers it was calculators. We had to use our heads. We were given mental-arithmetic lessons. You had nothing to write down or add up on, nothing but using your brain. To me it seems that if children can't press a button, they're lost.

I have worked with people from my country [Bangladesh] for many years. If I compare an old man with his son who has become a GP, a dentist, a computer professional, then there are two different pictures. The younger generation's issues have changed. They are born and brought up in this country, they have become professionals, but they move out to America or Canada. Who loses out? This country is losing out.

Our children are taking advantage of the changes in society. They think their parents are from a seventeenth-century background. 'What does my dad know? He can't speak English. Me, I'm a cockney, man.' As a result there are changed ethics in society, and problems which mean you and I have to pay more taxes.

How many children from our families [Indian] know about their responsibilities as a citizen of a responsible society? It is the mother, your house, who should teach all these things.

Your house should be the finest school for all those things.
The children are showing no respect for this.

There were other, more encouraging, hopeful comments, with
some people feeling that not all change was bad but could be a move
forward into a better, modern world.

Some things that have disappeared for the good? Children
playing outside pubs, waiting for their parents, in some cases
to be fed, and workhouses, where the elderly were put away
and forgotten, with very little done for their comfort. Poverty
caused by parliamentary mismanagement. Having to pay for
the doctor to visit.

In the field of health, I give thanks for the wonderful progress
that has been made. Even as children we were made aware of
the scourge of tuberculosis that was rife among all ages.
People spoke in hushed voices when speaking of someone
with it. It was commonly called consumption. I think the
medical profession did their best with the limited knowledge
of the time [but] people seemed to accept then what ailments
they had [and that] nothing could be done.

I've not been hungry for years. Not like we used to be as kids,
when finding that bit extra to eat was all you could think of.

Having a warm house and not having to chuck all the coats
on the bed to stop yourself freezing!

And not everything from the past has disappeared or is even
changing. The Widow's Son, or the Bun House, is a pub in Devons
Road, Bow, on what is known by older cockneys as the Widdersun
Bridge. Built on the site of a widow's cottage that once nestled in a
landscape of meadows and country lanes, the pub hosts an annual
ritual said to be over 200 years old.

The story goes that the widow had baked hot cross buns for her
sailor son, due home from sea, as a Good Friday treat. When he
failed to return, the widow did not despair; instead, she kept hoping

that one day he would turn up, alive and well, at her cottage door. She continued, each Good Friday, to add a fresh bun to those which were hanging from her rafters, ready for her boy to enjoy.

The pub, which had survived both the Blitz and the post-war developers' bulldozers, was burnt out in December 1995, but by Easter 1996 it was reopened and the widow's tradition was back in place, with a new bun being added to the few that had survived the fire.

Whether or not it is true, as some cynics have claimed, that the custom was invented as a marketing ploy in the late Victorian period, and whether or not it is true that there was a devoted widow who refused to admit that her child was dead, it is a good excuse for an old-fashioned knees-up.

In 1998, I arrived at the Bun House early, by mid morning, to watch the formalities that were going to be carried out by Able Seaman Russ Abbott, and the celebrations were already well under way, with everyone drinking, eating, singing and dancing.

The quaint, possibly hokey, ceremony in that little Devons Road pub is also a sign of hope for today: a worthwhile symbol of the East End itself, a place that, despite disruption, change and, too often, neglect and destruction, knows all about regeneration, and has been, and still is, the home of a sometimes unregulated people who are maybe not quite like others, but who enjoy having a good time, who can be generous and kind, and who will never, ever be ordinary.

PART 4

Post-war, Post-imperial, Post-industrial, Postmodern, Post-East End?

Things just aren't the same any more.
Isabel Pam

18

Do you know, Kelly's pie and eel shop in the Roman Road is doing a *veggie alternative*? I can remember the shock when they first started selling tea in the pie shop, and selling afters, and then putting knives in the cutlery tray instead of just spoons and forks. But vegetarian pies? That doesn't seem right to me.

The image of the East End as a place where extended families lived a street-centred, neighbourhood-based life has, for those whose relatives lived there for generations but who have now moved on, gone for ever.

It is hard to imagine the bustling scenes on the river of only a few decades ago and the romance of living in a place that, though shabby and down at heel, was the gateway to every port in the world, and where a young man could go down to the docks and jump on a ship just because he didn't want stew for his tea. With the world there for the taking, how could you feel you were isolated or were missing out on the good life?

The sounds of dock workers shouting to one another over the din of the machinery, as they loaded and unloaded ships from all over the globe, and the sounds of the workers in the victualling yards, the ship-repair works, the hostels, pubs and cafés, competing with the cries of the foghorns downstream, were familiar, commonplace noises. Now men and women travel into the area in a hushed, cocooned world of mobile phones and lap-top computers, on an automated train that doesn't even require the employment of a local person to drive it.

Aspirations for a better, if different life are not, of course, bad *per se*; any child or grandchild can hope that a more desirable place exists, somewhere nicer to raise their own children, with a little garden and a bit less street crime. But the nostalgic draw of the idea of the East End remains. Shopping malls, such as the Lakeside centre in Essex, offer just about everything that the dedicated consumer could hunger for, yet the street markets in east London flourish, and it is not only locals who are going there to shop, browse, gossip and have a laugh. As I queue in an eel and pie house for my take-away pie and mash, I am surrounded by similar ex-East Enders waiting to buy their own little bit of 'up home' to take back to their families; and while the stalls in the street outside might now take credit cards for their knock-off designer clothes, the barrow boys' patter is still as cheekily entertaining as ever.

But, as diverting and colourful as that might be, what, if any, is the future of the East End when a visitor, returning to look for the glorious Victoria Park lido, now finds only a tarmacadamed car park? And then experiences other changes that cannot be quite so easily identified, but which can be felt or sensed in other ways. We are discomforted, as we long for the 'good old days' when 'we was all one', had a knees-up every Saturday night and never locked the street door, when we realize it is a world that is fading fast, a series of sepia-coloured memories being swallowed up by change. It is not simply the fact that change occurs that is alarming but, as the people explained in the previous chapter, that it does so with such rapidity. One of the defining features of the twentieth century, this can both excite and cause great stress. Is it progress or destruction? Are there ever more marvellous improvements on the way or are we plummeting headlong towards consumer obsolescence? Having just mastered the answering machine, along comes the fax, and, before we know it, we are being given e-mail addresses to write to and websites to visit. If we can be nostalgic for just a decade or so ago, when those machines belonged only in offices, is it any wonder that we long for a slightly more distant past, when we knew the members of our local community and looked out for one another as a matter of mutual survival rather than being persuaded along to Neighbourhood Watch meetings, with people we have never spoken to before, a sticker in the window declaring our watchful, yet isolated participation?

But those who retain their community roots can be as disappointed as those who leave. I spoke to a man in Shoreditch who was fuming about newcomers in the area. He was Jewish and had lived there all his life, his grandparents having come to the East End at the tail end of the last century.

*

These people who have moved in round here, did you see in
the papers? They said there's more artists here now than
anywhere else in the world. Artists? Whatever they are, all I
know is it's obvious they don't come from round here. You
should see them. Terrible. People round here have always
tried to look nice, not like something out of the rag bag. Even
if you didn't have much, you can afford a bar of soap. They
poke about on the stalls for all sorts of old rubbish – things
we'd throw away. That's up to them, but where are our kids
meant to live?

In the introduction to his book *1963. Five Hundred Days: History
as Melodrama*, John Lawton wrote:

A common, corny opening for works of recent history is to refer to 'a
world we have lost' and then to dribble down into nostalgia – the world
as it was in 1962 is not a world we lost, it's one we threw away.

After speaking to the people who contributed their stories to this
book, I would argue that they do not believe that *they* threw away
their old world but that it was snatched from them – by bombs and
housing policies, other people's notion of progress and the pressures
of consumerism. It is these which have destroyed their communities
and left them stranded.

I was in an East End information centre, close to the City, when
a well-dressed man in his thirties came in to inquire about the
ownership of the 'derelict' houses in the area. When asked by one
of the workers why he wanted to know, he explained that he could
maybe 'pick up' one of the beautiful eighteenth-century houses 'for
a song' and 'do it up a bit'. When he learned that any property in
the area that wasn't either social housing or privately owned had,
long ago, been snapped up by property developers and speculators,
he seemed surprised that somebody had had the idea first. He was,
to his credit, shocked when we told him about the historical pressures
on affordable housing in the borough and the ever-present problems
for local residents and their families. He hadn't found the answer
he was looking for, but he had discovered something about the

community – that it is a place where people have always wanted to live.

> The old East End, it was great. The smell, sights, sounds. In the summer, you know, you could smell the smells coming from the river. Not bad smells. No, no, no. You could smell when the sun was on the tarpaulin sheets on the lighters, the barges . . . [*Sighing*] I'll never forget that smell. I can smell it now, after all these years. It was beautiful. And the bloody ships going up and down. The tugs. It was so good, the East End.

This woman recalled a resilience she feels is missing from the society in which she now lives.

> The thing I miss about the old days was the light-heartedness of the people. Most of my family and friends were fairly hard up, but they tried to make a living the best way they could. There were no free hand-outs . . . they knew there was 'nothing for nothing', so this gave them an ambition which came out of need. This purpose made them busy and, to a certain extent, content. This happy contentment is something I miss.

But the point she went on to make explained much about what she feels.

> I must express, however, that this was seen through the eyes of a child! I feel very nostalgic when I think about the East End, especially when sad events take my mind back to the past and my childhood. When my mother died a few years ago, I found I kept thinking about my time as a child in the East End, because it brought back happy memories. Words that crop up from time to time like 'pie and mash' 'wally' [pickled cucumber] or any rhyming slang which my uncles used. They take me back. This all sounds very nostalgic, which, of course, it is. But I do think I might have had a different view of things if I had been an adult living in the East End.

*

Her life would undoubtedly have been one of tougher choices and wider concerns, but there are those who have made their homes in east London as adults – like the people fleeing oppression and austerity in the past – who are more than glad to be part of their new community.

The first quote is from a political refugee, the second from a poet.

> People in this country are very friendly. Since [my family] has come here, we have never had a quarrel, never made an enemy. People ask you to go out on Saturdays. They don't say, 'These are foreigners', they just accept us as people. People are good to us. We are able to mix. They don't care who we are. There are houses where, if you have problems, you can just knock on the door and it will be opened to us.

> I love the East End of London. I came here in 1979. I love the down-to-earthness about the place. It's interesting that a lot of people from the artistic community want to know why I don't live in north London. I call them intellectual wankers. They don't want to mix in the real world. The real world is difficult sometimes – I've been chased down West Ham Lane by about twenty skinheads who came out of nowhere – but I like mixing in the real world. One day [one of the broadsheet newspapers] wanted to do an interview with me. They wanted to do it in the dressing room before or after one of my meetings. I said, 'I'll tell you what, come to a school and see the work I do in the East End of London.' They came, and they seemed OK at the time. They went away and the article that came out was terrible:

>> I woke up this frosty morning and went out to interview Benjamin Zephaniah, and I got my bacon and eggs down me, or my croissant, or whatever it was, and as I crossed over Tower Bridge and entered east London, I noticed the place was different. The people seemed hungrier. Staring faces into my car like they were going to rob me.

> He described the East End of London like it was a Third World country, where all the people were hungry. He said all

the people look thinner, like they were going to rob him. That all the kids at the school looked neglected. I got a call from the headmistress saying that all the kids wanted to write letters to the newspaper and I said, 'Let them do it.' People don't understand about the East End, about working-class pride.

There is still, however, a great deal of concern among East Enders themselves over what they feel is happening in the area – their area.

There is racism. Racism is about fear. About being driven out. I hate it when people demonize a whole race, as resentment is such a sad thing. Refusing to see that new communities, Asians for instance, can bring vitality and even wealth to an area. And other things such as family values and a real concern for educational standards. It's common to have people who are usually prejudiced confer a sort of honorary white status on individuals who have become known to them as friends and neighbours. They say something like, 'She's all right, it's the others. She's not like them.' They also tend to get sentimental over 'dear little babies', as though they become a different race when they grow up.

But hope gleams through.

I think on my little street the whole of life is there. When I was moving there, people said, 'That's a nice street, there's not many black people living there.' Black people said that to *me. Me*, a black man. There was one of my neighbours who was wonderful. He played for West Ham football team before it was even called West Ham. He died when he was gone a hundred. He was a great guy, had a sharp memory, and really independent. He would get up every day and walk down the road. I think about him. He was just so nice, had no animosity. He must have known this area, must have seen so many changes, then to see a black guy like me moving next door to him, and he thought nothing of it. The guy on the

other side came out and said, 'I'm telling you now, I'm a
racist and I don't like you black bastards. You park your car
there. I park my car here.' He really put it on the line. I kind
of took it as a challenge. The other day, he was talking to me
about the Queen. And there he was, she's English this and
English that. And I said, 'They're from German stock.' 'Yeah,
but she talks like an English girl.' Then he started talking
about her husband. He's Greek. And Lady Di, she was all
right, but what was she doing with a Paki? He is a real
modern-day Alf Garnett character. When I moved in, white
people came up and said, 'Oh, shit, you've moved next door
to him.' But there are lots of other people. They know me.
Their kids read my books, see my videos. The guy who lives
across from me, his daughter recognized me when I moved
in. His dad was one of the guys who fought Mosley's
Blackshirts. When he read my poetry and read the politics of
it and everything, he was so proud, he showed me all the
photographs of his dad being battered by the police. He was
really proud. I was speaking to my next-door neighbour the
other day. Another example. He wanted to know why I was
here. I explained how Britain colonized Jamaica, India,
wherever. We're here because you were there. That's why
people from Surinam are in Holland. The people from Chad
in France. It hit him. He had never thought it through. That's
what I like about the work I do, about being a self-educated
working-class man. I know the way working-class people
think. I couldn't live anywhere else. I couldn't live with all
these other artists. Where would I get my inspiration from? I
get my inspiration not only from the politicians, the big
issues, but by looking at normal, everyday people and seeing
their prejudices, seeing their aspirations, their wants and their
needs and their struggles. That is my muse. There are times
when, if I'm doing a tour and I'm with a group of
'Wonderful Darlings', I come home and still have to listen to
my next-door neighbour's ramblings. Racism is dumb, it's
wrong, but there are people who think like my neighbour, so
I listen to him. But I am optimistic for the future of the East
End. When I see the new generation of children that are

> coming up, I am optimistic. The people will lead the way,
> and then the politicians will have to catch up.

Optimism, as was seen in the previous chapter, is an important and powerful emotion, but, as in the see-saw life of any vibrant working-class area, there are undeniable problems related to living in the East End, especially if you are poor.

A Public Health Report published in autumn 1998, 'The Health of Londoners', concluded, with a point of analysis straight from the *school of the bleeding obvious*, that there is a link between poor health and poverty, and, regardless of what measures are employed, the inner east London boroughs are among the worst in the country in the league tables of deprivation.

But pessimism leads to impotence. Isn't it better to ask what can be done than to simply bemoan the problems? One route is that taken by the Bromley-by-Bow Centre, a voluntary organization with the specific aim of improving the quality of life – from health to education – of local people; or that of the Newham Parents' Centre and Bookshop, which plays a fundamental role in matters of education and access to opportunities in the lives of people from an area of the East End far wider than its immediate vicinity. But can it realistically be hoped that similar schemes will suddenly emerge fully formed in other neighbourhoods? No, they have to have inspired battlers behind them, people who will give their time, and ensure continued funding and support, to enable them to evolve and survive. In other words, they need a community behind them.

Again: community.

And community depends on decent, affordable, available housing for all who want to remain close to their families, preferably with a patch of grass where they can grow a few flowers, and put out the pram for the baby to get some fresh air; places without threatening alleys or crisp-packet-strewn walkways. Living conditions taken for granted by a large percentage of the British population – and rightly so – would ensure that the East End remains a place in which people aspire to live, and not just because it is so 'handy for the City'.

> I think it's important to try and encourage successful young
> people to remain in the area, so we can have our own

'home-grown' lawyers, teachers and doctors and so on. Some of us have chosen to return – to work in the community, and hopefully to develop it.

I love working in the East End and I love living in the East End. Nothing gives me a bigger thrill now – I've worked so long selling books – when kids who bought their first Ladybird book from me are now college lecturers. I've been through the whole education of a lot of children and I find that fantastic. Kids who started reading [went through] their GCSEs, then their A-levels and then a lot [went] to university. It isn't acknowledged enough just how many do go. I really think that this bookshop, me and my colleagues have been part of that education . . . We've gone out of our way to make it a place where people want to come. Not off-putting.

While I was taping the above interview, in a side room of the Newham Parents' Centre and Bookshop, a man came in asking for help with an official document. The recording then continued.

He felt he could just come in here. People come in with every possible problem. Unfortunately, sometimes quite severe social problems. They bring letters, forms they can't understand because they are so ridiculously formal. You are struck by just how absolutely desperate some things are for people. You'd be surprised though by the attitude of some people. They go, 'Good heavens, a bookshop like this in the East End?' Well, we've been here in Newham for twenty-two years. We've built a reputation. It's important that everyone who works in the shop is part of the community. Lives in it, works in it and have brought their children up in it – they've been to the local schools. It makes people know we've not just been imported from somewhere and are going to just leave. It's important . . . I'm known as a book lady at the schools where I do book stalls. There are two schools that I do every week, and have done for the last seven years. There's enough call for me to go *every week*. We sell huge amounts.

The children can save up for the books and we've got
stationery, so that if a child has only got 10p there is still
something they can buy.

No big city can remain static and London is no exception, but at
times the changes have been dramatic: invasions; plague; fire; bridges
spanning the great river; industry; docks; railways; canals; the beginnings of the commuter belt; wars; new towns and suburbs; East
Enders leaving the bomb sites and slums behind them; and now,
Docklands, with Canary Wharf's massive tower dwarfing, and sup-
planting, the spire of St Anne's as the great landmark rising above
all that surrounds it.

Where once the Thames was so densely packed with shipping,
you could walk from bank to bank across the decks of the vessels
crowding the waters without wetting your feet, where apprentices
had it in writing that they should not be forced to eat salmon more
than four times a week, and the pleasure boats took trippers down
to Blackwall to enjoy the sunset while feasting on fine whitebait
suppers, the river is now a much quieter, lonelier place. Its waters
are all but empty of craft, although the fish are returning, and rather
than drab riverside slums the vision is of a new financial quarter for
the new millennium, a glittering glass and steel extension of the City.
But the East End is still an area of acute poverty. Demolishing slums
doesn't demolish homelessness. Nor does it do much to dispel the
old prejudices about the place and its inhabitants.

A few years ago, someone asked my husband, who works in the
City, to play a game of five-a-side football at the nearby pitches in
the old Spitalfields Market, an area which butts on to the ancient
boundary wall at Bishopsgate, adding that he was welcome, 'If you
can stand going there.'

Two insults in one! Not only was his wife – me – born in Bethnal
Green, not that far away, but we had recently chosen to move back
there to live. My husband did, and does – just – manage to play in
an occasional five-a-side match, but he has chosen to do so with a
different team.

Among the thoughts on east London I received from abroad –
newspaper clippings about my research had been sent by families to
Australia, New Zealand and Canada – were firmly held convictions

that a leading supermarket chain employed only people from ethnic-minority groups and that East End streets are no longer fit to walk along. I was reminded of this when I heard a radio programme, in February 1998, on the differences between private and state education. A teacher spoke about feeling – morally – that he should teach in east London, but, as he wanted to spend his time teaching and not acting as a social worker, policeman and crowd controller, it was obvious, to him, that he should work in the private sector. It was also taken as obvious – and unquestioned by his interviewer – that his description of schooling in east London was accurate.

Prejudices about newcomers arriving and settling in the area also continue.

> As far as we Asians are concerned, people look on us as a problem. Jews, Irish, Europeans and others who have settled in this part of the country, at least they have got fair colouring or fair skin. It is a colour bias. I don't know why. I think it is probably historical, [to do with] British colonial rule. India was one of the most important countries. The jewel in the crown. Think of the Indian people who sacrificed their lives during the two wars, and those who were given Victoria Crosses. I think racism is the biggest problem that Asians face. With no racism, you can see how enterprising we can be. Nobody knows about the great many professionals here who are from Bangladesh. The contribution to the catering industry alone is enormous – £1.6 billion a year. Is this contribution appreciated? Who is taking advantage of this economy? Building societies and banks? Insurance companies? The Asian banks here generate many millions just transferring money. The question is, would the assistant at the counter of Barclays deal with an illiterate, half-educated, curry-smelling old Bangladeshi with the patience and courtesy he would extend to an Englishman? You know the answer. Many of the successful traders from the East End use the Asian banks for that reason. Who is losing out?

Maybe, as this person suggests, the 1970s idea of promoting a cultural melting pot, rather than a discrete cluster of communities within a multicultural society, could be the way forward in the twenty-first century.

> I am a Rastafarian. My wife is from Liverpool, her family is of Pakistani origin, and my mum's Jamaican. I love the East End because there is not just one community which dominates. I was thinking of learning a language and thought of maybe learning French, but then I thought, 'What use would French be in the East End?' so I learned Urdu. But all communities have their prejudices. The Bengalis are the latest immigrants from Asia, and the Montserratians are the latest from the Caribbean. They become the butt of the jokes. Amongst the Caribbean community, the people from Montserrat are treated kind of like the Irish are. The Bengalis the same. They just change the joke from Irish to Bengali. In the United States they call it the 'last-off-the boat syndrome' – to explain all these internal prejudices. I've been to Pakistan and the people there can't understand why this woman – my wife – who is beautiful and light-skinned, went and married a dark-skinned man. Once they get over that, they are great people. It's like here, on the whole we all kind of live together. We don't refer to the problems back in the Caribbean, or Africa, or Asia in order to negotiate our relationships here.

But all problems can't be so easily dismissed. There are moments of a rise in support for the extreme right, such as the ephemeral but still-alarming success of a British National Party candidate in Millwall who, like Mosley before him, tried to rally the poor unemployed and disaffected who were failing to find any other answer to their problems.

Such events can be analysed within the context of ignorance and bigotry, or be seen as arising from disappointed individuals lamenting the loss of their once-secure community, or simply as the reaction of people standing in post office queues for their giros and feeling resentment at the numbers of strange faces surrounding them, strangers who don't even speak their language. But communities do change, and probably always will, no matter what anyone might prefer.

I recently saw an elderly man in Brick Lane wearing what had, up until a generation ago, been the familiar outfit of the many Jewish men in the area – wide-brimmed hat, long dark coat and side whiskers. He was waving his arms in frustration at not being able to make himself understood by a member of the local Bengali population. 'All I want,' he was complaining, 'is for him to move his car forward a few feet.'

Perhaps it is too late for some to change, but ignorance of one another's lives, needs, desires and feelings can be countered with education and, more importantly, a shared pride in being cockneys.

When I was a schoolgirl – an eleven-plus success – I was encouraged at school to lose my accent, to *improve* myself. They didn't do much of a job on me, although, like generations of cockney kids, I became bilingual in order to save myself from getting into trouble; not exactly speaking another language, as the Chinese, Yemeni, German and other immigrant children have had to do, but speaking with a different accent, slower, 'nicer', in front of the non-East Enders, especially teachers, who could have punished me for doing otherwise. The teachers failed to understand, in my school at least, that there was a real importance attached to being seen as respectable in my East End, but it didn't depend on having a 'proper' accent – just on behaving in what was considered a proper manner. It involved taking a pride in yourself; working hard to get by; being there to help your neighbour during the bad times, and joining in their celebrations when they were good; feeling you were part of something bigger than yourself; and knowing that your kids could be kids, raking the streets and having a bit of fun, instead of becoming pasty-faced little mouse potatoes glued to their computers.

Corny and nostalgic? Maybe, but it's a way of life that many remember and a way of life that some wish they could still enjoy.

> If I had to say what I miss most, it would definitely be that gaslamp we used to play on in Mossford Street. In fact, I have such nostalgia for it, as does my sister, that we went back a few years ago just to take a look at it. Of course, it was gone.

*

I look back still and, it doesn't matter how old I get, I'll always remember – the swish of the skipping rope, the games of tin-can copper, the Gaiety Girls, the sights, the smells, the laughter, and not many tears. But I'll remember it. I'll be seventy-six next birthday and if I live any longer I know I'll never forget those days when I was young and just had everything to look forward to. We won't mention the bad times that the East End had during that bloody turn-out [the war], but this I know: whoever went away from this island, from the East End, and didn't come back will always be remembered. *I'll remember them all.* I hope you'll excuse me, my dear, I won't even tell you my name, because there's no need for that. I'm just an old East Ender who has looked back. The East End is where I was born and I'm proud of that.

Thank you all for sharing your stories. I hope I have done them justice.

Appendix: The Docks

From the end of the eighteenth until the mid-twentieth century, London's port, with its East End docks and close-knit communities, was the most important in the world. How, and why, this position was sacrificed is a disputed, controversial and often sorry tale that, eventually, might be seen by some as having a positive outcome. For others, though, it will never be anything other than a personal and a community tragedy. To say that controversy has surrounded the project to reconstruct the docklands is to misunderstand what has actually been the destruction of a whole way of life. It must be acknowledged that something had to be done, although exactly what is open to question.

There is a lot of bitterness about what happened, and a whole library could be written on the details without beginning to tell the complete story, but these are the bare bones of the events from a number of different angles.

The post-war period could have been seen as an opportunity for extensive modernization of the bomb-damaged docks, but failure to meet the challenge of increased containerization and the extension of the facilities downstream at Tilbury meant that the moment was ripe for a concerted assault on the power of the trade unions, and what was to become the lamentable, but inevitable, decline led to the transformation of the once-great docks into the Docklands.

In 1967, McKinsey and Co., Management Consultants, told the Port of London Authority (PLA), the main landowner in the docks, that containerization was the way forward and, as the inner London docks were not of a suitable size, that Tilbury should be expanded at the expense of the upstream facilities.

To understand how the docks came to be the centre of a prolonged battle needs the historical context briefly restating. As was described earlier, the docks were built in the nineteenth century as a direct result of the pressures which came with increasing imperial trade. Not only was more quay space required, but it had to be secure. The Committee of the West Indies Merchants founded the West India

Dock Company and opened their dock on the Isle of Dogs in 1802. Other dock companies quickly followed, all keen to profit from the burgeoning business based on the importing of cheap raw materials and the export of an ever-growing variety of manufactured and finished goods.

The old quays were now replaced by massive enclosed docks and, as had happened with the historical riverside trades, new dock-related industries and services soon appeared to process raw imports such as chemicals, oil, sugar, rubber, cereals for flour and animal feed.

Towards the end of the nineteenth century, the old ship-building trades were becoming obsolete as steam power came to dominate, and increasing mechanization in the ever larger companies, keen to exploit economies of scale, saw many workers unemployed or forced into casual work.

The exploitation of labour in the docks which resulted from this casualization reflected the experience of many other trades and industries throughout the East End in the nineteenth century, where the cheap, subjugated pool of workers were being abused in the sweated trades, with women and immigrant labour usually faring the worst.

As profits rose, there was a series of dock mergers and, with the increasing competition between the newly enlarged companies, the need was seen for an overall authority to settle disputes and to introduce order. The PLA (Port of London Authority) was set up in 1908. The first board was elected by merchants, wharfingers (wharf owners and managers) and the ship owners, each having one vote for every £10 of trade. The ship owners clearly dominated.

The PLA became well established and continued to operate into the twentieth century, but, having no subsidy, it depended solely on revenue and by the middle of this century that was declining. With investment and business increasing downstream at Tilbury, the PLA looked towards its considerable upstream property assets and took McKinsey's advice. Massive ships, being dealt with in a fraction of the time, became the future prospect.

A comment at the time, attributed to Bernie Steer, a shop steward with the National Association of Stevedores and Dockers, was that the PLA was acting as an estate agent rather than as a port employer.

But dock-workers also knew that, without change, closure was inevitable. A man I spoke to who had followed the family tradition of working in the docks most of his adult life was saddened by, but resigned to, the changes.

> The reason the docks *had* to close was because the ships were getting bigger and bigger. The trouble with these docks was that every one [of the ships] had to be locked into them. Take their turn to be locked into the docks. Sometimes that used to take a full day. The same going out. If they went to Tilbury, where they had more water, bigger ships, well, they could go straight away. It was a matter of modernizing the docks or else. They could also have spent money straightening out the river, taking away that bend, the one you see at the beginning of *EastEnders*. And the cranes could lift five tons, whereas the containers coming in from abroad were weighing twenty tons. So, what we had to do on the ship was dismantle the cargo, take it out of the container, send that ashore, then send the empty container on to the shore, where they would repack it. Whereas down at Tilbury, they've got a big crane that can pick the whole lot up and put it on the quay. We [some of the dock-workers] went to Rotterdam for a week and they were even more modernized. The ships come right alongside, and, as they do, they get worked on straight away, right round the clock.
>
> I've only been back down there a couple of times – to the Docklands – and I was amazed. Down the bottom of the lane, where the Connaught used to be, they've got a railway there that goes up over the top round to Woolwich. You can lose yourself there.

Containerization had an appeal for the employers other than that of economies of scale, however.

In 1947 the Dock Labour Board Scheme was set up, with each port having its own board jointly controlled by the employers and the unions. Workers who registered with their board were hired out to the employers on a casual basis. This continued for twenty years and then, in 1967, the work was decasualized and dockers were paid a regular wage. The boards were not popular with the employers; they objected to the 50 per cent power granted to the unions and to the levy they were expected to pay to their Dock Labour Board to finance the registration scheme. Containerization offered an alternative. Easily shifted by road, the containers could be dealt with outside the actual port area by non-registered workers and could also be shipped to non-scheme ports such as Felixstowe, lowering costs for the employers. The non-scheme ports made the upstream PLA ports even more uncompetitive, as they were forced to raise their charges to cover pay for the growing pool of surplus labour.

It was what happened during the late 1960s and 1970s that resulted in the 1980s jobs crisis in east London. The ill-feelings of the dockworkers were clear.

> Everything finished. I came out of the docks because I thought, 'I'm going to be the last one here and all the jobs will be gone. There'll be nothing. Fifty-eight I was when I came out. I should have been sixty-five. You could retire at fifty-eight, but on a reduced pension. My reduced pension when I first came out [in the 1970s] was eleven shillings a month. Now it's near enough £32 a month. Each October, I get £169 as a lump sum. That's through the National Dock Labour Board. It pays my television licence.

In 1967 there were 22,815 registered dock-workers and associated lighterage personnel employed in the Port of London. In 1980 there were 7,120. By the end of 1981 the last remaining enclosed upstream docks – the Royals – ceased to be operational, and with their closure came the job devastation in port-related local trades and services.

The social and financial cost to the old dockland area began in east London, with the London Docks being closed in 1969 and St Katharine's following. In south London, the Surrey Docks were shut in 1970, then, back on the north side, the East India Docks went in 1971 and the West India followed a few years later. The furthest east of the docks, the Royals, were the last to go. But the question remained: who, exactly, was benefiting?

In January 1973, Tower Hamlets had 6,200 people on its housing waiting list, at the same time that Taylor Woodrow were about to start work on the luxury development at St Katharine's Docks. Being on a waiting list is a very different matter from having your relative speak to the landlord about finding you a room or two to begin your married life, and locals on the list were interested to find that, when the development was completed, a prominent Member of Parliament moved in there.

A 1974 satirical pamphlet by Alun Gilbey of the Basement Writers illustrated what locals feared would be the future of east London's docklands, that there would be a moat separating 'trendies' from the 'genuine' East Enders, with the Isle of Dogs being used as a camp for deposed locals whose homes had been bulldozed to make way for glittering skyscrapers, fancy marinas and totally unaffordable housing.

What Paul Beasley, leader of Tower Hamlets Council in 1976, identified to a local reporter was, for locals, a glaringly obvious truth:

If the docker has got no work then everybody else is idle. This is one of the last base industries we have left.

And to quote Mr Rogg, who owns a delicatessen in Cannon Street Road:

> In those days [when the docks were operating] the dockers were good customers. They earned a pound, they spent a pound. Their sons and grandsons were the same. The real dockers, not like that lot over in Docklands now. People ask me what's happened round here. I say, 'The people are different.'

The Docklands Joint Committee, made up of members from the five boroughs affected (Tower Hamlets and Newham on the north bank, and Southwark, Greenwich and Lewisham on the south) and from the Greater London Council (GLC), plus government-appointed figures picked, some might say, from the usual suspects, organized the Docklands Development Team to work out a plan to decide what should be done with the area. Transport was rightly identified as being vital, and the Joint Docklands Action Group (JDAG), financed by the GLC and made up of all the local action groups, pointed to the ridiculous under-use of the river, and even how barges could be utilized to make containerization a viable way forward in the existing inner London docks. JDAG also came up with a plan which proposed that, rather than letting the workshops and factories crumble – almost a way of guaranteeing their future sole sale potential as yet more development land – they should, instead, be renovated, with existing skill bases kept and encouraged to develop.

However, there was still the establishment vision that the Docklands would become a second City, and eventually *the* site that finance and banking would flock to, even though this was failing to happen.

Covering the story of the apparent failure of the Docklands to 'take off', the *Financial Times* of 31 July 1978 suggested that the main reason why the area had degenerated into dereliction rather than rising in phoenix-like glory when the 'City would move east' had been the ill-thought-out policies of successive governments which had, in practical terms such as subsidy and development of infrastructure, forced firms and corporations to choose other places to site their businesses. This was written two years after the original planning report had first put forward the vision of the Docklands being the greatest opportunity for the reconstruction of London since the Great Fire of 1666, an urban development site, stretching east from the City on both sides of the river, totalling eight and a half square miles.

The government was already promising considerable investment in the area, but the fears, on all sides, remained. Where were the jobs and when would good, affordable housing schemes be created for the dispossessed locals?

By 1979, over ten years since the first dock closure, much of the area was derelict and had become, in fact, Europe's largest area of urban desolation. In February the *East London Advertiser* was reporting the fears of the House of Commons Expenditure Committee that locals would not be among those who benefited from the eventual Docklands developments, as their interests were being ignored in favour of a concern with profit.

The next major blow for the local community came when the government assumed the power to impose Urban Develop Corporations wherever it saw fit. The London Docklands Development Corporation (LDDC) was subsequently created in 1981.

These corporations had the power to circumvent local government controls over housing and planning, including the right of compulsory purchase. Urban Development Corporations could, effectively, become sole land-owners in an area – not a very comforting thought for locals, when they discovered the specific function of the corporations was to sell or lease such land as it considered 'expedient' for the purpose of development.

No one was disagreeing that something had to be done, but the question still remained, for whose benefit were these actions being taken? When the Dockland's Enterprise Zone, with a fixed life of ten years, was opened on the Isle of Dogs in May 1982 by the then Chancellor of the Exchequer, Sir Geoffrey Howe, releasing thousands of red, white and blue balloons in celebration, there were many protest groups at the ceremony. One, the Campaign to Restore Democracy in Docklands, was against the establishment of the Enterprise Zone, believing that it denied local people a say in what went on in their own neighbourhood and that the LDDC was able to operate without any accountability; while another group, from the new Billingsgate fish market in the Docklands, was protesting at being left out of the Enterprise Zone and so being excluded from the business benefits.

In the *Hackney Gazette* of 28 May 1982, Geoffrey Howe claimed that the Enterprise Zone was to be a 'test area' that would show how a 'return to free-market principles' would bring prosperity and jobs to the area, and that private initiative would prove to be the new heart of the local economy, and would thus play an important role in the LDDC's strategy for regeneration of the whole Docklands area.

There were local hopes, at one time, that the existence of the Enterprise Zone would weaken the arguments for the necessity of an Urban Development Corporation and that more control would be retained by the local authority, but these hopes, like many others, were not fulfilled.

As with the Enterprise Zone, there was persistent ambivalence regarding the value of other initiatives being implemented in the name of regeneration. In 1984, for instance, the *City of London Post* was comparing the area to Venice, while Connie Hunt, the secretary of the Newham Docklands Forum, in a JDAG press release, was saying that, after compulsory purchase orders had been served by the LDDC on 1,000 acres, it was time to take the gloves off and no longer listen to the 'soft soap', because the people were 'really against them now' and wanted their homes back. And the Docklands Community Poster Project, with money from the local authority and the GLC, placed massive photomontages on billboards to express the fear that the Docklands would be taken away from the community altogether and handed over to big business, big money and big buildings.

After generations of supplying their labour and, in the not so distant past, giving their health to making a success of the riverside economy which had contributed so much towards making the City the financial world power it is today, and after having carried on and survived, in varyingly fair shape, the ravages of the Blitz, there was little wonder that East Enders from the dockside areas should be angry, suspicious and resentful.

Community and trade union opposition continued. Meetings were held, pamphlets printed, industrial action taken. With the PLA's decision to scrap the upstream docks – the West India and Millwall Group in the Isle of Dogs and the Royals Group in Newham – it meant, according to the Action Committee on Jobs, that east London would lose an immediate 4,000 jobs and many tens more thousands throughout the community as a direct result of the closures. In an area already suffering from high unemployment, this would be a disaster. Instead of closure, the call from the community was for modernization that would not see government spending money to destroy their livelihoods, but would instead save taxpayers' money and create new employment opportunities. But the PLA claimed that this was not a viable option, even though there was a strong argument that investment in a rail-served heavy lift berth for specialized cargo for the new types of ship, along with upgraded servicing, would save this area in the heart of London's East End. But this was not to be.

From the mid-1980s, land prices began to rise and private capital began to be attracted. By 1987, a new airport specifically aimed at the business market had been opened. Offices, shops, restaurants and other leisure facilities began to attract home-buyers who could afford houses and flats that were not even a possibility for most locals, many of whom had been displaced – from both homes and jobs – for the redevelopment of the area. And much of the postmodern-inspired buildings of the Docklands were not intended for the existing community anyway.

There was a 'joke' around at the time that went something like this:

Tower Hamlets was so poor it couldn't even afford social workers to tell homeless families it had nowhere to house them. But with the coming of Docklands the council had lots of money. Unfortunately, all the land had been given away to developers. Still, it could now afford plenty of social workers to tell the homeless people there were no homes for them.

But the mini-boom was short-lived. When the stock market crashed, in October 1987, the newly lively Docklands property market slumped once more.

The roller-coaster of Docklands history, however, continued: following the general election in 1987, there was a change in the relationship between the LDDC and the local authorities, who decided to try cooperating more with the Corporation and to negotiate funding community programmes. This small sign of hope was also dashed when, in 1990, the LDDC made its first loss and the new funding strategy was one of the first to suffer.

The LDDC's problems had begun with a hike in mortgage rates and the City's continuing reluctance to move into the Docklands, and were then followed by so-called Black Monday and the subsequent recession. But, as is the way with high finance, optimism returned to the markets and, at last, businesses began moving into the Docklands.

Then, in February 1996, there was the tragic bombing at South Quay, when two people were killed and many more injured. Antagonism became very public after this terrible event, when local residents – the remaining members of the traditional riverside community – claimed that their rehousing needs following the devastation were being ignored while big business was being pandered to. This argument was still having to be put forward in the summer of 1998. A television crew, interviewing residents of one of the damaged blocks for a local news programme, found the same complaint: big business was the priority. And those who had been rehoused had not been put together; their close-knit community had received the final blow of dispersal.

The housing pressures in east London, exacerbated by the high cost of luxury developments, rising levels of unemployment and companies' reluctance to employ locals, have been described as 'growth accompanied by increasing inequality'.

In 1998, with the collapse of the so-called tiger economies and, despite the strength of the City and the buoyant pound, the threat of yet another recession just around the corner, many of the 'investment' properties bought in the Docklands over the past five years have been put back up for sale. That said, those with glorious river views and secure parking – many incomers never do feel *quite* safe in the area, according to the conspiratorial whisper of one local estate agent – are apparently still being snapped up if the sold notices are anything to go by.

An area without an established community needs to have purchasers who can afford to live there almost on a whim – because it's close to where they work or because the views are great – not because they want to live close to their extended family.

It has become increasingly accepted that the Docklands has a future all right, but not one which will benefit many of the people who were living there before the closure of the old docks.

Across the river, the situation is similar. The Hays Galleria has replaced the old Hay's Wharf, once a valuable source of work for local people, and is now a luxury shopping complex for tourists, popular as a place to browse after they've visited the London Dungeon.

Bibliography, Further Reading and Suggested Sources

All the books are published in London unless stated otherwise.

Banton, M. P., *The Coloured Quarter* (1953)

Barnardo, Thomas, *Three Tracts* (1888)

Barnett, H. O., *Canon Barnett: His Life, Works and Friends* (2 vols., 1918)

Beer, Reg, 'Matchgirls' Strike, 1888: The Struggle against Sweated Labour in London's East End' (National Museum of Labour History pamphlet, 1971)

Beer, R., and Pickard, C. A., 'Eighty Years on Bow Common' (pamphlet, no date)

Bermant, Chaim, *Point of Arrival* (1975)

Besant, A., *Annie Besant: An Autobiography* (1893)

Binder, Pearl, *The Pearlies* (1975)

Bishop, E., *Blood and Fire* (1964)

Black, Graham, 'The Archaeology of Tower Hamlets' (Inner London Archaeological Unit, no date)

Booth, Charles, *Life and Labour of the London Poor* (1892–7)

Booth, William, *In Darkest England* (1890)

Branson, Noreen, *Poplarism, 1919–1925* (1979)

Briggs, Asa, and Macartney, Anne, *Toynbee Hall: The First Hundred Years* (1984)

Brooks, Peter F., *Pearly Kings and Queens* (1974)

The Campaign to Restore Democracy in Docklands, 'Heseltine's Docklands: The First 6 Months (Joint Docklands Action Group, May 1982)

Chadwick, Edwin, *Report on the Sanitary Conditions of the Labouring Population* (1842)

Choo, Ng Kwee, *The Chinese in London* (1968)

Clayton, P. B., and Leftwich, B. R., *The Pageant of Tower Hill* (1933)

Clout, Hugh, ed., *The Times London History Atlas* (1994)

Coates, T. F. G., *The Prophet of the Poor* (1905)

Cunningham, Hugh, 'The Metropolitan Fairs', in A. P. Donajgrodzki (ed.), *Social Control in Nineteenth-century Britain* (1977)

Department of the Environment, 'The Proposed London Docklands Development Corporation' (memorandum, 1980)

East London Employment Study Group, 'The East London File' (GLC pamphlet, 1982)

Eddy, J. P., *The Mystery of Peter the Painter* (1946)

Farrell, Jerome, 'The German Community in Nineteenth-century East London' (Tower Hamlets Local History Library and Archive, May 1990)

Fishman, W. J., *East End Jewish Radicals* (1975)

Fishman, William J., with Nicholas Breach, *The Streets of East London* (1987)

Gartner, L. P., *The Jewish Immigrant in England, 1870–1914* (1960)

Gilbey, Alun, *Up the Docks* (1974)

Goodman, Jonathan, *The Christmas Murders* (1985)

Historians' Group of the Communist Party, *The Poplar Story, 1921* (1953)

Hitchman, Janet, *They Carried the Sword* (1966)

Hobsbawm, Eric, *The Age of Revolution* (1996)

Holme, Anthea, *Housing and Young Families in East London: Report of the Institute of Community Studies* (1985)

Holmes, Colin, ed., *Immigrants and Minorities in British Society* (1978)

Holroyd, J. E., *The Gaslight Murders* (1960)

House of Commons Expenditure Committee, Environment Subcommittee, Minutes of Evidence, session 1977–8, 'Redevelopment of Docklands'.

Huddleston, Trevor, *Naught for Your Comfort* (1956)

Jackson, John A., 'The Irish in East London', *East London Papers*, vol. 6, no. 2, December 1963

Keating, P. J., *Working-class Stories of the 1890s* (1971)

Kray, Charles, *Me and My Brothers* (1976)

Latham, Robert, ed., *The Shorter Pepys* (1993)

Law, John, (pseudonym of Margaret Harkness), *In Darkest London* (1889)
— *Out of Work* (1888)

Lawton, John, *1963. Five Hundred Days: History as Melodrama* (1992)

Lees, Lynn Hollen, *Exiles of Erin: Irish Migrants in Victorian London* (1979)

Leff, Vera, and Blunden, G. H., *The Story of Tower Hamlets* (1967)

London, Jack, *The People of the Abyss* (1903)

Lovell, John, 'The Irish and the London Docker', *Bulletin of the Society for the Study of Labour History* (1977)

McDonnell, Kevin, *Medieval London Suburbs* (1978)

Mackay, J. H., *The Anarchists* (Boston, 1891)

Massey, Doreen, 'Docklands: A Microcosm of Broader Social Economic Trends' (The Docklands Forum, April 1991)

Mayhew, Henry, *London Labour and the London Poor* (1851–62)

Merrifield, Ralph, 'Roman', in *The Archaeology of the London Area: Current Knowledge and Problems* (Special Paper No. 1, London and Middlesex Archaeological Society, 1976)

Morrison, A., *Tales of Mean Streets* (1894)

Museum of London, 'Summaries of Excavations Carried out in Tower Hamlets since 1985' (no date)

Nott-Bower, Sir William, *Fifty-two Years a Policeman* (1926)

O'Neill, Gilda, *Pull No More Bines: An Oral History of East London Hop-pickers* (1990)

Palmer, Alan, *The East End* (1989)

Pankhurst, Sylvia, *The Suffragette Movement* (1912)

Pimlott, J. A. R., *Toynbee Hall: Fifty Years of Social Progress* (1935)

Preston, William, *The Bitter Cry of Outcast London* (1883)

Reaney, G. S., article in Arnold White, *The Destitute Alien in Great Britain* (1892)

Rose, Millicent, *The East End of London* (1951)

Rumbelow, D., *The Houndsditch Murders and the Siege of Sidney Street* (1973)

Samuel, Raphael, *East End Underworld, 1887–1947* (1981)

Schama, Simon, *Landscape and Memory* (1996)

Shadwell, Arthur, 'The German Colony in London', *National Review* (26 February 1896)

Sheldon, Harvey, 'Excavations at Parnell Road and Appian Road, Old Ford, E3', reprinted from *Transactions of the London and Middlesex Archaeological Society*, vol. 23, part 2 (1972)

Sheridan, Michael, 'Rowton Houses, 1892–1954' (Rowton Houses Ltd, 1956)

Stedman-Jones, Gareth, *Outcast London: A Study in the Relationship between Classes in Victorian Society* (1992)

Stow, John, *A Survey of London*, reprinted from the text of 1603, with introduction and notes by Charles Lethbridge Kingsford (1908, reprinted by Oxford University Press, 1971)

Taylor, Rosemary, *Blackwall, The Brunswick and Whitebait Dinners* (1991)

Thompson, E. P., *The Making of the English Working Class* (1979)

Thorne, G., *The Great Acceptance: The Life Story of F. N. Charrington* (1912)

Thorne, W., *My Life's Battles* (1926)

Tillett, B., *A Brief History of the Dockers' Union* (1910)

— *Memoirs and Reflections* (1931)

Wensley, F. B., *Detective Days* (1931)
Williams, A. E., *Barnardo of Stepney* (1945)
Zangwill, Israel, *Children of the Ghetto* (1892)

The following newspapers and journals were of particular interest: *Bethnal Green News, City of London Post, Co-partnership Herald of the Commercial Gas Company, Daily Graphic, Daily News, Daily Telegraph, East End Life, East End News, East London Advertiser, East London Observer, Evening News, Evening Standard, Financial Times, Gentleman's Magazine, Guardian, Illustrated Police News, Independent on Sunday, Jewish Chronicle, The Link, Local Municipal Review, London Argus, Morning Star, Municipal Journal, New Statesman, Observer, Pall Mall Gazette, Punch, Reynolds News, The Sphere, The Star* (London evening paper, now defunct), *Tailor and Cutter, The Times, Women's Dreadnought.*

As to archives, exhibitions, public records, other printed materials, general information, suggestions and referrals to further resources and agencies, the following are useful, though some records can initially be difficult to locate as the notion of what constitutes the East End is constantly changing: Bishopsgate Library, British Library, Commission for Racial Equality, Corporation of London Records Office, Guildhall Library, London Metropolitan Archives, London Museum of Jewish Life, London Research Centre, Museum of London, Newham Local Studies Library, Newspaper Library, Public Record Office, Ragged School Museum, Tower Hamlets Local History Library.

refresh yourself at penguin.co.uk

Visit penguin.co.uk for exclusive information and interviews with
bestselling authors, fantastic give-aways and the
inside track on all our books, from the Penguin Classics
to the latest bestsellers.

BE FIRST

first chapters, first editions, first novels

EXCLUSIVES

author chats, video interviews, biographies, special
features

EVERYONE'S A WINNER

give-aways, competitions, quizzes, ecards

READERS GROUPS

exciting features to support existing groups and
create new ones

NEWS

author events, bestsellers, awards, what's new

EBOOKS

books that click – download an ePenguin today

BROWSE AND BUY

thousands of books to investigate – search, try
and buy the perfect gift online – or treat yourself!

ABOUT US

job vacancies, advice for writers and company
history

Get Closer To Penguin . . . www.penguin.co.uk